Born Fighter

Born Fighter

Ruqsana Begum

with Sarah Shephard

SIMON &
SCHUSTER

London · New York · Sydney · Toronto · New Delhi

First published in Great Britain by Simon & Schuster UK Ltd, 2020

Copyright © Ruqsana Begum, 2020

The right of Ruqsana Begum to be identified
as the author of this work has been asserted in accordance
with the Copyright, Designs and Patents Act, 1988.

1 3 5 7 9 10 8 6 4 2

Simon & Schuster UK Ltd
1st Floor
222 Gray's Inn Road
London WC1X 8HB

www.simonandschuster.co.uk
www.simonandschuster.com.au
www.simonandschuster.co.in

Simon & Schuster Australia, Sydney
Simon & Schuster India, New Delhi

The author and publishers have made all reasonable efforts
to contact copyright-holders for permission, and apologise
for any omissions or errors in the form of credits given.
Corrections may be made to future printings.

A CIP catalogue record for this book
is available from the British Library

Trade Paperback ISBN: 978-1-4711-8515-1
eBook ISBN: 978-1-4711-8516-8

Typeset in Bembo by M Rules
Printed and bound by CPI Group (UK) Ltd, Croydon, CR0 4YY

MIX
Paper from
responsible sources
FSC® C020471
FSC
www.fsc.org

Preface

November 2018

'Welcome to Las Vegas where the local time is 1.30 p.m. The weather today is mostly cloudy, and it's a chilly 58 degrees out there.'

I'm not even off the plane yet and I already know this trip is going to be different. The last time I was here, it was so hot it felt like walking into an oven every time you stepped outside.

Did I even pack any warm clothes?

Judging by the lightness of my suitcase as I lift it off the conveyor belt, the answer to that is definitely: no. Great.

Zipping my hoodie up as high as it will go, I wheel my bag out of the terminal and head to the usual Uber pick-up spot, bypassing the stream of Brits joining a taxi queue growing longer by the second.

As I walk, my pocket vibrates. Pulling my phone out, I expect to see a notification telling me the Uber I requested a few moments ago has arrived. Instead, I see one telling me that actually, it's not coming at all. It cancelled on me.

I let out a long sigh and request another one. A few

minutes later, there's another vibration: RIDE CANCELLED. What's going on?

I stop walking and stare down at my phone, my mind suddenly infested by negative thoughts. Fears. Worries.

What am I doing here? I've spent my life savings on this trip and I don't even have a fight lined up. I could have used that money to put a deposit down on a flat or do something useful. Instead, I'm chasing something I don't have any answer for. Something that might not lead me anywhere.

My body decides to join in with the negativity. Tightening my chest. Shortening my breaths. If I don't take control of the situation I know exactly what comes next . . . focus, Rox. And breathe . . .

In for three, out for four. In for three, out for four.

Sitting on a nearby bench I close my eyes and try to stop the tears from gathering beneath my eyelids. I desperately want to call my sister, but it's 5.30 in the morning at home. I can't call her now. Instead, I text Bill – my Muay Thai coach and a man who's been in my life for more than fifteen years: 'I don't know what I'm doing any more. Do I have what it takes?'

SEND MESSAGE.

Staring down at the screen once more, I tell myself he won't reply straight away. But I stare anyway – the screen offers a comforting sense of familiarity compared to the reality around it. No more than thirty seconds later, three flashing dots tell me Bill is awake and typing his response . . .

Another deep breath: in for three, out for four.

'You're in the right place. Think about all the times in the past you felt like this and you came out the other side. This is just another one of those. You'll get through it.'

Sinking back into the bench, I start to notice its hard metal seat chilling me through my jeans. Time to move. I take one more look at Bill's words and start wheeling my case back towards the taxi queue. Uber can do one.

At least the hotel feels familiar. I was in the same one a few months earlier – when the streets were warmed by bright sunshine and the picture in front of me seemed so much clearer. Then, I was building towards my first fight as a professional boxer. I had a manager and support team around me. And in my corner, one of the best boxing trainers in the world: Ismael Salas.

This time, it's just me.

Before going to bed that night, I say a prayer called *Salat al-Istikhara*: the prayer of seeking guidance. I ask God to let me know if I should be here. If it's good for me. Because if not, I will go straight back to the airport in the morning, fly home and be the traditional Bangladeshi daughter my parents always wanted me to be.

The next morning, I turn on the TV and get the direction I asked for.

America's former First Lady, Michelle Obama, is on a breakfast television programme, being interviewed about her time as a student at Princeton University in the early 1980s. I lie in bed and listen as she describes how out of place she felt. How she was judged on her background and the colour of her skin. And how she learned not just to survive, but to thrive in that environment.

I recognise every thought. Every feeling. And the mindset that didn't allow her to give in to them or to change who she was just so that she could 'fit in'.

It's what I've spent most of my life doing.

She came through all of those things to become a leader. Someone who makes a real difference.

As I listen, I understand that my path is leading me towards a similar purpose. That my story can help others to realise that there is no obstacle too high for them to climb. That there is something beautiful we can take even from the darkest moments. That those who persevere will always get to their destination.

Sharing it here is part of that.

My hope is that you will recognise some of your own thoughts and feelings in mine. And understand that if I can overcome these obstacles then there is hope for you, too.

This is my purpose.

Yes, I am meant to be here.

Chapter 1

Shit. Shit shit shit shit shit.

I'd known this moment would come. For three and a half years I'd felt like a fugitive living with the constant fear of capture. But I still felt unprepared for it. What should I say? What *could* I say?

I said nothing. I was frozen. Stuck halfway up the stairs with my father glaring at me from the bottom step.

A few moments earlier, he'd caught me coming home from training, attempting – as I always did – to make it upstairs to the relative safety of my bedroom without being seen.

'Ruqsana, why are you walking like that?'

His voice chased after me as I hurried further up the stairs.

'Like what?' The moment the words came out of my mouth I wanted to suck them back in.

'Like a boxer.'

I'd made it as far as the second to last step when I was paralysed. He knew. Shit.

I turned and stood there, looking at him, my mouth hanging open while my brain searched for a response.

Eventually I turned away – I could never look directly at him when I wasn't being entirely truthful – muttering something about the treadmill and my tired legs. Then I forced myself to move, picking up one leg at a time to inch closer to my room and further away from him.

Fight or flight? Outside of the ring, it's always the latter, especially when it comes to my family. Anything to avoid confrontation.

I don't know if he was still watching me but I made sure to move as calmly as possible, just in case. Internally, I was anything but calm.

A million thoughts whirred around my head. Did he really know? If not, why would he say that? And if he did know, then why not say something?

Back in my room I went straight to my bedside cabinet where I'd hidden my first-ever trophy. It was a golden figure of a boxer standing on a plinth. Beneath the fighter's feet was a silver plate bearing the words:

Ruqsana Begum
U21 Atomweight Champion

What if he had found it? I was so stupid. I should never have brought it home. I found a stash of old plastic bags in my wardrobe and wrapped the trophy in them. Next time I went out it was going straight into the neighbour's dustbin.

'What's that?'

I spun around, clutching what turned out to be a tatty old Tesco bag tight to my chest and glared angrily at my sister. She'd scared the crap out of me.

'It's my room too, you know,' she said, flopping down onto her bed. 'Anyway, what's in the bag?'

Ane (whose full name is Farzana – in our culture we have

a 'passport' name, which is used for formal things, and a nickname that we use at home. So while everyone outside of the family knows me as Ruqsana, at home I'm usually Tanni, or Tan) had known about the Muay Thai right from the start. She's only a year younger than me and we've always been really close. She was my best friend. We told each other everything. Even if that hadn't been the case, sharing a bedroom meant it would have been almost impossible to keep it from her.

I told her what Dad had said. That he must have found the trophy and that I was going to have to give up something that over the last three and a half years had become an important part of my life. An important part of me.

Ane wasn't convinced. 'If he knew, you would already know that he knew. You know?'

As she spoke, Ane came closer and motioned for me to turn around. After every training session she checked me over, looking for any cuts or bruises that I might need to hide from our parents. The backs of my legs were the usual spot – the kicks in Muay Thai can be more brutal than the punches – but they were easy enough to hide with trousers or a long skirt.

My arms often took a battering, too, from blocking the kicks aimed at my body or head. Long sleeves covered them up for most of the year, but in the summer it could be a real struggle. I'd sweat my way through a family meal, dressed for winter when it was 25 degrees outside.

So far, I'd been lucky. I'd never suffered any real facial damage. I often think that's one of the reasons my defence became so good – all I had to do was imagine my father's face when confronted by his daughter's puffed up, battered eye socket and my levels of concentration doubled.

This time, Ane found no visible signs of damage. I was given the all-clear to go downstairs and help Mum with the dinner. As the oldest daughter, I'd always felt it was my responsibility to help around the house, and that feeling was redoubled by my guilt.

In some ways, doing something that I knew went against my parents' wishes actually made me a better daughter. When I wasn't at the boxing gym, I was either in lectures at uni, studying in the library or doing chores around the house. No socialising, no partying, no boyfriends.

Outside of the ring, I was the perfect daughter.

Chapter 2

It all started a few years earlier, at KO gym in Punderson's Gardens.

Except that it didn't. Not really.

Where it really started is about a ten-minute bus ride from the sweaty stench of KO, inside a three-bedroom flat on Tapp Street in Bethnal Green. That was the Begum family home. The only home I knew for the first sixteen years of my life. And the home where my uncle Surath would often spend his Saturday nights, staying over after finishing work at a restaurant in town.

One Sunday morning, when I was about eight years old, I woke to find him watching something on our TV that I'd never seen before. It looked like people fighting, but it was more about movement than violence. More about speed. Balance. Awareness.

I was captivated.

Uncle Surath was a massive Bruce Lee fan, and from then on, so was I (although I didn't exactly know it at the time). It got logged somewhere in my brain as something intriguing.

As I got older, I'd flick through our local newspaper – *East End Life* – looking for snippets on martial arts. I don't think I really knew why, or what I was looking for. I just knew I was attracted to the words and the pictures that went with them. I wanted to know more, but I had no idea about how I could do it, nor did I think my parents would ever really allow me to find out.

Aside from the wonders of Bruce Lee, the flat in Bethnal Green was where I also learned the meaning of the word 'sacrifice'. Not because myself, my sister Ane, or my three brothers, Moynul, Mosh and Eklim, were left wanting for anything (well, aside from the things we didn't actually need, like designer clothes or the latest video games), but because that was where I watched my parents put everything they had into giving us the best life they possibly could.

That included giving up their own bedroom. Try dividing five kids, two grandparents and two parents into a three-bedroom flat . . . something has to give, right? For my parents, it was their bedroom, which they gave up to my younger brothers Mosh and Eklim. My sister and I had one of the other rooms and the third bedroom was shared by my paternal grandparents and eldest brother Moynul. All of which left Mum (Minara) and Dad (Awlad) sleeping on sofabeds in the living room (occasionally joined by Uncle Surath).

Now, I look back and wonder how we lived like that for so many years, but at the time it didn't seem that hard. Most of my friends were living in the same circumstances, so it was all I knew.

The only thing I really hated about it was the cold. Some of the flats in our building – including ours – had one room that was cantilevered, meaning it actually sat outside of the building structure. I suppose they wanted to make the block look attractive or different from the other council flats around us, but for those of us on the inside, it had a major downside: that room was freezing.

That was the room I shared with my sister. Even though we slept in the same bed, I'd wake up every morning with blocks of ice instead of feet. And when the temperatures got really low, I'd wake up with a nose bleed.

But it was home, and there was a lot I liked about it, too. For a start, it was right next door to our primary school, which meant Mum didn't have to walk us there. And we had a playground just outside where I'd spend hours riding my bike and playing. But once I got to about ten years old, Mum put a stop to that.

Playing with boys? Not any more. As the eldest daughter, I had to be the responsible one. My brother Moynul – the eldest boy – had responsibility, but my family wanted to give him all the opportunity, too. The traditional way of thinking is that: he's the male, he needs to really do well for himself. Whereas with the female, they're not really as concerned because they think: you're going to have someone else to look after you.

It was also my responsibility to set an example for my younger sister. We're only a year apart but the rules for Ane turned out to be pretty different from those for me.

You wouldn't think it to look at me now, but I was the one who grew too tall, too soon. While Ane was very skinny, I was an early developer – and the 'chubby' one – something that put the fear of Allah into my parents when I reached my teenage years. 'Cover your hair, cover your bum ... cover your boobs.'

I wanted to wear jeans and leggings and whatever my friends at school were wearing. But Mum liked me in long dresses with trousers or leggings underneath. If I had a shirt on, I needed a scarf around my neck to cover it. If I wore jogging bottoms, I needed a long jacket or shirt on to go over my bum.

It was part of our culture to cover up, I knew that. But having been called 'chubby' from about the age of five, it made me feel even more conscious of my body shape than I already was. My parents never used that word, but my brothers did, and so did my uncles.

I always felt like I was too big. Even as a teenager at school my friends – who were all slimmer than me – would point out the size of my thighs or my 'big bum'. I was so conscious of it. And every time my parents told me to 'cover up' it only intensified that feeling. The image of beauty in our culture was of someone who was petite, light-skinned and had sleek, straight hair.

Well, two of those three things definitely did not apply to me. My hair has always been naturally curly. My mum used to call it 'bird's nest hair' and tell me I should oil it to get it looking more like my sister's straighter hair. I would do it occasionally and, as I got older, I did try to straighten it when I could be bothered.

But when I was at university, I did something that I knew would not go down well: I cut my hair short, into a bob. I knew Mum was going to come down hard on me but getting into trouble for a few days was a price I was willing to pay. Shorter hair was in fashion and I wanted to see what it would be like to have mine short.

Mum wasn't happy: 'It's not very ladylike ... you don't look nice with that hair.'

Even now, she doesn't like my hair curly. But the difference is that as I've grown older, I've learned to love it. I've realised that it makes me unique. I am Bangladeshi, but I have attributes and features that aren't typical in our population, and that's not something I have to be ashamed or embarrassed about – I'm proud to be different.

That goes for my body shape too. It took a long time for me to rid my mind of those insecurities, though. And although I didn't recognise it at the time, it was a process that started when I first walked into a Muay Thai gym and began a journey of learning about what my body could do. As I improved and my confidence in the gym grew, it started to have a knock-on effect on how I felt outside of the gym, too. I started to see the benefits of having bigger, stronger legs and larger shoulders than more petite girls. I started to feel: *I'm made for this. I'm built for it.*

Over time, my belief systems changed. That doesn't mean I don't still have those moments – like we all do – when I look in the mirror and think my shoulders are too big or my legs too bulky. And there are still times when I'll get comments from women such as: 'You've got large shoulders . . .', which I'm never too sure how to take. But I just remind myself that, actually, these are my weapons. These are what helped me to become a world champion.

If someone tries to knock me out, my strong legs are going to hold me in place. And these shoulders are strong enough to keep my punches flowing for as long as necessary to get the victory.

In society we're constantly bombarded with images of what beauty 'should' look like and sometimes it's hard to fight against that. But whenever those thoughts come into my head, I shut them down. Because I know that, actually, I am beautiful. I know who I am and I love myself. It has taken time for me to get to this place, but now I'm here I can tell you it makes you feel so much happier and more confident in yourself.

Aside from the 'chubby' label I picked up as a child, I was fortunate to grow up in an extremely loving household. A huge part of that was down to my grandparents who, in some ways, were actually more modern than my parents.

My grandfather first came to England to fight for the British Army during the Second World War, and, afterwards, he brought my grandmother over from Bangladesh to join him. They lived all over London but really loved the time they spent in Marble Arch. My grandmother's face would light up every time she told me about the times she and my grandfather went out to the cinema or to walk around Hyde Park.

They weren't like a traditional Bangladeshi couple – they were genuinely in love. My parents love each other too, but it's in a different way. My grandparents were in love in a way that you could *see*. Bengali couples tend not to really show their spouse how they feel, but my grandfather didn't care: he loved my grandmother and he was never afraid to show it.

He was the same with his grandchildren. We were his world. He would take us to Victoria Park and kick a ball around with us. Or to Green Street (a famous Asian shopping area in east London) where he would take my grandmother every so often to buy a new sari. And every day he'd come back from mosque with chocolate bars – Aeros or Whispas – anything that came in a pack of five, so that there was always enough for all of us.

We had a lot of love growing up. I've always been grateful

for that. Some of my friends didn't have the same kind of love – not from their parents or their grandparents. Even years later, when my grandfather became ill with kidney problems, he was still determined to make his grandchildren happy.

I remember when my youngest brother Mosh wanted a pair of Nike trainers that were about £80. He asked my father for the money and, of course, he said no. So Mosh went straight to my grandfather. At that time he was really ill – housebound, in fact – but he didn't want to say no, so he called my father into his room, gave him his bank card and asked if he would go to the cashpoint for him.

'Why? What do you need money for?'

'Mosh. He needs shoes.'

Now, my father smiles when he remembers that story – his heart warmed by the memory of the lengths his own father would go to for his grandchildren. But at the time, he definitely wasn't smiling . . .

My grandmother wasn't quite as soft a touch; you couldn't get anything past her. I remember my sister coming home from college one afternoon and walking into the living room. Before she had even put down her bag, my grandmother said: 'You had your hair cut at Toni & Guy and you spent £70.'

She knew everything. When I was at college, I had a summer job working in a sports shop on Oxford Street and some nights I wouldn't get home until around midnight. The first time it happened, my father went crazy: 'You don't finish work at twelve o'clock, what are you talking about? All the shops close at seven o'clock.'

'No,' said my grandmother, 'not in the West End.'

She knew.

My parents were so different. I don't think my mum even

knew what Toni & Guy was and, still today, she has never been to the cinema. Although she did discover YouTube recently, and is now addicted to the cooking channels.

Sometimes I wonder if that difference comes down to the fact that my parents were the next generation on from the ones who first left Bangladesh. Maybe they felt as though they were drifting further away from their culture and wanted to do whatever they could to hold on tight to it. Maybe they were scared of losing their identity.

I was around eighteen months old when my grandfather decided to go back to Bangladesh for a while. He still had three daughters in the country (my aunties) and wanted to build a family home there in case my parents ever decided to move back. But he found it hard to leave his grandchildren behind for so long, so he asked my parents if he could take one of us with him.

At that time, there were three of us – my eldest brother Moynul, me and Ane, who was only around six months old. I was the chosen one.

For the next nine months I resided in Bangladesh, cared for by my grandparents, aunties and uncles. The one memory I have that has always stuck with me is from the day I heard the distinctive sound of a rickshaw coming down our road, accompanied by a less familiar noise: ding, ding, ding. I ran to the gate, knowing it was about the time my grandfather would be coming home, and found him with a present for me – my first bicycle!

By the time I started school, I'd been back in England for a couple of years, but my English still wasn't as good as some of my friends'. At home, we spoke mostly Bengali – my grandmother got offended if we spoke anything else – and the community we lived in was predominantly Bengali. So, I never really had to speak English that often.

That didn't change much even once I started school. Most of the kids there were Bengali too – it was just the teachers and a small number of pupils who weren't. I found English harder to pick up than some of my friends, though – maybe because I'd spent those nine months in Bangladesh at such a young age. For the first few months, my friends would often have to translate what the teacher was saying for me.

These days, it's the opposite – my struggle is to communicate with my parents in Bengali. I speak it so infrequently now that I find I can't express myself as well as I can in English. So, I'll often talk to them in a mixture of the two.

My father's English isn't too bad because he's had his own business – he used to make leather jackets for big brands like Topshop – and has had to communicate with a wide range of people. But my mum hasn't had that opportunity so her English isn't as strong. Outside of our community, she knows our neighbours, but, really, that's about it. She did sign up for an English course once, but it got put on the backburner because my grandmother still needed a lot of looking after and Mum felt she couldn't take the time to do it. I'm hoping she will go back to it one day.

Like I said, our primary school was right next door to where we lived. So close that Mum could keep an eye on us in the playground at breaktimes. It was there, outside of the classroom, that I really came into my own. I tried in lessons, but it sometimes felt like I had to work twice as hard to get a grade half as good as my siblings.

It was only years later, when I was in college, that I found out why that might have been – I am dyslexic. But at school, they just thought I wasn't as smart as Ane or my brothers. I struggled with reading and writing – sometimes the words would just come out in the wrong order. It was the same with numbers, too.

When it came to doing my GCSEs, the teachers decided they couldn't put me into the higher tier for maths, so they put me into the lower tier, where the highest mark I could get was a D. I knew I was capable of doing better than that, and I really wanted to get all A to C passes. So, I resat it as soon as I could, which was in my first year at college, and got my C grade. A few years later, I was doing some pretty high-level mathematics as part of my architecture degree – presumably something my schoolteachers would never have thought me capable of either.

It was quite a relief when I was actually diagnosed as dyslexic – I knew I wasn't as dumb as people thought, I just needed the right support. But I never really shook off that feeling; never rid myself of the voice in my head: *They don't think you can do it. No one believes in you.*

Even later on, when I was doing my A-levels, I think my family thought: what's she doing? Okay, if she wants to go to university, let her. If she can finance it herself, just let her get on with it. I was sure they all thought I was going to fail because I wasn't smart like my older brother Moynul, or as street smart as others in the family. I was just someone who had to work really hard.

Growing up, my view of myself was always: I'm not good enough.

Looking back, maybe that's one of the reasons I've always been so determined to prove everyone else wrong – so willing to push through the difficult times to find the better ones.

Inside and outside of the ring, I've always had that voice in my head reminding me of just how good it will feel to show the doubters what I'm really capable of.

The playground was the one place where I felt differently, especially at school. There, I was just as good as everyone else. Actually, I was better. I was the fastest girl in my year and used to love playing football with the boys at breaktimes. I wasn't one of the 'popular' kids, but I was good at sport, which in many ways was just as good. I was one of the few girls in my school who the boys wanted on their team during PE lessons and on sports day.

When the Spice Girls emerged a few years later, that meant I automatically became Sporty Spice among my group of friends. And that was fine by me. I always thought she was the best one anyway.

At the end of the school day, my learning continued at the East London Mosque. I was about nine years old when my grandfather enrolled us there and we started going most evenings after school. There, my siblings and I joined a huge group of kids for a two-hour lesson that mostly seemed to consist of learning verses from the Quran and doing recitations.

I hated it. Mostly because the teachers used to carry this little stick around with them, and if you didn't get the read-ings right, they'd hit you on the hand with it. I always felt that was unfair – I wasn't *trying* to forget the words; I just had a bad memory.

It didn't help that I never really understood what I was reading. So I could never become interested in the passages or learn anything from them. I was just committing them to memory (trying to, anyway).

As a child, that's what religion was to me – something I had to learn, but never fully understood. I actually used to go to school thinking, *I wish I wasn't Muslim*, because it felt like something that was imposed on me – not something I was actually a part of, or that was part of me.

When I moved on to Swanlea secondary school my parents were keen for me to start wearing a hijab (headscarf). It was never something they forced on me, but I wanted to please my mother (and I don't like confrontation), so sometimes I'd leave home with it wrapped loosely around my head. Of course, once I actually got to school it was straight onto my shoulders – or stuffed in my backpack.

That first year, I was still what I guess you'd call a tomboy – playing with the boys and being 'Sporty Spice' with my female friends. But it was then that I first started to feel a sense of being dragged in two different directions. At home I was very Bangladeshi. That meant being respectful. Being very honest. Helping my mum cook. Not really having a life outside of the house. Studying hard, but not being overly ambitious. And probably getting married once I reached my early twenties. That was how I envisioned being a 'good Bangladeshi daughter'.

But in school the message was different. We were supposed to be ambitious. Encouraged to follow our dreams and be who we wanted to be. I felt like all those things contradicted each other. Like I was living in two separate worlds, and I had no idea how they could possibly fit together.

But towards the end of my first year at Swanlea, one of those worlds started to come into sharper focus, and present me with a sense of direction I'd never had before. A sense of purpose. A sense of who I thought I really was.

I found the Prayer Room by accident, really. It was in the music corridor where I used to go for my weekly violin lesson, but I'd never ventured inside it until this particular afternoon when circumstances – mostly my violin tutor running late – led me to do just that. While I was standing around in the corridor waiting for him, I saw a girl I knew – she was a teaching assistant who worked with a disabled boy in my class. I gave her a little smile as she went into the room next door and she beckoned me in.

There weren't many people in there. Maybe two or three other pupils and an older Muslim woman who seemed to be leading the conversation. It was one I couldn't help but be drawn into (silently, that is). I stood just a few inches inside the doorway and listened as this small group discussed religion and God. But this wasn't like any religious discussion I'd ever heard before. They were talking about whether God actually existed. I'd never thought about that before, and I'd certainly never allowed myself to question it.

I wasn't raised to ask those kinds of questions. I was raised to think: I'm Muslim, I follow Islam and that's it. You don't ask questions. If we did ask anything as kids, we got told off because you were meant to 'just do it'. But here it was being encouraged. Recommended, even.

I was twelve years old and following Islam, because that's what made my parents happy, but in terms of actual belief, I wasn't quite sure if I believed in anything at that point.

I only stayed by the doorway for a few minutes, but it was long enough to spark my curiosity. I wanted to know: is there a God? And, if there is, then why does he punish people?

I went back to the Prayer Room at lunchtime a few days later. They were discussing something different, but the openness was still there. Questions were encouraged. Opinions allowed. For the first time, I felt like I was really learning about and understanding my religion.

I fell completely in love with it. Everything I'd learned from my parents about Islam had been: 'Do this' and 'Don't do that'. My parents had simply taught me what they themselves had been taught: to blindly follow. Whereas now, I was asking the right questions and finding out so much more as a result. A whole new world opened up to me. And it wasn't about 'doing' or following instructions. It wasn't about blind faith. It was saying: God wants you to ask questions. God wants you to find out what it's all about.

Over time, it led to a realisation: I did believe. For me that meant I needed to start praying. I'd pray as soon as I woke up for school, then in the Prayer Room at lunchtime, again when I got home from school and then once more before I went to bed. If I ever did miss one, I'd always make it up. I was more observant than my family. My parents were thrilled (apart from those times I took it a bit far and would say things like: 'Mum, can you do this properly please?' or 'This is not how you pray').

From the start of the next school year, I decided to wear the hijab. The sisters encouraged me to, and I felt that, as a good Muslim, it was something I should do. Mum and Dad were so proud. They could hardly believe it when my sister started wearing one too – her enthusiasm for it only lasted about a term, though.

At school, I started to isolate myself from the boys. I asked the head teacher if we could have separate PE lessons, and would sit by myself in class if I had to, just to avoid getting involved in any of the sexual jokes teenagers like to throw around. I didn't want to feel like I was doing anything wrong. I was so caught up in the religion and what I was learning that when the sisters started talking about what was expected of me as a Muslim, I accepted it. I was young and passionate about what I'd found. I didn't want to put it at risk.

It took me a few years to realise that this path I was on wasn't mine. To understand that, actually, I am human – God is not going to be angry with me for doing PE lessons with boys or sharing a joke with my schoolfriends. The sisters were expecting me to be in a place that I wasn't ready for.

By the time I went to college, I'd started to feel like a hypocrite for wearing the hijab. I hadn't put it on out of my own desire. I'd put it on to fit in. Gradually, I wore it less and less. I'd find excuses like 'my scarf doesn't go with it' when going to a wedding where my mum wanted me to wear a beautiful outfit. Other times I would wear it, but not fully. Not really tight.

My father was heartbroken. He'd been so proud of his daughter, teaching him and my mum things that even they didn't know about our religion. I felt like a disappointment. But I also knew that I'd found my own path. I'd come to understand that God doesn't judge you based on what you're wearing; it's about the intention behind it.

But when I took the scarf off, the Muslim sisters I'd become so enamoured of completely lost contact with me. It felt as if they'd judged me. And that taught me something valuable: that people portray Islam in different ways and you can't judge it on their beliefs or actions. It took time, but eventually I became comfortable with the fact that I was still a good person and still making the right steps to get close to God. I just felt that wearing the hijab didn't make any difference for me – I was still me. I was still a good person. Still a good daughter. Still respectful. Still praying.

Others will feel differently, and that's completely understandable too. You have to find your own lane – one where you are comfortable.

I don't feel any resentment towards the sisters. I'm actually grateful to them in a way, because even though I missed out on some of those teenage years, that period in my life helped to make me who I am today. It taught me principles and values. Gave me resilience and inner strength.

Little did I know then just how much I would need all these things, as I climbed the ladder of a sport where people like me (female, Muslim) were a rarity. Indeed, it's only in recent years that I've come to understand what those things really mean. And how they have made my journey a far more positive one than it might have been.

Chapter 3

'I want to train. I want to be a fighter.'

As the words came out of my mouth, I could see Bill's brain whirring. He was sitting in his office upstairs at the KO gym in Punderson's Gardens when I knocked on his door. When he'd asked: 'How can I help you?', I don't think my statement was quite what he was expecting.

I can't blame him. At that time, it was pretty rare to see a female in his gym, let alone one like me: a 5ft 3in Asian girl wearing baggy tracksuit bottoms, an oversized long-sleeved top and a scarf wrapped around my head like a bandana.

'You want to train here?'

He pointed incredulously to the room below us that housed a sweat-stained boxing ring, a collection of decaying heavy bags and a pile of gloves that had been used so many times they sagged open, waiting for the next sweaty hand to be inserted.

The doors to this world – one that I never imagined being allowed to enter – had cracked open a few weeks earlier, when I'd seen a sign pinned to the notice board at my college: 'Try Thai Boxing! Thursday 4 p.m. in the gym'.

I had to go.

That morning I told Mum I was going shopping with a friend after college – I hated lying to them but there was no way my parents would approve of me doing something that was so male-dominated. And it was just this once. I walked the 2 miles to college with an excited buzz in my stomach. I had no idea if I'd like it, or even if I'd be any good at it, but at least I was finally going to get to try it.

By 3.45 I was already in the gym and ready to go. I was also the only one there . . .

Bang on four o'clock, a young-ish guy, in his mid-thirties, walked in wearing a black adidas tracksuit – hardly the bright-yellow jumpsuit I remembered Bruce Lee wearing. But the bag of gloves and boxing pads he was carrying confirmed it: this was the coach. By then there were around six of us all nervously shifting from one foot to the other as we waited to see what he had in store for us.

For the first fifteen minutes or so, it was mostly sitting while Kru Zeeshan (*kru* means teacher in Thai) told us about the history of Muay Thai: how it was originally designed as a warfare art by the Thais, who used it to defend their country. Why it's known as 'the art of eight limbs' (you can strike your opponent with punches, kicks, elbows and knees) and what it looks like in full flow: 'It's full pace, full speed, full power.'

There was so much to learn.

The rest of the session was spent mastering the basics, starting with our fighting stance: 'Get this right and everything should flow from there. Get it wrong and you'll always be off balance and out of position.

'Feet slightly wider than shoulder width apart. Dominant foot half a step back. The other foot half a step forward. Knees slightly bent. Weight on the balls of your feet.'

I listened intently as Kru Zeeshan talked us through it.

'Now, bring your fists up to your cheekbones, keeping your wrists straight, knuckles facing outwards and palms facing in. If you're right-handed, you should have your left foot and hand set forward, with your right side ready to throw the more powerful shots. If you're left-handed then . . . yep, you guessed it, it's the other way around.

'From here, you should feel in complete control of your weight and able to attack, defend or move out of your opponent's line of attack without losing your balance.'

Standing there with my hands raised up to my face and my feet ready to kick out, I felt powerful. Like I was in control.

Next up: how to actually throw a punch.

'Remember, any strike comes from the ground – not from your arm or your shoulder, but from the earth.'

Zeeshan explained how we had to transfer the force from the ground, up through our legs and into the hips, which twist to increase the power of a strike from any of the eight points.

His eyes scanned our small group of confused-looking schoolgirls, then settled on me: 'What's your name?'

'Rox . . . Ruqsana.'

'Okay, Rox, come up here and hold this pad for me, so I can demonstrate how to throw a jab.'

He wasn't a huge guy, but he certainly had quite a few inches on my 5ft 3in frame . . .

'Okay, hold the pads up a bit, Rox, and set your feet in the position I showed you earlier. Don't want you flying backwards across the gym now.'

I smiled nervously, got into the position he described and waited. I was watching his left hand all the time, but it came shooting out towards the pad so quickly it was like my brain didn't have time to react to what my eyes had seen. Before I knew it, his jab landed hard, sending me stumbling backwards, just as he had warned.

Zeeshan apologised profusely, but I felt like I was the one who should have been saying sorry. I'd messed up.

'Do it again,' I said, setting my feet once more and this time bracing myself for the shot.

'Next time, Rox. Now it's your turn.'

Zeeshan put us into pairs: one held the pads while the other practised throwing the jab and then we'd swap. None of us could get it to make the same sharp sound as Zeeshan's had, though – his was like a gunshot. Ours were more like the faint thud of someone punching into a pillow.

In the final part of the session he showed us one more punch: the cross. A power punch that starts right from the toes of your back foot, and travels through that hip to explode into your opponent (or a pad, in our case) with as much force as you can generate.

I held the pads first and watched as my partner struggled to get her timing right. It was like her toe, hip and arm were acting completely independently of one another. Instead of forming one fluid motion, they created something jerky and forced – and powerless.

My turn. As I took the gloves from my partner and pulled them on, I visualised the way Zeeshan looked when he demonstrated the shot. The way his back foot pivoted. The speed with which his hip twisted inwards. The effortless way his fist followed, producing a crack that echoed around the gym.

I set up my feet, lifted my back heel off the ground and

twisted, throwing my right fist towards the pad as hard as I could.

Thud.

I left my hand out there for a moment, confused. Why hadn't my noise matched up to Zeeshan's?

'Relax your shoulders, Rox. You're forcing it. Don't think about throwing the shot with your shoulder or your arm, think about throwing it from the hip . . .'

Okay. Shake out the arms. Drop the shoulders. Reset.

CRACK!

Wow. That was weird. I threw my arm out with nowhere near as much force as I had the first time, but it hit the pad with twice the power. Zeeshan walked over, grinning proudly: 'See? That's what happens when you stay relaxed.'

My face too was fixed in a broad smile. I wanted to go again. And again. And again. But all too soon it was over. The session had come to an end and Zeeshan was stuffing the pads and gloves back into his bag.

'When's the next session?' I asked, reluctantly pulling off my gloves.

'Actually, this is the last one.'

I stood there looking at him. How could it be the last one? I'd only just discovered it. Zeeshan told me the school had said they didn't have the funding to pay for his sessions any more, so he wouldn't be coming back. I was devastated.

Seeing the look on my face, Zeeshan reached into his pocket and pulled out a business card with the name of his Muay Thai gym on it. Handing it to me he said: 'Why don't you come along to a few sessions? It's not that far from here.'

I was desperate to say yes, but I knew I could never afford to pay for something like that. Wouldn't I have to be a member?

'Don't worry about that,' he said, picking up his kit bag and walking a few steps towards the door before looking back over his shoulder: 'Just come along and I'll look after you.'

On the walk home, I pulled out Zeeshan's card and looked at the words embossed on it in bright-red lettering: WARRIOR MUAY THAI: THAI BOXING GYM OF CHAMPIONS! I had to go, but there was no way Mum and Dad would let me and I didn't want to lie to them again. I'd felt guilty all day after telling Mum I was shopping so that I could go to Zeeshan's class. I wasn't sure I wanted that feeling again.

At home I went straight to my room to change and found Ane in there, lying on her bed reading a magazine and chain-eating strawberry laces (our sweet tooth is one of the few things we have in common). She looked up mid-chew: 'Where've you been?'

I told her about Zeeshan and the Muay Thai, how I'd learned to throw a punch and that I was gutted it was something I wasn't going to get to do again because of the school's funding issues. I spat it all out, threw myself down onto Ane's bed next to her and took a strawberry lace from the paper bag.

'You said this guy has his own gym, right?'

'Yeah.'

'So, why don't you go?'

'How can I? Mum will never let me . . .'

'You don't have to tell her, you know? Just make something up, like you did today.'

My parents were always much more lenient with Ane than with me. I was the eldest daughter – so I was the one expected to be the role model – while she could get away with wearing and doing things I never could. In some ways

I guess that made her a bit braver when it came to pushing the boundaries.

There were times when Mum would ask us to bring something back from the supermarket on our way home from school and both of us would forget. I'd be the one saying: 'We better go back and get it.' Ane would be the one saying: 'Don't worry about it. We'll just tell her they ran out . . .'

We've always been super-close, though. We're in our thirties now but we still speak on the phone every other night. I think it's because we are so different that, even though we're only a year apart in age, there has never been any competitiveness between us. She has always supported my journey and I hers.

Ane convinced me that I should go to Zeeshan's gym, just to see what it was all about and if it was something I really wanted to do. But there was no way I felt ready to go that weekend – I needed a bit of time to build up to it. To get my head straight and to figure out how I was going to get out of the flat without arousing suspicion.

The following weekend was the one. On Sunday morning I made sure I was up early enough to help Mum with the housework. I cleaned the bathroom. Chopped vegetables. Did the washing-up. Hoovered the entire flat. By 11 a.m. everything was done. I took a deep breath:

'Mum, can I go to the gym?'

It wasn't something I'd ever asked before, but it also wasn't that strange coming from me. I'd always been the sporty one in the family (along with my younger brother Mosh, who loves football), and this was just me saying that I wanted to be a bit more active – now I was doing my A-levels, it wasn't like I had PE lessons to go to any more.

It wasn't really a lie. I just didn't specify what type of gym I was going to. I guess Mum just thought I was going to the gym to run on a treadmill or sit on an exercise bike. She looked a little surprised but said okay. Seeing as I had done everything else, I could go for an hour or so.

Warrior Muay Thai was only a ten-minute walk away from the flat, so by midday I was already standing outside a shabby-looking building that gave no clue as to what lay behind its corrugated-metal door. The number and street name matched those on Zeeshan's card, though. It had to be the right place.

I looked around me to see if there was anyone else heading this way. Anyone who might give me some clue as to whether I was right. There was not a soul in sight. But I did start to hear a noise – a rhythmic *tap, tap, tap* – coming from inside. Once it started, it didn't stop. Gradually the taps speeded up, getting faster and faster until they were so close together they emerged as one constant *tapppppppppppppppppp*.

I pushed open the door, stepped inside and saw a tall, muscled figure through the blur of a skipping rope whipping swiftly around him. Before I could take in anything more, I was struck by a stench so thick it felt like it was stuck in the back of my throat. I coughed.

The tapping stopped. The source of it was glaring at me: he looked a few years older than me and was wearing all black – the only splashes of colour coming from the red Warrior logo on his t-shirt and the whiteness of his bare legs and feet.

'Yeah?'

'Is Zeeshan here? I'm here for the class.'

He raised his eyes upwards, towards a mezzanine level.

'Thanks.'

Tap, tap, tap, tap. He was clearly done talking to me. I watched for a moment, captivated by the way the skipping rope seemed to pass just millimetres beneath the soles of his bare feet, before making my way towards the staircase at the back of the gym. My nostrils were gradually coming to terms with the smell, but it was still pungent enough to taste. I tried to take fewer breaths, holding each one for longer than usual. The only problem with that was that I ended up gulping in a giant mouthful of stale air every time my lungs required refilling.

The gym was dimly lit and made darker still by black rubber mats covering the floor and walls plastered in old fight posters. The ring in the centre of the gym provided the only spot of brightness, courtesy of its white ropes and blue canvas. As I passed around its perimeter, I noticed a collection of spots spattered across the ring's canvas – dry blood.

As I climbed the stairs, I heard muffled voices. There wasn't much space up there but once at the top I saw there were three rooms. The doors to two of them were propped open, allowing me to peer inside. One was a small changing room that probably had just enough space for two people (providing they knew each other pretty well). The other was a shower room – home to a few filthy-looking towels and a collection of half-empty shower gel bottles. It clearly hadn't seen a bottle of bleach in years. Maybe ever.

The third room, where the voices were coming from, had its door firmly shut. I knocked.

'Yeah?'

I went in to find Zeeshan sitting behind a desk opposite a guy I didn't know. In between them was a pile of paperwork.

'Oh hi. It's Rox, isn't it?'

I nodded.

'Well, you're a bit early for the class. It doesn't start until 2 p.m.'

There was no way I could stay that long. Mum was expecting me home in an hour.

'Oh, okay. I'll come back next week,' I said, stepping back towards the doorway.

'Great,' said Zeeshan. 'Though I should probably tell you that I'm selling the gym.' He looked at the guy sitting opposite him. 'I'll still be here for a few weeks, though, while we finalise the details, so come down and train. Beginners' sessions are Wednesday night at seven or Sunday, two o'clock.'

As he was talking, I could feel my eyes watering. Maybe I just wasn't meant to do this. Maybe this was a sign that I should be at home with my family, not wasting my time in a dark hole of a gym trying not to breathe in its toxic fumes.

I left quickly, thankful to get back outside into the fresher air, and started walking slowly back home. My brain was in a whirl. Maybe I could go back at two o'clock ... nah, that was stupid. Making it there once was pushing it. Twice in one day would be impossible.

By the time I got home, my mindset had changed. Of course I was going back – just not today. I'd go again next Sunday. While Zeeshan was still there I should make the most of it. Who knew what the next coach would be like. Maybe he wasn't even planning to keep it as a Muay Thai gym. I cursed myself for not asking the question.

The following Sunday I repeated my routine of waking early, helping Mum with all the chores and then asking if I could go to the gym a bit later in the afternoon. Walking back into the gym a week later, this time I was prepared for the smell, but it still felt like my nostrils had been assaulted as soon as the door opened.

Putting my bag down next to a poster advertising a fight from 1995, I cast my eyes around the room. There were six guys there all busy either wrapping their hands, skipping or shadow boxing. So much for 'beginners'. I started to think I was going to be the only girl there, but just as the class was about to start, another one walked in. She was about 4 inches taller than me, a good few kilos heavier, and made her way straight to the opposite side of the room from where I was loitering.

Not up for a chat, then.

A few minutes later, Zeeshan appeared from upstairs. I made a beeline for him and asked if he would show me how to apply the hand wraps everyone else was wearing. He grabbed a pair that were hanging over the side of the ring and started winding one around my left hand and wrist. It was cold, and still damp from the sweat of the last person who'd worn it.

'Yeah, you might want to get a pair of your own,' smiled Zeeshan. 'At least then you know they're clean. And if they're not, then at least it's only your own sweat.'

He took me over to four punchbags of varying shapes and sizes that were lined up on the other side of the ring and showed me a few simple drills using the two punches – the jab and the cross – we'd learned at college.

'What about the class?' I asked.

'Maybe in a few weeks,' he said, glancing over at the others getting warmed up. 'Let's get you up to speed with the basics before we chuck you in with that lot.'

For the next two Sundays, that was my remit: throwing

shots on the bags and observing the rest of the class whenever I took a breather, which was frequently. And every now and again Zeeshan would come over to give me some pointers and encouragement. I found it so satisfying – working hard on the bags, trying to recreate the *CRACK!* of the power shot I'd thrown during my first session. My whole week was spent looking forward to that one hour on Sunday afternoon.

But those feelings of excitement and anticipation were always accompanied by another feeling. One that sat deep in my stomach and gave me a sense of uneasiness about what I was doing. It came from a question that I didn't know how to answer: was I allowed to do this? Of course, I already knew that my parents wouldn't be happy about it. But what about my faith? I'd learned so much about my religion during my early teenage years and felt like my faith was a big part of me.

What if doing Muay Thai – the dress code, the mentality of being violent towards another person – was something that went against the principles of being a Muslim? Something that violated the principles that are an integral part of who I am? The debate raged in my head in between each session. I'd spend hours going back and forth in my own mind about whether I was doing something inherently wrong. Something that went against the things I valued most in life.

If I'd known for sure that it was wrong then I probably would have walked away. Because if I do something that goes against my values, then who am I? But because I wasn't sure, there were so many grey areas in my head.

It was hard to put the debate to the back of my mind – it was there every day, eating away at me. But every day, I talked to myself, trying to give myself the courage and wisdom to carry on. I saw the sport as an art. A game of chess. And I could already feel how happy it was making me when I was there learning so many new skills. I was in love with it.

It would take years before I was able to accept that I wasn't doing anything wrong. Until then, it was something that ate away at me, always.

My third visit to KO was different to the previous two. I arrived to find a massive banner stuck to the wall above the doorway reading: KO MUAY THAI. Warrior was gone. Zeeshan, the man I had to thank for getting me started, whose support had been crucial, had sold up. I stood outside, unsure of what to do. Zeeshan had never asked me for any money for the class – maybe because he knew he was leaving – but the new owner didn't know me. He had no reason to help me out.

I couldn't bring myself to walk away, though.

Inside, nothing had changed except there were only a handful of fighters there warming up. Certainly fewer than there had been for Zeeshan's sessions. I put my bag down in the usual spot and looked upstairs. There was a light on in the office.

I went up and knocked on the door. The man inside was Bill, someone who would become one of the most important people in my life. But at the time, he was just a middle-aged man with the whitest hair I'd ever seen and a stern expression.

'How can I help you?'

His face suggested he didn't really want to help me at all.

I said the first thing that came into my head: 'I want to train. I want to be a fighter.'

The words took me by surprise a little, but saying them out loud felt good. It felt right. I *did* want to be a fighter. I wanted to learn how to move and control my body like I'd seen Bruce Lee do in the films Uncle Surath watched. I wanted to feel that sense of power and confidence that had flooded through me when I landed that right hand in my first class with Zeeshan. And I wanted to do something that took me far away from that traditional Bangladeshi girl I had to be at home – something that felt more 'me'.

Bill looked a little uncertain about my declaration, but I explained that I'd been going along for the last few weeks and was happy just hitting the bags. He didn't have to train me (i.e. please, please don't ask me for money . . .). There was a softening in his face. It wasn't a smile, but something just gave me the sense he was intrigued by this young, fragile-looking female who wanted to spend her Sunday afternoons in his gym.

Knowing Bill the way I do now, I understand what that look on his face was. It was recognition. Recognition of everything I had already overcome to walk in there. Recognition of the guts it took to say those words to him. Recognition of someone who was prepared to push the boundaries and step outside of their comfort zone into an extremely challenging one. He saw someone who went against all the norms and boundaries of the macho world of Muay Thai – size, shape, culture, gender, age – and yet looked him straight in the eye and said: I want to be a part of it. I want to train. I want to fight.

For the first few weeks, Bill mostly left me to it. I started saving up my pocket money so that I could at least give him something after the sessions, but every time I looked for him to pay, he'd disappear. And whenever I did see him to offer, he'd just say: 'Don't worry. Pay me next time.'

He'd always come over for a little chat at some point during my session, though. It unnerved me a little to start with: why is this man talking to me? I just want to train. But as time went on, I realised he was interested in me. I got to learn a bit about him, too. He'd travelled the world, studying the arts of judo, kickboxing and Muay Thai under the guidance of the most respected Masters. Been a world champion. Trained countless world champions and amateur gold medallists.

He knew about other cultures. Other traditions. When he spoke, I learned to listen – even if it was sometimes not what I wanted to hear.

Bill's sessions were two hours long, but I was the only one he ever allowed to leave after an hour, because he knew I had given my word to my mum that I wouldn't be gone for too long. But one week, when I was packing up my stuff to rush home, he came over to me and said: 'You're living a double life.' I didn't like him saying that. It made me feel like a liar. Like I was doing something wrong. Like I was deceiving my parents.

That summer, life became even more complicated when we finally left the flat in Bethnal Green. The council had actually offered to move us a few years earlier – putting Mum, Dad and us five kids into a slightly bigger flat and my grandparents into a sheltered one, but my father refused. Splitting up the family wasn't something he was prepared to do.

Now, he'd bought a house with room enough for all of us: four bedrooms and a garden! I still shared a room with Ane, but this one was a lot bigger and so much warmer than our room in the flat. There was enough room downstairs to create a bedroom for my grandparents too, so they didn't have to worry about climbing stairs.

The complication came from the fact the house was in a place called Seven Kings in north-east London. It's about 11 miles away from Bethnal Green, which doesn't sound like much, but when you don't drive, and trains and buses cost money you don't have, getting between those two places requires some effort. And cash. I was already skipping lunch at college most days to save my pocket money for the gym (now that Bill had started letting me pay). There was no way I could afford travel costs too.

My dad would usually give me a lift to college on his way to work (which meant having to leave ridiculously early so we could spend hours sitting in rush-hour traffic), but it wasn't like I could ask him for a lift to the gym on a Sunday. Instead, I had to get on a train to Stratford and then the underground. There was only one option: a Saturday job. My dad was actually quite open to the idea. I think he liked the fact that I wasn't just asking him for more pocket money, but trying to earn my own – he often talked proudly about how my grandfather had worked four jobs at the same time when he first came to England, and that work ethic is something he always wanted to pass on to us.

As soon as we moved, I handed out my CV to almost every shop in Seven Kings. I ended up in the local chemist's, earning around £35 a week, which was enough to travel to the gym, pay Bill and start saving a little bit, too.

Week by week, Bill was watching me improve. I was hitting pads and holding them for partners in the class. Shadow boxing. Practising my kicks. Getting better at moving around the bag. He could see the passion I had for the sport: even after the house move made getting there so much more difficult, I never missed a session.

Eventually, the day came: 'I think you should join in with sparring today, Rox.' Bill paired me up with a more senior girl who'd been training for quite a while. Anna had short, blonde hair, thick shoulders and calf muscles as wide as my thighs.

I wasn't scared. This was what I signed up for. What I wanted.

It might sound odd, but the fear only came later, once I had more experience and knowledge. The fear only creeps in when you start thinking about the bad things that can happen – that's when you start feeling nervous and anxiety kicks in. At this point, I was still a fresh canvas. I wasn't projecting a bad outcome because I'd never experienced or really seen one.

Anna and I started to move around the ring. She tried a couple of kicks, one of which caught me painfully on the thigh. A few seconds later, I threw a right hand that landed harder than I really expected, or wanted. At that stage, I didn't really know what sort of power I had, or how to control it.

Anna went absolutely berserk on me. A fierce explosion of punches, combinations, power shots all started raining down on me for what felt like ages before Bill stepped in and told her to calm down: 'She's only young.'

It was the first time I'd been hit. But it wasn't a shock to me. Anna had serious power, but it wasn't anything that made me feel I was out of my depth or scared to try again. I had no fear. This was how it was meant to be. I just thought: *Okay, how do I control the situation next time?*

It took Bill by surprise. The moment I got hit, he thought that would be it for me. That I wouldn't come back.

When I walked back through the door the following Sunday, I swear I saw a hint of a smile on his face. Another recognition: this time, of someone who can take a hit, pick herself up and come back for more.

Chapter 4

I wasn't scared in those days.

Before my first fight, I had no fear of getting in the ring. Maybe because, like I said, I didn't really know what I was getting myself into. I suppose I was a bit naive, which allowed me to be fearless. Well, mostly fearless. The one thing I was fearful of was my parents finding out what I was doing and putting a stop to it.

It was only as I got older that the fear started creeping in, especially during those quiet moments in the changing room before a fight. But the first time I did it? The only thing I remember feeling then was excitement.

I'd been training with Bill for around six or seven months when he entered me into my first inter-club competition towards the end of the summer in 2002. These are like mini-tournaments, where two Muay Thai clubs get together and match up their fighters of similar size and weight. I was up against a girl who was also new to the sport, but she wasn't new to fighting.

Her background was in taekwondo – a Korean martial art that's focused mostly on kicking. Especially to the head. Head kicks are allowed in Muay Thai, too, but they're a notoriously difficult skill to master – you need seriously flexible hips, excellent balance and the strength to support yourself on one leg while the other lands a powerful shot to your opponent's head. I definitely hadn't ticked all those boxes off just yet.

At that stage, I was really reliant on my boxing. I had naturally fast hands, which gave me the confidence that I'd land my punches, so I was much more inclined to use my hands rather than try too many kicks or knees, which I still felt needed a lot of mastering in terms of technique.

As soon as I walked into the gym that day, I felt the buzz. I'd never seen it so full before. Never experienced the sights and sounds of so many fighters in one place. Never inhaled so much Deep Heat before.

I spotted Bill on the far side of the gym. He was deep in conversation with one of our more experienced fighters. I wandered over and stood a few paces away from them, hoping to grab a few words with Bill before things got underway. I should have known it was a silly idea – if Bill's in the right mood, he can talk for hours.

I started getting myself warmed up; doing the shoulder- and hip-mobilising drills we'd usually start our sessions with, stretching out my back and hamstrings. I even found a few square centimetres of space to start skipping in. Finally, Bill's fighter moved away and I had my opportunity to jump in.

'Okay, Rox?' said Bill. It wasn't so much a question as a statement, suggesting he'd made all his small talk for the day.

'Yeah, I just wondered if you'd seen the girl I'm fighting?'

Bill shrugged. 'Not really, but you'll be fine. I don't have any worries about you . . .'

'Why's that?'

'Because you can't teach someone to fight.'

I knew what he meant. Some people have that instinct. Others don't. You can have all the skill, be the biggest, strongest fighter in the world, but if you don't have that instinct, then you won't make it. Bill's belief in me that day gave me all the reassurance I needed. I was more than ready for what lay ahead.

Mine was the second fight in the ring. I was too busy getting my hands wrapped and shin pads on (these protect both you and your opponent from too much bone-on-bone damage) to watch, but I heard the roar of encouragement for the fighters. I was excited to get in there.

Our bout was to be a 'non-decision' fight, which basically means it's a practice run between two inexperienced fighters, to give them a taste of what it's like. A dress rehearsal, I suppose. At the end, no one 'wins', but you both walk away with a bit more knowledge about your own strengths and weaknesses. That's the idea, anyway.

Helping me to get ready was Nic – a British champion at the time and one of the top female fighters in our gym. She'd be in my corner for the fight, too, because Bill was too busy running around the gym and organising everything. That didn't bother me – I just saw it as further proof of his belief in me.

We were only scheduled to fight for three two-minute rounds. Just six minutes to show what I could do.

As soon as I got in the ring, I felt calmer than I had done all day. This was my time, now. I walked to the centre of the ring to touch gloves with my opponent. Size-wise, we were a good match. She might have had a few pounds on me but that was nothing compared to most of the fighters I'd been sparring in the gym. There weren't many female fighters around at the time, and those who were there tended to be bigger than me, so I was generally sparring stronger women or guys who were around my height (but naturally carried more weight).

We walked back to our respective corners and waited for the bell. This was it.

The next two minutes passed by in a blur. She definitely landed a few kicks on me, because I had the bruises to show for it, but I don't remember any of them hurting at the time. What I do remember is the grimace on her face every time I landed a blow of my own. I was too strong for her.

After the first round, the judges at the side of the ring told me to 'power down', meaning they wanted me to take some of the sting out of my shots. In my corner, Nic smiled as she poured some water down my throat and told me to take some deep breaths. Easier said than done when a heady mix of excitement and adrenaline are making your heart race at a million miles an hour.

For the next two rounds I kept my cool (mostly), and tried to treat the bout more like a sparring session.

After the final bell, the referee raised both our hands, but I felt triumphant. It was such a buzz to know that everything I'd been working on could come together in the ring. Not only that, but I had real power. I was still grinning as I climbed out of the ring and went over to Nic to thank her for being in my corner. Enveloping me in a big hug, she told me how proud the whole gym was of me: 'Why don't you come to the pub afterwards? We can have a celebratory drink.'

I had warned my parents that morning that I would be out for longer than usual today. I said I was meeting up with my sister after the gym to go for a late lunch (Ane was in on it, of course – the plan was that I would text her when I was done so we could meet up and arrive back in Seven Kings at the same time). After checking with her that she would be okay to stay out a bit longer, I told Nic I'd love to buy her a quick drink to say thank you.

As I was packing up my kit to leave, Bill came over: 'Off home, Rox?'

'No, I'm going to the pub.'

He looked at me, eyebrows raised in disbelief. 'You're going to the pub?'

Bill was always so protective of me. Even when the gym had Christmas parties, he'd be wary of inviting me along. Scared he was taking me away from my world, and of the consequences that could have.

I reassured him: 'I'm not drinking. I'll get an orange juice but I just want to say thanks to Nic.'

I also wanted to feel like a part of the team. I wanted to be there to celebrate with them and show my appreciation – not just take their help and then walk away.

On the way home I found myself thinking about Bill's words to me at the beginning of the day: 'You can't teach someone to fight.' If he was right, and I did have that fighter's instinct, where had it come from?

My mind settled first on one man: my grandfather. He had left his home in Sylhet, Bangladesh, to fight for Britain in the Second World War. Worked for the railways, the NHS and in a hotel, all at the same time, so that he could send money back to Bangladesh for my dad's sisters, as well as paying rent and taking care of the family here. He was so strong-minded. And so physically strong, too. One of my abiding memories is watching him carry a huge, heavy wooden table home from the Sunday market one weekend. He was like a superhero to me.

So it was hard to get my head around the fact that he was ill. When we moved to Seven Kings he was actually in hospital. His kidneys weren't working properly so they put him on dialysis. It had been about eighteen months since he first became unwell. He was in Bangladesh at the time and my father decided we should all be out there with him, including me. But I was in my final year of GCSEs at the time. I didn't know what to do – part of me wanted to go and be with my grandfather, but part of me wanted to stay at school. It was the last term before my exams and I knew I couldn't afford to miss anything.

When I went to speak to my head of year, Mr Cotterill, about it, he looked at me, worried: 'Ruqsana, are they getting you married?' In our school, it was quite normal at that time for girls to be taken out of school for that reason. A look of relief flashed across his face when I explained exactly why my dad wanted to take me to Bangladesh. But he was still concerned: 'Rox, if you go, you're putting your future in real jeopardy. No GCSEs means no qualifications.'

The week before we were due to leave, I rushed to get all my coursework handed in – at least I could get part of my marks for that. But then, at the last minute, my dad told me I should stay. I found out later on that he'd had his own conversation with Mr Cotterill, who repeated his fears: 'This is a crucial period. If she goes, she might not have a future.' I still think it was really brave of my dad to leave me by myself. That was a big step for him.

We had a lovely elderly neighbour who lived on her own, so in the evenings she would come and stay in the house with me. In a few weeks' time it was Easter, so I would fly out then and spend two weeks with everyone in Bangladesh. The first thing my grandfather did when I got there was grab me in his arms: 'How could you leave my little darling there? How could they have left you on your own?'

He got well enough for my parents to bring him home shortly after I came back. But things took a turn for the worse not long after I started college. Eventually, the hospital took him off dialysis. They said he was too weak for it. That he only had six months left to live.

We didn't believe it. Once we got him home, he started feeling a lot better. We were lulled into believing that everything was going to be okay. Getting on with our lives as normal. So, when he did go, it was a real shock. We were all devastated. But I found the worst part of it was seeing my grandmother so heartbroken. The day they came to take his body away I couldn't even bring myself to look at her.

Because of his hard work, Ane and I are living a better life. We've been to college, and university. We can work. We have so many rights that we might not have if we were in Bangladesh. If we were there, I think I'd be a completely different person. The battles he fought are what allow me to fight my own. The day we lost him, I vowed to always try to approach them with the strength, values and respect that I always saw in him.

That first inter-club tournament made me feel more like a fighter than I ever had. I loved it. I was learning about mental toughness, self-discipline and focus – things that would help me in everyday life just as much as in the ring. I was also getting to meet people from all walks of life and seeing how, despite our differences, a sense of unity can be created just by having one thing in common – the sport. Best of all, I was discovering that I was capable of more than I ever imagined, and that was giving me a sense of self-belief like nothing I'd ever felt before.

The feeling of empowerment was addictive. At the end of every session I'd walk out of the gym feeling a foot taller than when I went in. I loved the way my body felt. The aches and pains reminded me that I'd worked hard. The mental fatigue told me that I'd been learning new skills and techniques.

But that all came with a downside. Each time I left the gym, I did so with an anxious knot in the pit of my stomach. Did I have any bruises to hide from my parents? Had I remembered to leave my gloves in the gym? Would this be the day they found me out? With every session I completed, I felt more conflicted. I wanted to be myself – to do the things that made me happy – but I hated the thought that I was doing something that would upset my parents.

The sense that I was doing something wrong went against all the values my father had drilled into us from a young age.

One of the stories he loved to tell us was about my grandfather's determination to keep a tight hold on the teachings of Islam when he first moved to this country. There was such a look of pride on my father's face when he told us how, at the time, most of his father's peers were setting up restaurants as a way to make a living – many of them making good money. But my grandfather had refused to follow the crowd. He knew that setting up a restaurant business would mean selling alcohol, and that wasn't something he was prepared to do, given that alcohol is forbidden in our religion.

I saw the way my dad lived his life too: the ridiculously long hours he worked to make sure we grew up with the best that he could provide. My mum used to say to him: 'Why don't you just do what some of your friends do and go on the dole?' I think she felt bad, watching him work so many hours, and, even then, not earning a lot. But he always said no: he would rather carry on working.

Their work ethic and refusal to follow the crowd are things I now recognise in myself – and in the decisions I've made over the years to put everything I've got into achieving a dream not many people around me could understand.

My father's values are what made us who we are. One of the things he'd always say when we were growing up (and something I still say now) is: 'If it's not right, then walk away. God will give you something better.' He always taught us that. And it's funny, because if I ever did anything wrong (I mean, wrong in the legal sense as opposed to something that would upset my parents), then I would get caught straight away.

Like the one time, when a friend and I thought we'd buy a child travelcard instead of an adult one. We were in our first year of university, and everyone else was doing it so we thought we would too – we still looked about sixteen anyway, so we were sure we'd be fine. As it turned out, we weren't. We got stopped at the ticket barriers and given the worst punishment I'd ever heard of for travelling on a child ticket. Most people got handed a fine at the train station – maybe £20 or £30. But not us. We got taken to court, put in front of a judge and fined £300: a huge amount of money for me.

I was so scared to tell my parents, but there was no way I could keep it from them, especially when I received the court summons through the post. I can still hear my dad's exact words as I stood in front of him in tears after showing him the letter: 'When you do something wrong – the littlest thing – you will get caught. That's God's way of protecting you, because it's not in your nature.'

Those words stayed with me.

A year or so later, I went for lunch after lectures with one of my best friends, Samina. We had a lovely meal in a café that was really close to London Central Mosque near Regent's Park, so we decided to go and pray afterwards. We were next to each other finishing our prayers, when at the exact same moment, both of us stopped and looked at each other: We forgot to pay!

I could hear my dad's words ringing loudly in my ears. It made it even worse that we were in God's house. We rushed back to the café and paid our dues. I knew that kind of life was not for me: even if I'd got away with it, I couldn't have lived with myself knowing I'd done something unequivocally wrong.

Having the support of Ane was so important to me during those times when I was conflicted over whether I was doing the right thing by carrying on with Muay Thai. Whenever I was panicking about Mum and Dad finding out, or feeling bad for not telling them the truth, she was the one I could talk to. She was the one who covered for me when I came home exhausted from sparring.

There were a couple of occasions when I came home with a bit of a black eye and had to run upstairs to my room as soon as I got in to avoid Mum seeing me. For the next few days I'd stay out of her way as much as possible and wear a scarf or hoodie to try to hide it. I guess I was helped by the fact that Mum wasn't expecting anything and she wasn't looking for anything, so even if I made her a cup of tea, I could put it down in front of her and be out of her eyesight before she noticed anything.

The worst pain was always from the bruises. While I was still learning and figuring out which weapons to use at what time, I'd block a lot of shots and end up with loads of bruises all over my shins. It wasn't like taking a blow to the stomach in sparring, which would be painful at the time but not leave any lasting damage. These bruises could hang around and be painful for up to four weeks.

Once, I had a humongous one on my shin. I felt it when I walked. And even touching it lightly would leave me wincing in pain. It hung around for so long, the boys in the gym were saying I might have to go to hospital to get the fluid released.

But one week I just put my shin pads on top of the bruise, prepared myself for the pain and started practising my kicks on the bags at the gym. Every kick hurt like hell, but I tried to just block it out. At the end of the session, I sat on the gym floor and carefully took off my shin pads. Glancing down at the spot where the huge purple mass had been, I was amazed to see how much better it looked. The bruising had actually gone down – it was as if the pressure of me kicking the bag had actually eliminated the fluid. It's not a method I'd recommend to most people, but it worked!

Aside from Ane, my brothers knew about my training too, but we never really discussed it. My big brother Moynul had that protective role of being the oldest sibling, which meant he sort of fell into the same category as my parents. The younger two, Mosh and Eklim, were always more forward-thinking and very supportive, but sharing a room with Ane just made us that much closer.

As I went through university, the gym – and Bill – took on an even greater importance for me.

I was at Westminster University from 2002 until 2006, studying for a degree in architectural technology – a four-year course (the first year acted as a foundation level) that I quickly learned was going to challenge me in my weakest areas. I was really into design – art was one of my A-levels along with history and media – and had thought the course was going to involve more of that creative side. But once I started, it became obvious there was going to be a lot more of an engineering focus. And that meant lots of maths and physics – two subjects I'd struggled with at school.

But I wasn't about to walk away. I'd worked so hard to get here, not to mention to cover the cost of the course (as well as the Saturday job in the chemist's, I'd had a summer job in JD Sports and been a receptionist at a local leisure centre to save for uni over the last few years). And I knew that everyone was expecting me to fail anyway, so I felt like I had nothing to lose. I might as well just keep going.

I was lucky in that I have one aunt who is a physics and maths teacher, so once a week I'd go to her for some tutoring. Each year, I gave it my best shot, and each year I surprised everyone by getting through it.

It wasn't easy, though. Throughout those four years, Muay Thai was my release. It helped me to cope, not only with university stress but with family stress, too.

During the years I was at university, I was evolving into more of me. I'd been brought up in a traditional household, but I don't think I was ever traditional as a person. So, once I got to university I started slowly moving away from those elements and discovering who I really was.

The training kept me sane. Even if Mum shouted at me or stressed about things at home, I didn't react. I was able to handle it much better, and stay calmer because the training made me so much happier in myself. And it was the same with university. I was able to apply myself and concentrate more on my studies because I had an outlet.

My training was the body of everything – the core that everything else stemmed from. Without it, I'm not sure I would have been able to cope. There was a gap growing between the person who my parents wanted me to be and the one I was realising I really was. Without the outlet of the gym, I think there would have been so many more arguments between us – training was the one thing giving me the balance I needed to cope with both worlds and find a medium.

When I was in my second year at uni, Bill had also given me the responsibility of helping to run a women-only class in the gym. One of the female instructors led it every Sunday afternoon, so after I finished my own session I'd stick around and help out (now that I was a bit older, my parents had become a bit less strict over how long I spent at the gym). It wasn't exactly a big group – usually between two and four women would show up.

After a year or so, the main instructor left KO and Bill wanted me to take over the class. I'd only been doing the sport a couple of years, but I didn't want to let Bill down and I'd already built up a good relationship with the women who came, so I said yes. The class didn't really make any money, so whatever I got, I'd give straight to Bill. Sometimes he'd let me keep it.

He also got me a ladies-only class at King's College, so

I started teaching there once a week as well. It was every Wednesday evening and much more popular than the one at KO (it also paid me a set rate which was great, as I knew I'd get paid no matter how many people showed up). Usually, I'd have about ten to fifteen girls there, unless it was an exam period when I'd get about half that.

I loved it. It helped me in so many ways – it gave me the skills to lead and made me more confident about talking to people from walks of life I'd not really come across before. At King's they were all medics or pharmacists, some were even doing PhDs. I'd never thought I would be the one standing in front of such a group and teaching them.

As well as the confidence it gave me, it was also helping with my own training. Because I would analyse and take note of my own sessions, so that I could understand the way I was being taught and become a better teacher myself. It also gave me the chance to reflect on my own skills and understand which ones I needed to work on – there's no quicker way to realise you don't understand something than trying to teach it to someone else.

I competed in two more inter-clubs during the time I was at uni. The third one yielded my first-ever trophy – the one that ended up wrapped in a tatty Tesco bag a few months later when my dad caught me walking 'like a boxer'. But the sport was about more than competing and winning for me. It was the one area of my life that I felt belonged to me. The one area where no one told me what I could or couldn't do. Should or shouldn't do. And in Bill I felt I had someone who really believed in me. Someone who would always give me the chance to improve. Inside that gym I developed my strategy for life.

It was like there were two Ruqsanas: one outside of the

gym, who was constantly trying to please her parents. Who would sit on the train home worrying about how her mum was going to react because she was home five minutes late. And another Ruqsana inside the gym, who wasn't afraid of anything. Who believed she was capable of achieving whatever she put her mind to.

Muay Thai is such a tough sport that my thought process was: if I can do this, then I can manage the rest of my life. All I had to do was follow the principles that Bill taught me: never give up. Inside the ring, that's not an option. There's no one else who can get in there with you and help you through it – you have to find the self-belief to do it alone, and take responsibility for your own actions.

Quite often, athletes blame their coach or are quick to look at other people if they lose, but over time I understood that, actually, I lost because *I* didn't do something right. Others are there to lend support and help, but it's up to you to control and manage your own thoughts, which in turn control your actions. Where your mind goes, your body follows.

From the very first time I met Bill, I was going through this process. Learning that if plan A doesn't work, then you move on to plan B. You never give up.

I was like a sponge, soaking up everything Bill said. He could have come out with the most insignificant thing, just in passing, but I would hold on to it as though it was the most valuable insight I'd ever heard. I learned so much, not only from listening to him but from watching him, too. His life experiences gave him the ability to communicate with people from any walk of life and taught him never to judge a book by its cover. He would always give people a chance.

The open-mindedness probably came from his own

fighting career. Bill's not a huge, muscular guy. He doesn't really look like the typical Muay Thai fighter. But he was able to succeed in the sport because he had the intelligence and grit to be able to adapt and find whatever way he could to win. He taught me that life outside of the ring is no different – you need to have a strategy where you're not relying on just one thing to get you through.

I was going through a particularly stressful period towards the end of my third year at university when Bill pulled me aside one week after training. He'd noticed that I wasn't as focused as I usually was during the session and asked if there was anything wrong. I told him that my head was in a mess. That I was stressed about the next couple of weeks because I had a series of deadlines to meet. He came straight back at me: 'It's two weeks. You can work in a chemist's for the rest of your life, or you can work really hard for the next two weeks and that's going to define you for the rest of your life.'

Those words made such a difference to me. Bill knew I was hard-working anyway, but he just put everything into perspective. For me, that degree was everything. If I had to pull all-nighters to get it done, then that's what I'd do. Because this was about the rest of my life.

There was one other place I'd go to whenever I felt like things were getting on top of me: London Central Mosque (or Regent's Park Mosque, as I always called it). There is something about that place that makes me feel at peace from the moment I walk in. It was only about ten or fifteen minutes from the university, so on certain days – when I was struggling with coursework and really panicking – I would go and sit in the mosque for an hour. Sometimes I'd go to listen to the *Khutbah* (a sermon from the imam on a Friday afternoon). The topic would vary from week to week – one Friday it might be a story about the prophets; the next, a discussion about our purpose in this world – and I found it really helpful.

I was still afraid that I was somehow going against my religion by doing the boxing. But despite that, prayer and the mosque were still things that went hand in hand with the sport in helping me to get through my university days. They kept me grounded. Helped me to find some peace within. As soon as I walked into the mosque, I could feel a shift in my mindset. I might not have been wearing the hijab every day any more, but religion was still a focal part of my life. Not in the sense of being fully practising and praying five times a day every day, but in that it was the main part of my mind and body.

The journey of getting close to God is a work in progress. It's something I'm still working on now. Sometimes you have days when you're closer, other days you feel a bit distant and disconnected.

But I'm always grateful to have religion in my life because it's such a powerful thing. And it's something that, along with Bill's teachings and those of the sport, equipped me with the fortitude I would desperately need over the next few years. Because when everything else is stripped away, all you have left is your faith, and hope.

Chapter 5

I was in the university library when my phone started vibrating its way across my desk. The word 'HOME' was splashed across the screen in bold capitals. I glanced at the time. It was only three o'clock; I wasn't due home for hours yet. And my parents knew I was in the midst of writing up my dissertation – 10,000 words on damp-proof membrane and condensation in buildings stood between me and the degree in architectural technology I'd spent four years sweating over.

I let it ring out and waited for the voicemail message to come through. It was Mum. She had something to talk to me about urgently. My brain did that thing where it skips through all the elderly members of your family, thinking: what if? But then, I hadn't detected any hints of sadness in her voice. Quite the opposite, actually. The words had tripped out of her mouth like she could hardly bear to hold them in.

I asked my study partner, Lai Ping, to keep an eye on my stuff while I headed outside with my phone, intrigued to find out what had got Mum so excitable. It barely rang once before she answered.

'Ruqsana?'

'Yes, Mum. What is it? Is something wrong?'

'No, no. I just thought you should know, your father and I have met someone for you. He's from a nice family. We think you will be very happy with him.'

I looked around for somewhere to sit down. I felt weak. Unsteady. Like my knees had suddenly turned to mush.

'But Mum, can this not wait? I'll have my degree soon, a qualification. I'll be able to get a good job. Start a career . . .'

I wasn't allowed to finish.

'This is perfect timing, Ruqsana. Studies are over and now you are free to start your own family. What time will you be home?'

I hung up the phone and slumped down onto a low wall just outside the entrance to the library. It was the smokers' favourite spot – somewhere I wouldn't normally linger for too long, just in case I took the smell of cigarettes home with me. Today I didn't care.

I'd known this could be coming because I'd seen the proposals start coming in. I can't remember exactly how many there were, but I'd definitely seen a few around the house in recent months. It's just how it works in our community: guys (or their families) put together a sort of CV, where they write about their family background – where their family is from in Bangladesh, their class and status – how many siblings they have and what they all do for work. And, of course, there is a picture attached so you can at least see who you might be marrying. I guess it's a bit like Tinder, just without the option to swipe.

I saw a CV from one guy who went to Queen Mary University in London and was doing a degree in IT and was a similar age to me (twenty-three, I was twenty-two at the time). I thought, okay, maybe I can talk to this guy. He could be on my level. But I never met him – he never got past the CV stage.

I'd always known that I would probably have an arranged marriage – it's part of our culture – so I was open to my parents exploring the idea. I'd even had a conversation with my dad about what I was looking for in a husband: 'I need someone modern. Bangladeshi, but modern.'

I gave him the example of a couple who lived a few doors down from us. They were Bengali but they had a very modern lifestyle – they were both lawyers and the wife was still dressing in Western outfits. 'That's what I need,' I told my father. 'Because I'm not suddenly going to start wearing a sari at home.'

Even after that conversation, I still thought it would take them one or two years to find potential candidates for me to meet. I didn't think it would happen overnight.

And I certainly didn't feel ready for it yet. I was on the brink of becoming a qualified architect, something that could open up so many exciting opportunities for me. What if I married someone who didn't like the idea of me working? What if his family didn't like the way I dressed? What if I wasn't allowed to go to the gym? I had been able to hide my training from my parents but could I hide it from a husband?

My stomach started to hurt. It felt like there was a rubber band wrapped around it that tightened with every breath. Squeezing my insides until I felt sick.

By the time I went back inside, Lai Ping was packing up to go home. She took one look at me and sat back down. 'Are you okay? You look . . . not okay.'

I nodded, stuffing my books into my bag. 'Fine. I'm

fine.' I wasn't capable of saying anything more and Lai Ping seemed to understand. We'd become friends in the first year, along with a few other Chinese girls who were on our course. Their work ethic was like nothing I'd ever seen before. It really showed me how to raise my game in terms of studying hard.

We left the library together, her chatting away about the assignment we were working on while I drifted in and out, nodding and making noises of agreement whenever I sensed I should. But inside my head, I was in full-on panic mode.

On my way home, I stopped to pick my sister up from work as I usually did. Ane was now also working in a chemist's while she completed a pharmacy course on the side. Sometimes I felt a bit envious of her. She was the complete opposite to me – loved dressing up in Indian outfits, going to weddings and doing all the traditional things that I would rather forego if it meant I could get in a training session instead.

For her, life seemed so straightforward. If she had received the news that I had earlier that day, I knew she would have felt entirely differently about it. Even so, Ane was as supportive as always. After I fought back the tears that had been threatening to flow ever since I'd hung up the phone to tell her about my chat with Mum, her words were exactly what I needed to hear:

'These things always take a long time to actually happen, you know? It will probably be at least a year until anything really gets going in terms of an actual wedding. And, you know, Mum and Dad won't make you go through with it if you really don't like him.'

By the time we got home I was feeling a little bit calmer.

The tightness in my stomach was still there but it no longer felt like my organs were being compressed into one solid mass.

I headed straight up to my room while Ane helped Mum with preparing dinner. It was usually my role, but I'd been spending such long hours in the library lately that she would often step in for me (just as she did whenever I came home from sparring too exhausted to stand in the kitchen and chop). I lay down on my bed, stared at the ceiling and tried to imagine what it would be like to be someone's wife.

When the distinctive aroma of Mum's fish curry started to waft upstairs, I steeled myself for the conversation to come and headed downstairs. We didn't always eat together – often my parents would wait until we (the 'children') had eaten before taking food for themselves. And it wasn't unusual for at least one of my brothers to be elsewhere at dinner time at least a few nights a week.

This time, though, it was a full house. With the boys all there, I relaxed a little. They normally dominated the conversation with chatter about computer games or football so, with any luck, the 'news' about my future wouldn't get a look-in.

I made it as far as the clearing up.

'So, have you thought about what I told you on the phone, Ruqsana?'

Mum's question silenced the room. I looked down at my hands, buried deep in hot, soapy water and muttered something about being too busy with my dissertation to really think about it.

My dad frowned at my lack of enthusiasm but said nothing. And before my brothers could start asking questions,

Ane changed the subject, allowing me to finish clearing up in peace and escape back to the sanctuary of my bedroom.

For the next few weeks, I heard nothing more about it, which was fine by me. I kept my head down. Spent as much time as I could out of the house, whether that was at uni or in the gym – trying to fill my brain with anything but thoughts of weddings or husbands.

Muay Thai gave me the perfect escape. Four years in, I was still learning and improving so much in every session. I was obsessed with improving my kicks and knees, because in Thai boxing they're the shots that score the highest. I'd spend hours standing in front of a bag, visualising the perfect kick: rotating my hips, coming onto the ball of my back foot, pivoting correctly.

Thwack! The sweet sound of the perfect connection – there's nothing quite like it.

Practising knees was something I looked forward to a bit less, because to do it, you have to spend time in what we call the 'intimate range'. Basically, that means physically touching another person; feeling their aura. It takes time to get used to – especially if they have a certain aroma … Sometimes I'd have to practise with guys, but I preferred to train with another female, or even one of the younger teenage boys who was just learning and would be a bit less confident, so maybe not come so close to me.

With the knees, you don't start in the usual guard position, which is slightly side-on to your opponent, but instead stand straight-on to them, as if you're 'squaring up'. Then you lock your elbows in, grab them by the neck with both hands and pull their head down. You're essentially aiming to get your knee to their head. And if you can't do that, then to the stomach where you're looking for areas like the liver or the kidneys. The trick is to angle your knee in slightly, so it digs in even harder. It's horrible, I know.

You also have to remember that when you're in that range, your opponent can do the same to you, so it's about manoeuvring their body weight until you sense you have the advantage and then grabbing them just at the right moment, when they're slightly off balance.

I was getting better at landing knees, but I was still wary of being in that range too much. Not only because you have to be prepared to take one back, but because with the knees come the elbows – and that's when you're most likely to get cuts around the eyes. I preferred to play it smart, and keep my range a bit longer.

With so much still to work on and improve, my weekly visits to KO helped take my mind away from everything that was going on at home. For a while, at least.

At the beginning of 2006 I was entering my last six months of being a student and gearing myself up mentally for a tough term. It was the final stretch that would take me one step closer to achieving something no one thought I was capable of.

One Wednesday evening, I got the train home from uni with Ane as normal. As I put my key in the front door, Mum pulled it open before I could even turn it. She'd clearly been standing in the porch waiting for me. Looking me up and down – as she usually did when I came home from university wearing a hoodie and jeans – she allowed herself a sigh of disappointment before telling me to: 'Go and get changed . . . put on something nice.'

As I kicked my trainers off, I noticed how tidy the porch

was: everyone's shoes arranged into neat pairs and coats hung
tidily on hooks. Mum had the hoover in her hand when she
opened the door, too. It was six o'clock in the evening – she
never left the housework that late. She was obviously expecting guests. Guests that she wanted me to dress for.

Ane and I rushed upstairs. As soon as the bedroom door
was shut, I said what we were both thinking: 'Do you think
this is anything to do with . . .?'

She tried to convince me it wouldn't be. That Mum and
Dad would have given me some sort of warning before inviting a potential future husband into our home. I hoped she
was right. I mean, they often had friends over for dinner –
Mum loves cooking for lots of people – so maybe that's just
what this was.

But this felt different. The house felt different.

About an hour after we got home, the doorbell rang and,
seconds later, my name was being called from downstairs.
Dressed in an Indian outfit I knew Mum liked, I went to the
top of the stairs and listened. I heard a male voice speaking.
I could tell it wasn't my dad, but I couldn't quite make out
what he was saying.

I took a deep breath and made my way down to see if my
suspicions were correct. They were gathered in the living
room – my parents, another older couple and a smartly
dressed guy who looked a few years older than me. The five
of them were arranged in a sort of semi-circle, leaving a small
gap for me to slot in, right next to the man I immediately
knew was the one my parents had decided would make a
good future husband for me.

I felt the tightness in my stomach returning as I walked
into the room, fixing my eyes on my dad with a look that I

hoped communicated exactly how I felt about this situation. He ignored me, instead introducing me to our visitors: first, Atif and Nazia Lohani – the husband and wife – and then Tareq. For the first time, I looked at him properly. He was tall and slim with hair smoothed into a side parting and a dusting of designer stubble, to ensure he fitted in with the rest of the male population of east London. On looks alone I thought it could have been worse.

We smiled at each other. Maybe this wasn't going to be so bad.

They stayed for about an hour – just long enough to share a cup of tea (I noticed Mum had the posh cups out) and some Indian sweets. Neither Tareq nor I said much in that hour, though – it was the parents who did most of the talking. So, by the time they left, I didn't really know much more about him than I had an hour earlier. His parents seemed okay, though. They were educated and successful, and even mentioned that Tareq's sisters were studying at university, which I took as a good sign. They obviously had a modern way of thinking.

After that first meeting, the Lohanis came over a couple more times. Mum cooked dinner for everyone (and made me get dressed up again) and each time Tareq and I got to know each other a little better. I discovered he'd studied economics at university, enjoyed eating out and going to the cinema. It seemed like he could be a good fit.

But it was difficult to get to know each other in any real way while we had two sets of parents listening to our every word. Watching every interaction. How was I supposed to know if I liked him if we couldn't even have a proper conversation?

The second time they came over, we managed to exchange phone numbers without anyone seeing, and a few days later I messaged him to see if he wanted to meet up – audience not included. He was keen, so we arranged to meet up at a café in Wanstead for a chat over coffee. And it was okay. I found out that he worked in banking and we had similar tastes in films and music. And for the half an hour or so that we spent chatting, the conversation seemed to flow pretty well.

So we arranged to meet up again. This time we went out for dinner – nothing fancy, just pizza. Gradually, I felt like we were getting to know each other a bit better. But meeting up outside of the family home wasn't something we were really supposed to be doing. It wasn't acceptable then for me to be seen out with a guy. Even if he was just a friend, it was seen as something that would set tongues wagging among the community.

Now, things are different. My parents would be happy for me to date someone these days. But ten years ago, it wasn't acceptable for me to date or be seen outside with a guy. They cared about how the community would view it, so they were cautious.

Tareq and I got found out. Someone who knew our families saw us, either at the café or the restaurant, and let on to them that we'd been meeting up in secret. Mum wasn't impressed. She was worried that people would get the wrong end of the stick (even though it was really the right one, considering we were being lined up for marriage) and think we were up to something.

'If you like him, then you need to tell us,' she told me, my father nodding in agreement alongside her. 'You can't be seen outside with him. You're not married to him.'

I tried to explain: 'But I don't know if I like him yet. I'm just trying to get to know him without everyone else sitting there.'

It fell on deaf ears. Both families seemed to view our two dates as a sign that they should move things along. They assumed that because we'd met up outside of the house, we were obviously madly in love and desperate to get married as soon as possible. It also emerged that Tareq's dad was ill and his family wanted to speed things up to make sure he was well enough to come to the wedding.

'The wedding . . .' I didn't know what had hit me. I wanted to shout it: 'Take a step back. I'm just getting to know this guy. I DON'T EVEN KNOW IF I LIKE HIM.'

But it was pointless. His parents approved of the marriage because he liked me. And my parents approved on my behalf. Everyone agreed that this was going to happen, and that it was going to happen sooner rather than later.

I was trapped.

I remember trying to have an open and honest conversation with Mum about it one evening during the next few months. But she didn't want to hear it. She just walked away from me with a dismissive wave of her hand: 'What are you talking about?' About ten minutes later I saw her go and sit on her prayer mat, presumably to have a few words with God about her troublesome daughter.

I was afraid that if I tried to speak to my father, he'd just get angry with me. I guess, deep down, I somehow felt it was my fault anyway. I was the one who'd met up with him outside of the house – twice. Maybe I encouraged the situation. Maybe I was the one to blame.

It wasn't that I didn't like him at all. I thought he was

okay. He was quite a nice guy. He had a good job. He was educated. And he was reasonably okay-looking … But the pressure was too much. I didn't feel I could say: 'Hang on a minute, I need a bit more time. Let's be engaged for a year and see how it goes.' After I tested the water with my mother and she brushed it off so completely, I knew there was no point even trying.

Over the next few months, Tareq made his feelings for me pretty clear. He was always trying to call or text me to see how I was, or asking to come over to the house to spend time with me. He was really attentive, and gradually that did start to change my mind a little bit. I liked the fact he was making so much effort with me. I think I enjoyed the attention. It was seductive.

He even came to pick me up from the gym a few times. He was into fitness, and loved the fact that I was as well (he assumed I was training mostly to stay in shape, as opposed to actually competing, but at least that was a start). I thought that would make my life easier once I got married – that I might even have more freedom to train than I did now.

The narrative in my head started to change: okay, so I'm not attracted to him, but looks aren't everything … and maybe this is what marriage is about, the husband taking care of the wife. Being supportive and interested and always there for me – which he was.

Planning a wedding was still the last thing I wanted to do, though. I was on the final stretch of my university degree and still had a dissertation to write, which required all of my time and focus. I didn't have hours to waste talking about venues, catering or guest lists.

Eventually, I snapped. The two families had started getting

together more often in the evenings, trying to entertain one another and get to know each other a bit more. There were siblings to meet, then cousins, uncles and aunts . . . Every time they came over, I had to get dressed up and spend my entire evening downstairs with them all, when I knew I should be in my room working.

I got more and more frustrated until it reached the point where I couldn't smile through it any more, where even the time I spent at the gym, injecting all my frustrations into punches and kicks, was not enough to quieten the feelings building up inside me. I'd had enough.

One night, after everyone had left and I was clearing up (again), I had a real go at my dad, telling him I couldn't keep doing this: 'I need to focus on my studies. Let me finish my degree, at least.'

I think that scared my parents a little bit. What if I changed my mind?

After that, everyone tried to make my life as easy as possible. They didn't want to give me any stress, just in case. So, as winter turned to spring, my evenings became clearer. There weren't as many gatherings in our house (and I didn't have to attend all the ones in theirs). And all the wedding plans were taken out of my hands.

Normally, the bride would get involved in the organisation, but my parents and my brothers did all the running around: they organised the hall, the food, the decorations, the transport . . . All I did was choose my own outfits. Apart from that, I really didn't care about anything else.

For both families, the wedding was a momentous occasion. There hadn't been a wedding in either family for a long time (I would be the first among my siblings to get married). So absolutely everyone wanted to be there. The guest list seemed to gain another fifty people every time I looked at it.

This wedding was going to be huge. And expensive – by the end, my father had spent something like £50,000 on it! He was so pleased that they had found someone nice for me, and that I was going into a family where he thought I would be happy, that he was willing to go all out to make it an occasion to remember.

The date was set for late July, but, before that, there was the engagement party. Somehow, this turned into a serious event, too. It was like everyone got so excited about the wedding that they decided they couldn't wait and would just have to have a dress rehearsal a couple of months earlier.

My father hired out a church hall close to where we lived, which ended up being just about big enough for the hundreds who came (around 400 in the end). I got to choose a beautiful traditional outfit (a skin-tone flowing skirt and blouse, with Swarovski crystals and shades of blue lining the bottom of the skirt). And there were endless platters of food on offer – samosas, kebabs, rice, loads of different curries and a massive cake.

None of which I ate. I was far too nervous about meeting so many members of Tareq's extended family for the first time. Plus, I had to spend most of the evening sitting up on a stage alongside my future husband – not exactly the most comfortable arena in which to tuck into a curry.

By the end of the night I was exhausted. My face ached from smiling constantly at the streams of people keen to congratulate us and gush about how much they were looking forward to that summer's big event. All night, they kept on coming. I didn't even know who half of them were.

Afterwards, I went home with the soles of my feet burning from the heels I was so unused to wearing, and desperate to clean off the thick layer of make-up that had been slathered over my face. If this was just the warm-up, what was my actual wedding day going to be like?

As we got ready for bed that night, Ane asked me how I was feeling about everything. Was I ready for the wedding now that I knew Tareq a bit better? Did I feel prepared for starting a new life away from home?

'Yeah . . . I think so.'

'You sure?'

I nodded, before turning off the lamp next to my bed so that she couldn't see my face through the darkness.

'I do like him. I mean, I care about him. But I don't know . . . is that enough for a marriage?'

I wasn't sure. I felt like the root of the marriage just wasn't there from my side. And I was worried about how I would fit into their family. As the only son, Tareq was really close to his parents, which was something that I admired about him, but at the same time I wondered where I figured in that situation. Would he support me in the same way he supported his family? I couldn't picture myself being happy in a place where I was basically a 'plus one' as opposed to a real part of the family.

I'd spent the last four years discovering who I really was, beyond the traditional Bangladeshi girl my parents had so wanted me to be. Learning how much I was capable of by going into the gym every week and pushing myself physically and mentally.

The conflict I'd felt so many times before – between the values instilled in me by my upbringing and the ones that

society told me I should have as a Western female – was
tearing me in two. I wanted to be the independent, ambitious
female I saw the other women in the gym and my university
friends becoming. But I'd always known this was the way it
worked in my culture, and it felt wrong for me to be questioning it.

When I told Bill I was getting married, even he didn't
see anything wrong with it. He understood that it was part
of who I was, and he respected that. He was no stranger to
seeing female fighters drift away from the gym after getting
married and I guess that's what he thought might happen
with me, too.

So, I tried to convince myself that I was worrying about
nothing. That life wouldn't be that different to how it was at
home. And that I would give everything I could to make it
work. Because it was true, I did care for him. And my parents
had put so much time and effort into this wedding, I didn't
want to let them down.

Over the next few weeks, the wedding preparations
stepped up a notch. Now that the engagement party was
over, there were only a couple of months left to go and I still
needed multiple outfits (one for the ceremony, one for the
day after and one for the ceremony at the registry office), a
collection of jewellery and, most importantly, the right hair
and make-up artist.

Every day there was something else to decide on.
Something else to think about. Sometimes I found myself
getting caught up in the excitement, picturing myself as a
bride and thinking about how the day might play out. Other
times, my mind went wandering into a world I didn't recognise. One where my life was completely different from the

one I knew. From the one I'd known for the last twenty-two years.

I couldn't dwell on those thoughts now, though. It was too late. This was happening. There was no rewind button. No option to 'undo'. This was my future now. I would just have to do whatever I could to make sure it was a positive one.

Chapter 6

It's quite a strange feeling, knowing you are spending your final night at home. Realising that you will never be sharing the same room as your sister again, waking up to the noise of your brothers arguing over the PlayStation or coming home to the smell of your mother's cooking at the end of a long day.

Throughout the whole build-up to the wedding day I had tried so hard not to let my mind go to *that* place. One of the reasons I never really spoke to anyone at the gym about it was because KO was the one place where I could almost pretend it wasn't happening – where I could swap endless chatter about guest lists and decorations for discussions about technique and punch power.

But now, the moment had arrived and I couldn't avoid it any longer. It was happening. I had to accept it.

I also had to put on my happiest face for one more pre-wedding-day ritual: the Mehndi (or henna) party. Traditionally, it's an evening of fun and celebration, where the bride is given all the secrets to a happy and successful marriage by her closest female family members and friends.

I suppose you could compare it to the Western custom of a hen party, but instead of playing drinking games, going out dancing or doing anything my parents would *definitely* not approve of, the bridal party spends the evening having intricate patterns drawn onto their hands and arms with a paste made from dried henna leaves. It's a ritual that's believed to bring you blessings, luck and joy: the henna that's drawn onto the palm of your hand signifies you are open to receive and offer blessings, while the designs on the top signify protection.

Initially, I told my parents I didn't want a henna party. I really didn't want them to spend more money than they already had done on something that I wasn't that fussed about. But my parents insisted on throwing one for me. So, we compromised. Instead of going down the usual route of organising a big party held in a huge venue with catered food, decorations and music, I had mine at home.

It was just a small gathering of close family and friends. My mum prepared all the food and my sister put together a playlist for the music. It was a really fun, relaxed evening. And a useful distraction from the anxiety that was bubbling away in the back of my mind about what was to come ... I mean, how do you prepare for a new life that you know next to nothing about? I honestly had no idea.

Once our guests had left, Ane and I sat on our beds talking long into the night. It was as if we'd decided that as long as we just kept talking, nothing would ever change.

I couldn't tell you who fell asleep first (so it was probably me), but I do know that from the moment I woke up, the rubber band around my stomach was back. Every breath reminded me it was there, squeezing my insides like a corset. There was no way I would be able to eat breakfast, but Ane made me go downstairs with her anyway: 'Just have a cup of tea. The warmth will help relax your stomach.'

Mum had laid out so much food: fruit, croissants, Indian sweets, Asian rice pudding. I sat down and watched everyone else get stuck in, while I sipped on my tea. We'd been sitting down for a few minutes when the doorbell rang. Guests were already arriving! Over the next hour or so a constant stream of family members came through the front door, bringing different foods and decorations to help with the *taals* (a Bangladeshi wedding tradition is to create food platters – *taals* – for the spouse's family and friends to share).

When the doorbell rang for what must have been the tenth time, my dad went to answer it and returned with something other than another distant relative – a huge bunch of red roses.

'These are for you, Ruqsana,' he said, passing them across the breakfast table.

I pulled out the little card from the bunch: 'Love Tareq'.

I actually smiled. Amid all the stress and anxiety of preparing for that day, I hadn't really thought about one thing: Tareq. Maybe I should concentrate on him and the feelings he had for me. I'd heard stories of other girls marrying guys who never really showed their emotions. Never let them know that they cared for them. So, in that respect, maybe I was lucky.

The next few hours were spent locked away in my bedroom with Farah, my hair and make-up artist, and Ane. I don't think I will ever look quite as glamorous as I did that day. I decided to go fully traditional – on the basis that it's the only time I would get to wear that outfit – and went for a classic maroon *lehenga* (which is a long, flowing skirt), with intricate gold embroidery and a blouse and headscarf to match.

The whole thing was studded with semi-precious stones,

metal sequins and diamantes. It was absolutely stunning to look at, but wearing it was like putting on an extra 3 stone. The headscarf alone felt like it weighed about 10kg.

Then there was the gold. Jewellery is one of the most important aspects of a bride's outfit in Bengali weddings. It's not about accessorising so much as it is a form of investment – a sort of financial security that is bestowed on the bride as she steps into her new life. I was dripping in gold rings, heavy necklaces and thick bangles.

Looking at myself in the mirror, I hardly recognised the woman looking back at me. I'd never worn anything so exquisitely beautiful before. Or been adorned with so much gold. A picture of an alternative me flashed into my mind – one where my head was concealed by a headguard, as opposed to a crystal-studded scarf, my gold-free fingers encased in sweaty hand wraps and my legs hidden beneath a baggy pair of old jogging bottoms, with not a stitch of embroidery in sight.

'Pfffft.' I tried to stifle the laughter but it squeaked out anyway.

'What's up with you?' said Ane. 'What's so funny?'

'I was just wondering what Bill would say if he saw me like this,' I said, smiling at the thought. Ane laughed. She used to come and meet me after sessions sometimes, so she knew that, while Bill understood much about our faith and culture, he was not exactly one for any kind of extravagance.

From the moment Farah and Ane had finished putting me together, I was fighting a constant battle to avoid breaking into a sweat. The sun had been blasting through my bedroom window for the last two hours. And now I was buried beneath what felt like the weight of a thousand sequins. I wanted to go downstairs, where it would be a little cooler and I could stop worrying about beads of sweat leaving trails of make-up across my face. But I also knew what going downstairs meant.

The imam had already arrived. So, as soon as I went downstairs, it would be time for the formalities to begin, with the *nikah* ceremony, where the marriage contract is signed. It's something that the bride and groom do separately, with the imam going to the bride's house first. That way, she feels she is able to say no, if she wants to. If it is done the other way around and the groom has already said yes before the imam speaks to the bride, that could make her feel she has no choice but to say yes, too.

Mum's tears started as soon as she saw me coming down the stairs. And seeing hers made my own eyes sting. I looked away, fixing my gaze on my dad instead, who was waiting for me by the bottom step. Kissing me on the forehead, he led me into the living room, where my uncle and my closest friend from university, Sumina, were waiting with the imam. Mum and Ane followed, both of them now weeping. The more Dad mouthed the words 'Stop crying!' at them, the worse they got.

My parents' marriage was an arranged one too, so Mum had been through everything I was experiencing. She knew that I was walking into a different world without really knowing what to expect. And she knew that, once I was married, I would no longer be living under her and Dad's rules, but under those of my in-laws. And as much as she and Dad had gotten to know the Lohanis over the past six months, they didn't *really* know what my life would be like once I was living under their rules – or how free I would be to come back and see them.

I think that was the first moment since I'd met Tareq that Mum really felt it. I kept my gaze firmly focused on the imam, trying not to succumb to the same emotions that were overwhelming Mum and Ane.

Focus on what's in front of you. Block everything else out. It was just like being in the midst of a tough training session, when everyone around you is struggling. At that point, you can either give in and join them in collapsing in a sweaty heap, or turn your focus inwards. Concentrate on your breathing. Tell yourself you're too strong to succumb.

There, in the living room, all I had to do was listen to the imam's recitations and respond with one word: '*Qabul*' – 'I accept' in Arabic. It passed by in a flash, leaving me to sign the marriage contract along with my two witnesses (Dad and Uncle Surath). I was a married woman, and it felt like it had all happened in the blink of an eye.

With the formalities ticked off, the house was buzzing. The wedding was on.

As we pulled up outside the vast expanse of La Royale in Tottenham, I took a deep breath and looked at Ane, sitting next to me. She squeezed my hand. Things were about to get very real.

We were taken into a huge banqueting suite upstairs, where my family and guests were gathering. At the same time, Tareq's family and their guests were assembling in the suite directly below us – for the first part of the afternoon at least, we would be kept apart.

I looked around the suite in awe. Everything was unbelievably fancy – chairs draped in silky white fabric, each one adorned with a delicately tied golden bow. Huge silver vases emerging from the centre of every table, each sending a bouquet of perfectly white roses soaring high up towards the ceiling. And, of course, the room's grand showpiece: a stage draped in the same silky white as the rest of the room, in the centre of which sat a stately white-and-gold-trimmed chesterfield; a wall of white roses positioned just behind it providing the most opulent of backdrops.

As my eyes came back to centre, I grabbed Ane's arm and breathed one word into her ear: 'Wow.' Putting her hand on top of mine, Ane smiled, but her eyes betrayed her; still showing signs of the sadness she felt at waving off her big sister and lifetime roommate.

Everything was so far beyond what I had expected – so distant from how I'd imagined my wedding to be (not that I had devoted much time to visualising it over the last six months, given that I'd spent much of that time trying to pretend it wasn't actually going to happen). But, in a way, I think it helped that everything was so grandiose. Because I could almost separate myself from it all. Pretend it wasn't really happening to me, but to someone else – and it was she who would go back to Tareq's house at the end of the day, while I went back to mine with Ane and my brothers and continued to live the life I knew.

That surreal feeling only intensified as I perched in the middle of the stately chesterfield, overlooking a room filled with around 600 of my 'closest family and friends', all of whom had turned up looking like a 'Bollywood-ised' version of themselves. Everyone had put in so much effort – splashed out on fancy outfits, had hair and make-up done. It was the most glamorous collection of people I'd ever seen in real life.

I sat up there for hours, greeting friends and family who came over to pass on their congratulations, and pretending to join in with the feasting that was going on around me. In reality, there was no way my stomach was up to welcoming any food, not while it was still locked in the grip of that elastic band.

My only wobble came when my brother Mosh made his way over to speak to me. He gave me a hug (a pretty rare thing to get from any of my brothers) and I held him tight. 'You okay?' he asked, looking slightly concerned as I let him loose.

I nodded, keeping the smile that had been fixed onto my face for the last few hours in place. But his kindness unlocked something in me that I had been desperately trying to shut away ever since we arrived at the venue. Before I knew it, my eyes started to water. Mosh put his arms back around me, returning the tight hold I'd had on him moments earlier.

'Don't worry. You know I'll support you.' For a teenage boy, Mosh was pretty good at knowing the right thing to say.

The biggest moment of the afternoon was to come after the food. That's when I would make my way downstairs to join Tareq on the 'main' stage, accompanied by my bridesmaids and backed by my very own entrance music.

It was almost like a ring walk. Your whole body feels like it's buzzing with a strange mix of fear and exhilaration on the walk that takes you from dressing room to boxing ring before a fight. Well, my feelings at that moment of my wedding day were not much different.

I trod carefully down the stairs, conscious of the weight of my *lehenga* trying to pull me forwards. As I slowly descended into the sound of hundreds of people cheering my entrance, I saw Tareq – my husband – for the first time that day, standing in the centre of the stage that was decorated in similar fashion to mine (except the colour scheme was reversed, so that everything was more gold than white).

He was dressed in a cream wedding sherwani (a long top that comes down to the knees and trousers that are baggy around the thigh and narrow at the ankle) and a traditional flat-topped hat. I thought he looked pretty good. We caught each other's eye, and shared a smile as I made my way over to the stage amid the sound of more than 1,000 people going crazy. After spending the last few hours feeling pretty lonely (despite being in the presence of so many), it was a comforting feeling to have him by my side.

The rest of the afternoon passed by in a blur of posing for photographs, cake cutting, gift receiving – all of it seemed to go on for hours. The one thing that I do remember clearly, though, is the moment I threw the bouquet. It's normally an English tradition, but it was something I really wanted to incorporate. The girls all went absolutely crazy trying to get their hands on it – they were so desperate to be the next one getting married. I wanted to tell them there was no rush. Everything will happen quickly enough.

It was still light outside when the moment I had been dreading arrived. It was time to leave the venue and go to my new home – the one that Tareq shared with his parents and three sisters in Essex. It was time to say goodbye to my family.

As they kissed me goodbye, Mum and Dad were both in tears. I would see them again in a few hours' time when the party continued at my in-laws' house, but we all knew what that moment signified: the end of our chapter together and the beginning of a new one, in which their role would always be secondary to that of my new family.

I could hardly bring myself to look at Ane, but hugged

her and my three brothers in turn before making my way to the car that was waiting for us outside. As we pulled away, I couldn't stop the tears from rolling. I'd held them in for so much of the afternoon but, now, I just let them flow. Tareq took my hand, but he knew that there was nothing he could say. He just had to hope that, with time, I would feel like his home was also my own.

As we pulled up outside the house, the front door was wide open. Inside, I could see a crowd of people had beaten us to it. I asked Tareq to give me a moment to compose myself and make sure there was no evidence of the tearful journey we'd just endured. 'Do I look okay?' I checked, before getting out of the car. 'Amazing,' he said, kissing me softly on the cheek.

We were cheered into the house and ushered into their back garden, where a huge marquee provided the setting for the next stage of the party. It was still really warm and I was desperate to change out of my wedding outfit into something that wasn't quite so heavy. But I couldn't – not just yet. There were still formalities to fulfil. Meeting and greeting to do. Photographs to pose for.

It got to about ten o'clock, when I decided I had to do it and plucked up the courage to ask my mother-in-law if it was okay for me to take off the outfit. The relief when she said yes was only surpassed by the feeling of freeing myself from the weight of those clothes: much like the 'aaah' moment of taking off your bra after a long day, but about a million times better.

Upstairs, in the bedroom set aside for us, I found a wardrobe already filled with most of my clothes (thanks to one of my brothers, who had delivered them earlier in the day). I hung up the *lehenga* and headscarf, sat down on the bed and was suddenly struck by a feeling of overwhelming tiredness. Every single part of me wanted to lie down and close my eyes. But I knew I couldn't just disappear like that. Going to bed without saying goodnight to everyone still gathered downstairs (including my new husband) would not be a good start to my new life as a daughter-in-law.

It was almost three o'clock in the morning by the time we made it to bed. Exhaustion was good, though – it meant little capacity for thinking about what the morning might bring.

When my alarm went off, there was a brief moment when I thought I was at home, in my own bed. A moment when I thought I'd wake up to see Ane straightening her hair on the other side of the room and hear the heavy footsteps of my brothers echoing around the house. But it didn't last long. The movement of Tareq stirring next to me cut straight through that comforting vision and prompted me to sit bolt upright in bed.

I had to get up, get dressed and help my mother-in-law, Nazia, to prepare the house for the day's festivities. Mum, Dad, my grandmother and all my siblings would soon be arriving at the house, armed with plates of food. It's a tradition for the bride's family to bring over breakfast the day after a wedding and it's one I was thankful for that morning, as I adjusted to my new surroundings.

The house was more spacious than ours; his sisters each had their own bedroom and downstairs there were two large reception rooms, a separate kitchen and one of the biggest gardens I'd ever seen – at least half the size of a football pitch, although it would be taken up by the marquee for another day or two yet. The rituals of a Bengali wedding go on for days after the ceremony, so extra room for friends and members of the extended family is always useful.

For the next forty-eight hours I barely had a moment to myself. Nor did Tareq and I – at most, we probably exchanged about ten sentences a day for the first two days of our marriage. I couldn't wait for the festivities to be over so we could finally have some time to ourselves. I was also eager to get started with looking for a job.

At the start of the month I'd received the amazing news that I'd passed my degree in architectural technology. Amid all the wedding build-up, it got overshadowed pretty quickly but the actual moment that I showed my parents the letter was one I will never forget. They couldn't have been prouder. After all those years of not believing I was capable – thinking I wasn't the smart one out of the siblings – now I was the one to get a degree (and a husband, as Mum reminded me: 'And you are getting married!'). Finally, they believed in me. I even got a hug (neither of them is really a 'hugger').

Now I was keen to get a job as soon as I could, not only to show them that I wasn't going to let the last four years go to waste, but to make sure I had some form of independence in my daily life. Otherwise, I feared a future of being stuck at home helping Nazia with the chores all day, every day.

As soon as I had a little time to myself, I sent out loads of CVs and started scouring the internet for opportunities. There was only a week or so until we were due to go on honeymoon (thanks to my brother, who bought us some travel vouchers as a wedding present), but I wanted to get out there as much as I could before we left, knowing that every other graduate would be doing exactly the same (and probably more).

The idea of a holiday with Tareq both excited and unnerved me at the same time. It would be nice to have the chance to get to know him more, but a week was also the most time we'd ever spent alone together. What if we didn't have anything to talk about? What if he just wanted to sit on a beach all day? (I like to explore.) What if we ended up hating each other?

For the first couple of days it felt a bit like we were on a blind date: 'What do you want to do?'

'I don't mind. What do you want to do?'

'I don't mind . . .'

It took until halfway through the week for me to start to relax a bit and enjoy myself. I realised that we actually got along really well. And I loved having our own space where I felt free to be myself. It made me happy.

A couple of days before we were due to fly back to London, though, I started to feel anxious about going back to his family's house. I knew it wouldn't be the same as it had been that week and I was worried about the expectations his mother had of me. On our last night, I decided I had to say something: I told him I was a little scared about how his mum was going to treat me.

'Why are you thinking about that? We're not even home yet and, anyway, of course she's not going to treat you badly.'

He thought I was worried about the dress code.

'My sisters are allowed to dress how they want, so I don't see why it will be a problem if you want to wear jeans or something . . .'

That wasn't my main concern, though. Deep down, I had the feeling that his mother was apprehensive about having another female in the house – one whose concerns and opinions Tareq might consider before her own. I'd only been in the house for seven days, but it already seemed pretty clear to me that everyone in it followed her lead without question.

Of course, it was her house and I was willing to do all the things expected of me – I wanted to be a good daughter-in-law. But I also wanted to still be me. I'd spent the last four years at university and in the gym, making myself stronger, in every conceivable way. I'd reached a place where the self-conscious girl who'd grown up with so many hang-ups about her body and her brain was almost a distant memory, replaced by a young woman who knew who she really was and what she wanted out of life. Someone who held her head high as she walked down the street. Someone who was following her own dreams.

The thought of giving all of that up made me feel ill. Like I was being suffocated.

How could I say all of that to Tareq on the last night of our honeymoon, though, before I'd even given things a chance? I couldn't. Instead I smiled at Tareq's reassurances and tried to push everything else to the back of my mind.

It was late by the time we got back from the airport the next day. The house was already in darkness, so we snuck in as quietly as we could, trying not to wake anyone. In the kitchen, his mother had left some food out for us – chicken kebabs, rice, samosas – and Tareq got stuck in while I made us some tea and looked for something a bit lighter.

'You don't want any?' Tareq asked, in between mouthfuls.

'It's a bit too late for me,' I said. 'Just tea will be fine.'

The next morning, Tareq left the house early for work. In my semi-conscious state, I listened to the sounds of him getting ready to leave: the shower pump running, suit taken out of the wardrobe, footsteps descending the stairs … and the front door closing.

Just like that, I was alone. The rest of the house was in

silence. I guess that was when it really hit me: this was for real. All this time it had just been a bit of fun – I didn't have to live with Tareq or be at his family home. It was just like dating someone: going for coffee; going for dinner. I still got to be with my family and have my own life. But now, I was in his environment. My sister wasn't there for me to talk to. My brothers weren't there making a lot of noise. And my mum wasn't calling me to come and help her in the kitchen.

I was alone.

I lay there for a while listening for signs of life. Eventually I heard voices. It sounded like the two eldest girls, Sadaf and Poorva. Gradually, their voices faded as they must have gone downstairs. I rolled out of bed. Knowing that they were down there felt less intimidating than the idea of sharing breakfast alone with Tareq's parents.

When I walked into the kitchen ten minutes later, I found Nazia alone. She was standing by the hob, with her back to the doorway as I entered, so I wished her good morning to let her know I was there.

There was no reaction.

I said it again, this time a little louder: 'Good morning, Ma' – a more polite way of saying 'Mum' in Bengali.

'Oh, morning,' she said, turning to look at me just for a second, before going back to what she was cooking.

'Can I help you with anything?' I asked.

'You can get the bowls out of the cupboard for breakfast. I've made porridge for you.'

I took a step further into the kitchen before stopping, realising I had no idea where she kept anything.

'Here.' Nazia pointed to a cupboard next to the sink.

She seemed unhappy with me, but I had no idea why. I hadn't even seen her since before we went away.

She served up three bowls of porridge and instructed me to deliver two of them to her daughters who were sitting in the living room. When I returned to the kitchen for mine, she nodded to the table, suggesting I should eat there, instead of joining my sisters-in-law in the other room. I took a seat.

'Are you going to eat this?' she asked as she put the bowl down in front of me. 'Your mother told me you are very picky about your food and Tareq told me you didn't eat any of what I left for you last night.'

'Oh, well, it was a bit late and I didn't really want anything too heavy just before going to bed . . .'

Her expression darkened with every word I spoke. Should I apologise? I didn't feel I'd done anything wrong, but it seemed like she did. So I said I was sorry. That the food all looked lovely and I was very grateful to her for taking the time to prepare it for us.

Nazia had filled the bowl almost to the brim. It felt like a challenge.

Slowly, I worked my way through it. Forcing down the final few mouthfuls despite my stomach churning in such a way that I knew I was going to regret them later on.

It was not the best of starts to our relationship, but at least I was in no doubt as to what not to do when presented with Nazia's food. Mum was right, though; I was picky, in the sense that my training had given me a desire to fuel my body with the right kind of foods. I enjoyed eating pretty healthily. That didn't mean I never ate Mum's dishes, just that I tried to balance them out with lots of fruit, salads and vegetables. At that moment I didn't dare to even imagine what Nazia's reaction would be if I tried to explain that to her.

It was seven o'clock by the time Tareq got back from work. I had left the house just once in that time, to fetch a few things that Nazia wanted from the little supermarket around the corner. Otherwise, I had spent the day sorting out our holiday clothes – washing, drying, ironing. And trying to stay out of Nazia's way as much as possible.

As we got ready for bed that night, I asked Tareq if he thought it would be okay for me to go and see my parents the next day. I hadn't seen them or my siblings since the day after our wedding and I missed them terribly.

'Check with Mum,' he said. 'I'm sure that will be okay, as long as she doesn't need you here for anything.'

I let my head drop back onto my pillow and stared up at the ceiling wondering if this was the way it was always going to be from now on – my life dictated by someone else. No freedom to go to my parents' house when I wanted to, or to meet up with Ane for a coffee. And what about KO? I'd had visions of being able to spend more time there than before – maybe even with my husband's blessing. It was a vision that was fading fast.

I rolled away from Tareq, so he couldn't see the tears dropping onto the pillow. One word kept coming into my head. It was the only way I knew how to describe the way I felt. And it was exactly what I had feared: suffocation.

Chapter 7

I had just got out of the shower one morning when my phone rang: unknown number. Normally, I would let it go straight to voicemail but, for some reason, I thought I should answer this one.

'Hi, is this Ruqsana Begum?'

'Well . . . yes. Who's calling?'

'This is Peter Shields from BPTW. We received your CV and would like you to come in for an interview. How does next Thursday suit?'

BPTW . . . BPTW . . . Wow. It took me a moment to put the name into context, but then it came to me: they were a big architectural firm in Greenwich. They'd won awards. Had really smart offices. Of course, Thursday was fine.

Arrangements finalised with Peter, I hung up the phone and proceeded to walk round and round the bedroom, too excited to sit. Too excited to blow-dry. I had to tell someone. I called Tareq . . . straight to voicemail. I should have known; he never answers his phone at work. I left a garbled message, but it still didn't alleviate my need to tell somebody. I needed someone to share the excitement with.

I called Ane.

Voicemail again! What was wrong with everybody? I mean, what's the point of having a mobile phone if you're never going to answer it? I sat down on my bed and thought back to the day I had spent handing out CVs to all the posh architectural firms around Tower Bridge. At the time, it had only been a few days since we finished uni, but I knew that, with the wedding coming up, there was no time to waste. So I put on something smart, printed off a load of CVs and headed down into the City with my friend Sumina.

After delivering the first one, I remember her saying to me: 'Oh my God, you're so confident. You just walk in like that.'

It's something I'd learned in the gym: even if you don't *feel* confident, make sure you look it. Not only does it tell your opponent you're there to win, but it can also impact on you, too. Act like you believe in yourself often enough and, before you know it, your mind gets the hint and actually does.

From the moment I handed in my dissertation, I'd been optimistic about getting a job in architecture. Some of my friends doubted themselves. They'd pull back from applying for certain things – say things like: 'I don't know if I'm good enough for that job ...' Whereas my attitude was always: 'I'm going to apply anyway. Then they can interview me and decide for themselves if I'm good enough.'

I'd rather go for it and try to make an impression during the interview than rule myself out of it before I've even had the opportunity to get in there. After all, what did I have to lose?

With my excitement somewhat diluted by Tareq and Ane's elusiveness, I finished getting myself ready and went downstairs to find out what my day held. Perhaps, if Nazia didn't need me for too much, I could head over to my parents' house. I knew they would be just as thrilled as I was with the news.

I found her drinking a cup of tea with Tareq's father Atif in the living room. His illness meant that he was at home pretty much all of the time – something that no one seemed particularly happy about. She gave me a few chores to get on with, but nothing that would take all day, so I asked whether I might be able to go and see my parents, once I was finished.

Nazia said that it would be better to bring them over here. That way, I was sure to be at home when Tareq got back from work and could help her with preparing dinner. I hesitated in the doorway, knowing that I should tell them about the interview, too, but not wanting my excitement to be completely wiped away by what my gut feeling told me would be a lukewarm response.

I'd stood there too long, though. Nazia was looking at me expectantly.

'I have a job interview next week,' I said, finding myself smiling as I said it. 'It's for a really good firm in Greenwich.'

'So far away?' asked Nazia, combating my smile with a frown that suggested I should have stuck with my gut.

But, once I reassured her that the company had an office in Epping, too (which was a lot closer to where we lived in Barking), she took the news really well. She even seemed quite pleased.

At last; a positive sign. Maybe a job would mean more flexibility – more freedom – when it came to my time outside of the house. So far, weekends had been so busy with family commitments that I hadn't even been able to think about getting to KO for training. But maybe if I was working, there would be a way to fit something in one evening during the week.

When it came to the interview, my optimism paid off. It was only a few days later when they called to say I had the job and I could start the very next week. I'd spend the first few months training at their main office in Greenwich, but after that I would be based in the Epping office. It was perfect.

I had worked so hard. And now I had the degree no one thought I would be able to get and my dream job with a top architectural firm. Mum and Dad might not be the most expressive people in the world, but I could tell from their faces how proud they were. For the next few weeks, I was on a real high – we all were.

The job was great. Every day I was learning new things and meeting so many new people. The vibe in the office was really welcoming, so, right from the start, I felt like I was part of a team.

I was about two weeks into the job when Ane and I arranged to meet up one night after work. I was desperate to spend some time with her. We spoke on the phone as often as we could but it wasn't the same. I missed our nightly chats. Our morning routine. I missed having someone around who I could connect with.

That evening, I left work with a smile on my face. I was so excited to see Ane, I think I'd spent the whole day talking about her to anyone who'd listen. When we saw each other outside Ilford station we launched into each other's arms as though we'd been separated for years. It felt like we had.

We headed to a little café not too far from my parents' house where we used to go all the time for tea and something sweet. We did exactly the same now, splitting a chocolate muffin between us as we caught up on everything that was going on in the other's life. Before now, I hadn't told her much about what it was like living with Tareq's parents; it wasn't something I could really go into on the phone while I was there (Nazia always seemed to want me for something whenever I was mid-phone call, anyway) and typing out long text messages has never been my thing.

I tried to describe how different it was to our house. How it felt like there was no life in it. I was used to my brothers messing around, cheering over football in one room while Ane and I chilled out, sharing a bag of sweets and deciding who would be the one to help Mum out with dinner that day. Now, there was mostly silence.

'Maybe that's because of his dad being unwell,' Ane reasoned.

I nodded. 'There's something else . . .'

'What?' she asked, looking at me with concern.

I shifted in my seat, suddenly uncertain about whether I should have said anything. This wasn't something I had spoken about to anyone before and I wasn't sure how it would come out; I was worried it would sound stupid, like I was getting upset over nothing.

'Afa' – a Bengali term for older sister, which Ane often calls me by – '. . . what is it?'

I took a deep breath. 'It's Nazia and Atif . . . they don't seem to like it if I sit next to Tareq.'

'What do you mean?'

'I mean, we're not allowed to sit next to each other. Like, on the sofa in the evenings . . . they said it makes them uncomfortable.'

Ane was silent. Maybe she didn't know what to say. I carried on, telling her how Tareq's parents had no issues with the friends of my sisters-in-law sitting next to him whenever they came over. He would even hug them hello and goodbye, give them lifts home and spend his days off from work driving them around. I didn't get it.

Nazia would tell me how many girlfriends he'd had and how many of his sisters' friends had a crush on him. She showered them all with compliments, too – these friends of my sisters-in-law were always 'so beautiful ... a gorgeous girl'. It was constant; even when we watched the wedding video, she spent half the time commenting on how beautiful they all were. But with me, there was nothing. It made me feel like *I* was nothing. Like I was ugly. Like I wasn't good enough.

As I spoke, I felt myself getting more and more upset. So far, I'd tried not to let any of it get to me; just told myself I was being paranoid or too sensitive about things. But saying it out loud in front of Ane made me realise how much it was affecting me.

Ane suggested I should talk to Tareq about it. Let him know how I was feeling, and maybe then he could have a word with his mother. I wasn't so sure he would have the nerve. And even if he did, I didn't think Nazia would listen to him. But Ane was right about one thing: I should talk to Tareq.

We stayed in the café for longer than we should have, given that I had already decided I wanted to go back to my parents' house with Ane so I could see everyone else. By the time we got there it must have been about seven o'clock – dinner time. As soon as the front door opened the smell of Mum's cooking filled my nostrils. I'd missed that, too.

Not everyone was at home – Moynul was out somewhere and Mosh was playing football – but I got to see Eklim and my parents. They were pleased to see me but Dad was worried about me staying for too long. He kept looking at the clock on the kitchen wall, saying: 'You better go back now . . . Why did she bring you here? You need to go back.'

My own parents were worried about upsetting my new family.

I spent the thirty-minute walk back to Tareq's house thinking about how I could broach the situation with him. But everything I rehearsed in my head made me sound like a crazy woman. By the time I walked through the door I'd talked myself out of it. We'd only been married for a couple of months. Maybe it was just going to take a bit of time for everything to settle down. And, if not, then I still had hopes that, one day, we might be able to get a place of our own.

As soon as I walked in, Nazia wanted to know where I had been. So I told her. She never really said anything directly to me when she was unhappy with something I'd done. But it felt as if she found lots of other ways to let me know: barely looking at me when she spoke to me; giving me extra errands to run at the weekend so I had no time to see my sister; getting Tareq to tell me I should always come straight home after work to help out with things around the house.

It wasn't only Nazia who I felt didn't like me keeping a strong bond with my family. It was Tareq's sisters, too. When I got my first wages from work, I wanted to buy something for Ane with the money. When I was at university, she was earning a salary from working at the chemist's and would always help me out if I needed money for anything. So, now that I had an income, I really wanted to get her something.

I decided on a pair of trousers from Topshop – nothing extravagant. The day I brought them back to the house, Poorva (Tareq's middle sister) saw me coming in with the bag and asked what I'd bought. I told her that it was just a little gift for Ane; that I wanted to buy her something with my first wage packet. Poorva stood there for a moment, seemingly processing what I'd just said, before muttering something about *her* being my sister now and storming into the living room, closing the door behind her.

I couldn't win. It felt like I wasn't getting any love or affection from anyone in that house (except for Tareq, on the rare occasions that we had some time alone together). So any comfort I was getting was coming from my own family. But I couldn't always see them and even when I did, they were scared to show me too much affection in case it upset my in-laws.

Week by week, month by month, it was wearing me down.

Every evening I came back from work and steeled myself for the most difficult part of my day. Shutting the front door behind me didn't feel like I was shutting out the world. It felt like the world was shutting me out.

All I wanted was the freedom to get back out there. And the fact that I hadn't been able to get to the gym since before the wedding only made things worse.

I missed the training immensely. I'd started to feel lethargic and weak. Every day it felt like I'd lost a little more of the strength I'd worked so hard to build. Training was a part of me. And I'd gone to such lengths to keep it in my life over the last few years. Now it had come to a sudden halt.

At one point, I tried to get back to the gym. I knew I couldn't go there on a Sunday so I tried booking private sessions with one of the instructors during the week instead. But every time I booked one, something came up at home that I had to be there for – Nazia having guests over or a family visit to some relatives. So I kept missing the sessions – and I was paying for them. I wanted to train so badly, but it just seemed impossible.

Before the wedding, I had overcome so many obstacles to get to the gym each week. But now, I was so mentally and physically drained from trying to fulfil my role as a daughter-in-law that I had less energy to think – less energy to come up with creative ways to get to the gym and certainly less energy to have a conversation with my in-laws about it.

This was a whole new life. I just had to try to adapt to it.

And I backed myself to do that. I knew I'd built up a certain amount of resilience in the gym and thought that would be enough to help me through this period of adjustment. I was so unhappy, but I just kept telling myself that it wouldn't last for ever – that one day, Tareq and I would have our own home and then everything would be okay.

Living with his parents was so different from living with mine, where, by the time I was at university, I had a certain amount of flexibility. In fact, it wasn't like my parents' house in lots of ways. When I walked in Mum and Dad's front door, I immediately felt the warmth of being 'at home'. Of being safe.

Here, I felt like I was treading on eggshells all the time. It seemed I was constantly being reminded that I wasn't at home. If I walked up the stairs it was: 'Where are you going?' If I wanted to make a snack, it was: 'What are you eating?' If they saw me coming home with anything new, it was: 'What are you spending your money on now?'

Once I was earning a wage, it quickly became apparent that my money was also theirs. Nazia never asked me for it directly, of course, but Tareq's youngest sister, Afsana, used to deliver bills up to my room. The first time it happened I was completely taken aback: what am I supposed to do with these? Tareq was already paying the mortgage. Did they want me to pay for everything else, too?

I understood that as a daughter-in-law, there were certain things expected of me: you do have to be attentive to your in-laws' needs. You do need permission to go out. You do need to dress in a certain way. And I really was trying to do all of those things – while also being a good trainee at work. But it felt like the expectations had gone way beyond what was required of me. It was becoming exhausting.

When guests came over, I was the one serving and cleaning up after them. It didn't matter if I was tired after a long day at work – I couldn't go to bed until all the guests had gone home. If I wanted to cook some food for myself, I had to time it so that Nazia was out of the house. Otherwise I was accused of taking up too much room, using too much food or trying to force her son to live off salad leaves. When I did my washing, I couldn't hang it out to dry in the garden because she wanted to hang hers out. Eventually, I figured out that if I got up at the crack of dawn on a Saturday morning, I could wash my clothes and hang them out for a few hours, quickly bringing them in before she came downstairs around nine o'clock.

Even that had its dangers. One weekend, I'd done my washing early in the morning as usual and brought it in after a couple of hours. But it was still damp, so I left a few things spread out on the bed and over the heater to dry while I was out running some errands. When I came back, Atif was waiting to speak to me. He told me he'd needed to go into my room to get a file from the wardrobe and wasn't happy to see I had left my 'bits and pieces' lying around everywhere. I didn't have any answer for him. What else could I do when his wife wouldn't let me dry my clothes outside?

I was overthinking every single situation. Where am I going to eat? What am I going to have? Before long, I found myself living an almost solitary existence whenever I was within those four walls: I would go to work, come home and sit in my room. Sometimes Tareq would come and join me. But more often than not, he would be downstairs with his family.

I felt completely isolated. Alienated.

Eventually, I wasn't even thinking about the gym any more. Instead of waking up in the morning and longing to train (as I used to), I was simply thinking about surviving another day. I would lie there, keeping my eyes closed for as long as possible, thinking: *How do I cope with this situation? How can I make today a better one than yesterday?*

It was a survival mechanism. Every day was a series of challenges. Just as I used to approach training by thinking: I just need to get through the next round/interval/session, I'd start the day with: I just need to get through work today. Then, when I was coming home, it was: I just need to get through this evening. Rather than thinking about a long-term goal or what I was going to do on a Sunday afternoon, it was a day-to-day battle.

Looking back, I'm sure that those hours I'd spent in the gym helped me to persevere longer than most people would have been able to. Whenever I felt things were completely hopeless, all I had to do was remember Bill's words to me at that first inter-club tournament back in 2002 – four years ago: 'I don't worry about you, Rox ... because you can't teach someone to fight.'

If he believed I had that fighting instinct, then so did I.

On a couple of occasions, I tried to speak to Ane and my parents. I needed someone to open up to. Someone to confide in. But every time I tried to explain what was going on and how I was feeling, they couldn't quite understand. They were seeing things from the outside, where everything looked really pretty: nice house, good husband, great job ... but they didn't realise how much of a toll the situation was taking on me mentally. And I really struggled to articulate it.

It turned out that my great job was causing some damage of its own to Tareq's relationship with his mum and dad; something I only found out when I returned earlier than expected from a day trip to France with work. Initially, the plan had been to get a late train back from Paris, which would have seen me arrive back at the house around midnight. But when one of our last meetings got cancelled, we managed to catch an earlier train.

I got back to Barking around nine o'clock, expecting the house to be as quiet as usual. But as soon as I opened the front door, I heard raised voices coming from the kitchen. I paused in the doorway, trying to listen in without letting them know I was there. The first voice I heard belonged to my father-in-law. I guessed he was speaking to Tareq when he started talking about money and control – asking why Tareq didn't have control over mine, because everything I earned was his ...

'I'm trying . . .'

Tareq had occasionally asked me for money since I'd started working and I'd thought, okay, £200 here and there is not an issue. But I didn't think he wanted my whole salary. Now I started to believe that having a second income in the house had been on his parents' agenda all along: a wife for their son and some extra cash for them.

I shut the door with a bang and went straight upstairs. I didn't care if they knew I'd heard them.

As we were getting ready for bed that night, I tried to talk to Tareq about things. I didn't mention the conversation specifically, just tried to explain a bit about the way I was being treated and how it was making me feel. I reminded him that when we were on our honeymoon, he'd told me that it wasn't going to be like this. As I spoke, he was looking just as upset as I was.

He felt sorry for me. Told me he never thought they would treat me this way. That he thought they would treat their own daughter-in-law – the only one they'll ever have – with more love. But he wasn't strong enough to actually do anything about it. He pointed out that his dad was ill . . . his mum had enough to deal with. Basically, he didn't have the confidence to stand up to his parents.

Now, more than ever, it felt like there was no way out. So, I told myself I just had to try harder. Handle the situation better. Please them more. Fight.

Over time, the strain on me started to tell. One weekend there was a family function – we were going to visit a newborn – and at the last minute, Nazia asked me to rush out and buy some outfits for the baby before we left. I only had about an hour to buy the outfits, then get back and get ready to go. I knew that if I kept them waiting, she'd be fuming.

I got everything I needed, went back to the house and ran upstairs to get changed. At that point a wave of extreme exhaustion hit me. I couldn't help myself – I lay down on the bed. Just for a moment . . .

'We're leaving.'

Shit. It was Tareq's sister, Poorva. I must have drifted off. I told her I'd be there in two minutes and quickly threw on an outfit, tied my hair up and left the house without doing my make-up. As I sat in the back of the car, I felt myself waning again. I was like a kids' toy whose batteries were on their last legs.

I dragged myself through the afternoon, thankful that we were at somebody else's house and I wouldn't be expected to run around clearing up after everyone. Instead, I found a quiet corner to sit in and made sure I got my fill of the food on offer, thinking that might give me a boost of energy.

But it made no difference. I felt much the same on the journey home as I had on the way there. Once we got back, I told Tareq I wasn't feeling well and went straight upstairs for a nap. It wasn't exactly a lie – the only explanation I could think of for the way I was feeling was that I must be coming down with something. A few days later, I was definitely ill. I got up for work as usual but, as soon as I went downstairs and smelled everyone's breakfast things, a strong sense of nausea flooded over me. I ran back upstairs and into the bathroom to be sick and sat on the bathroom floor, waiting to see if the nausea would pass.

After ten minutes, I felt confident enough that nothing else was coming up to leave the bathroom, but the nausea hadn't shifted. I filled a bottle with water and sipped from it slowly on my way to work, trying to avoid all sights/scents of food along the way. By lunchtime I felt brave enough to try a plain bread roll from the work canteen (which I asked someone else to get for me – there was no way I could go in there while the nausea was still hanging around).

That evening, I cooked myself some plain rice for dinner and ate it upstairs. I hadn't been sick again but I definitely didn't feel quite right. The next day, it happened again – only this time I made it to work before actually being sick. When I told my line manager that I thought I should probably go home, she looked at me and smiled.

'Do you think you might be . . . you know?' She nodded down towards my stomach, just to make sure I knew what she was suggesting.

'Pregnant? I hadn't even . . . no, I don't think so. I'll go to the doctor's this afternoon and get checked out.'

Pregnant. Once the word was in my head, I couldn't get it out. My periods had been so all over the place for the last six months or so that I hadn't even realised I'd missed one. I left the office and headed straight home, stopping in the chemist's along the way to buy a pregnancy test. My hands were shaking as I opened the packet in the bathroom. A few minutes later they were shaking even more as I read the result.

Pregnant.

Shit.

My head started working through the consequences. Maybe this was the best thing for Tareq and me. Surely, now we would have to leave his parents' house and get a place of our own? There was no way his mum and dad would want a crying baby around.

I sent Tareq a message, asking him to call me urgently. Then I called the doctor's. They couldn't see me until the next morning, so I was going to have to wait to get it confirmed. I didn't have any doubts, though. The tiredness, the sickness ... now that I knew, it all seemed so obvious. Even so, I didn't want to tell anyone – apart from Tareq – until I was 100 per cent sure.

It was late afternoon by the time he rang me from work to see if I was okay: 'Are you still feeling crap?'

'Sort of ... I think I'm pregnant.'

'Oh, wow. That's brilliant news ... but, listen, I can't really talk right now. I'll be home around seven, okay?'

That was hours away. Until then it was just me and my thoughts. I had so many questions: what would I do about work? I'd only been there six months – would they be okay with me taking time off to have a baby? How would it feel to grow a big belly? Would we move into a place of our own before or after the baby was born?

By the time Tareq got home my brain was fried. He wasn't great at expressing his emotions, but he seemed pretty happy with the news that he was going to be a father. I asked him to keep it quiet from his family for now, though. Once the doctor confirmed it, then we could tell them.

The next morning, everything was made official. My GP confirmed I was pregnant and booked me in for a scan in a few weeks' time, when they would tell me the baby's expected due date. As soon as I left the surgery, I called Ane to tell her. She was so excited she wanted to see me straight away, but I had told work I'd only be off for the morning. Now that I knew what was causing the feelings of nausea, I was just going to have to get on with it as best I could.

Ane and I arranged to meet up at the weekend instead; I would ask Tareq if we could go over to my parents' house and tell them together. Those few days were the happiest I'd been in months. Everyone was thrilled with the news that there was going to be a baby in the family and it gave me such a lift to feel that sense of positivity and love.

But if I thought it was going to change anything just yet, I was mistaken. My life still felt like it didn't have an off switch. The days at work were long and, when I got home, Nazia and Atif were still there, seemingly waiting for their every demand to be met. This, coupled with the pregnancy tiredness I was already feeling, meant I wasn't sure quite how I was going to get through the next few months.

It was the Monday of the week I was due to go for my scan that something changed. Actually, everything changed.

I noticed a few spots of blood when I went to the toilet. It wasn't much, but enough to make me worry that something could be wrong. I didn't really know what, but I planned to mention it to the nurse when I went for the scan. A few days later, I found myself lying down on an examination table, looking at the face of a nurse whose eyes told me everything I needed to know.

I'd had a miscarriage.

I saw the nurse's mouth moving but I wasn't hearing anything. My mind was filled with too many questions. Too much confusion. Why? What had I done wrong? What was going to happen to the baby now? Was it my fault? It must be my fault . . .

I could see Tareq touching my hand but I couldn't feel it. It was like I was watching someone else lying there sobbing. It wasn't me, it couldn't be. I was only just getting used to the idea of becoming a mum. It couldn't be gone already.

The nurse explained what I could expect to happen over the next week or so, before asking me if I had any questions. I wanted to scream, but I was too empty to produce any sound. Instead, I shook my head, took all the leaflets she handed me and followed Tareq out of the room. We walked to his car in silence, neither of us really knowing how to process what we'd just been told. None of the words that came into my head felt like the right ones to express what I was thinking or how I felt. Mostly because I wasn't even sure I knew either of those things.

The days that followed were filled with pain: debilitating stomach cramps. Like being stabbed in the stomach over and over and over again. For a week I couldn't get out of bed. I simply lay there, waiting for the agony to be over.

Emotionally, I was broken. But I wasn't sure if I had any right to feel that way. I'd only been attached to the idea of being pregnant for a few weeks. I thought of all those women who go through months of pregnancy and getting attached to the idea of a new life before losing a baby and felt a sense of guilt. I told myself that they had more of a right to feel this way than I did.

But I couldn't help it. From the moment I'd found out, I'd started envisaging a different life for myself. A different purpose. It felt like there was something positive in my life – something that gave me hope. Now, all of a sudden, I was back to square one. From such a high to such a low within a matter of weeks.

I don't think anybody in the house knew how to deal with it, really. Nazia and Atif mostly stayed away and Tareq was busy in his normal routine of work and life. When I did see him, he didn't seem to know what to say or do. Emotionally, I got almost nothing from him.

Life seemed so normal for everyone else. But for me, it couldn't be. I wasn't sure if it ever would be again.

Chapter 8

A week later, I was back at work and right back at square one. People around me saw the same Ruqsana from the outside, but inside I felt different; vulnerable. Weaker. It was like an integral part of me that had been eroding ever since my wedding day was now completely destroyed: finished off by the emotional trauma of the last month.

I decided that the only way to start the rebuild was to bury the sadness deeper and deeper within me; to internalise the pain of losing something that, for the short time I'd had it, had shone a beam of light into my life. Without it, I was plunged back into the darkness of a lonely existence.

I desperately tried to find a reason to be hopeful. I hadn't had the chance to speak to Tareq about moving out into our own place over the last few weeks, but maybe that was still a possibility. 'You would still be able to visit,' I said, after tentatively raising the idea as we lay in bed one night. 'I just need a bit of breathing space. I feel like I can't even sit down next to you. Like I'm being judged all of the time . . .' Even as I spoke, I could see his face already forming into a frown.

It wasn't happening. He shut me down completely, saying that his dad was unwell and that it was simply out of the question for us to live anywhere else. And that was the end of the conversation. He turned away from me, switched off his light and went to sleep.

So, what hope was I left with? Divorce wasn't something I could contemplate because of the consequences within our community. I'd heard enough stories to leave me fearful of being scarred for life by something like that. And no matter how badly treated I felt, no matter how isolated and alone I had come to feel in that house, there was always a voice in my head asking: what have they really done that's so wrong? No one was hitting me. No one was swearing at me.

In my lowest moments, I almost wished they would hit me. Bruise me, just so that I had something to show people. Just so I could say: 'Look, this is what they're doing to me.' Instead, I had nothing apart from how I *felt*. Which was lost. Broken.

Stripped of everything that Muay Thai had given me. Confidence. Independence. Ambition. A sense that, as long as I worked hard, I could achieve whatever I wanted with my life.

All of that was gone now.

'You need to get that Western girl mentality out of your head. This is marriage.' Those were the words of my friend Kaniz as we lingered in the shallow end of our local leisure centre swimming pool. I had lost touch with so many friends since moving in with Tareq, but still managed to see Kaniz occasionally. She was Bangladeshi and in an arranged marriage too. So when I told her a bit about how I was feeling – like I couldn't please my in-laws whatever I did, and felt like a slave sometimes in that house – she had some understanding of what I was going through.

But she didn't agree with my resistance to it: 'You know

what, this is your life now. This is how marriage is. You need to just accept it.'

Her words echoed around my mind as we swam a few more lengths before going to get changed. If my own friends were telling me I wasn't Bangladeshi enough, that I was too modern-thinking, then maybe that voice in my head was right. What had Tareq's family really done that was so wrong? Maybe they were just doing what all in-laws did. Maybe I was the one in the wrong for still trying to be the Ruqsana that I was before I was married – open-minded. Modern. Westernised.

The last drops of resistance drained out of me after the conversation with Kaniz. I couldn't fight any more. The only hope I had left of making this marriage work was to give everything I had to trying to be a good daughter-in-law. To work harder than ever to try to earn their approval.

That week, I did whatever I could to make them happy. Every single minute that I was at home, I was attentive to all their needs. Shopping, cleaning, cooking, tidying – whatever they needed doing, I did it. The one thing I allowed for myself was an arrangement with Ane, that we would spend Sunday afternoon together. My plan was to get up early, help Nazia with anything she needed doing in the house and then go to meet Ane for an afternoon of shopping, cake-sharing and catching up. I couldn't wait. It was the highlight of my week.

But I never made it that far.

When my alarm went off that morning I was straight up and out of bed. I wanted to get started with the day's chores as early as I could to make sure I'd finished them in time to meet Ane. I wasn't the first one up, though; Tareq had left at the crack of dawn to get to a wedding up north. Initially, I asked if I could go with him, so we could spend some time together, but he said it wouldn't be worth it – that he was just going to show his face and then come home.

Downstairs, Nazia was nowhere to be seen so I made myself a cup of tea and threw some fruit and yoghurt into a bowl for breakfast. I'd just about finished when I heard her footsteps coming down the stairs. She wanted help with preparing the food for some guests they had coming over in the evening, so I made a start on that – cleaning some corns – while she disappeared into the living room to see Atif.

A few moments later I was lying on the kitchen floor, my whole body shaking. Nazia must have heard the thud of me hitting the floor and came rushing into the kitchen with Atif and Afsana following. The three of them picked me up, Atif taking hold of my arms, Nazia and Afsana my legs and carried me into the living room where they laid me down on the sofa. I was still shaking. My eyes were open but rolled right back into my head.

For three or four minutes, I lay there while the three of them discussed what to do. They were still talking about it when I came to, before Nazia sent Afsana to fetch me a glass of water. I was awake but not really 'there'. All I knew was that my entire body was aching. It felt like I'd been hit by a truck. The idea of getting up off the sofa, or even just sitting upright, seemed like a physical impossibility.

They decided to call a cousin of theirs, Hasan, who is a doctor, to see if he could come and check me over. Within half an hour or so, he was standing over me in the living room asking if I knew what had happened. Did I have any history of fainting? Had I felt ill before I collapsed? I answered him as well as I could but my head felt like it was filled with cotton wool. Nothing was clear.

Hasan didn't want to diagnose me with anything without any proper tests being done so said he thought I should go to hospital to get checked over. The next thing I knew, I was being loaded into an ambulance and driven away from the house that over the previous nine months had come to feel more like a prison than a home to me.

They tested me for all sorts of things at the hospital. I had scans on my head, an ECG to check my heart was working properly, blood tests, urine tests. But they couldn't find anything that told them what might have caused me to collapse like that. They even kept me in overnight, so that a different doctor could take a look at me the next morning.

That was when my parents arrived. Whether my sister had called Nazia to find out where I was or Nazia had called my parents to tell them what had happened, I never quite found out. What I do know is that Mum and Dad couldn't understand why Nazia and Atif hadn't been with me at the hospital in the first place. I think it was the first time they really started to understand what I had been trying to explain – that the family wasn't all that it seemed from the outside.

It was early afternoon by the time the nurses said I was allowed to go home. In the car, my parents hardly said a word as they drove me back to Tareq's. I hadn't seen him since he'd left for the wedding on Sunday morning and my mobile didn't make it to the hospital with me so I had no idea if he even knew I was there – though, presumably, Nazia must have told him something about my whereabouts.

Mum and Dad came into the house with me. I'd found it hard to take in everything the doctors had said, so my parents recounted what they'd heard to Nazia and Atif (not that there was much to tell, with no clues as to what had happened uncovered in any of the tests). The doctors at the hospital advised us to make an appointment to see my GP as soon as possible, to tell them what had happened. So, Dad called them the moment we got back to Nazia's and a few hours later I was sitting in the doctor's waiting room with my parents alongside me.

'Ruqsana Lohani?'

I looked up to see a petite Indian woman standing by the door to her office. She watched as I slowly stood up and moved gingerly across the waiting room towards her. Each step required every ounce of energy I had. Inside her office, I slumped into the chair next to her desk as if I'd just run a marathon.

We talked about what had happened as Dr Sharma did some routine checks on my pulse and blood pressure. I told her as much as I could (it was all pretty hazy) and she listened intently, looking away from me once or twice to make a note on her computer. Then she started asking me lots of questions: what did I do for work? Who did I live with? What was my life like outside of work? How had I been feeling in general over the last few months?

After noting down all of my answers, Dr Sharma shuffled towards me until she was close enough to take hold of my hand. Holding it in hers she looked me in the eye and said: 'You remind me of my daughter ... Can you pick yourself back up?'

I didn't really know what she meant, but her warmth and kindness were enough to set me off crying. She handed me a tissue and said she would give me a few minutes while she went outside to have a chat with my parents. When she came back in, she sat back down and said mine was the most severe case of a panic attack that she had ever come across. That I had been trying to stay strong for so long that my body had to find some way to release the pressure I was putting it under. 'Go and pack your bags and move back in to your mum's house for a while. Rest there. Recover.'

The look of concern on Mum and Dad's faces when I walked out of Dr Sharma's office was one I hadn't seen before. Not even when they'd come to see me in the hospital. There was nothing I could say to make them feel any better, though. I was mostly numb; couldn't fully process what was going on. The only thing going through my mind was an acceptance that I would go to Mum's house for a few days to get some rest, then go back to Tareq's when I felt better.

We drove back to his house first so that I could grab my overnight stuff and let Nazia and Atif know what was happening. My parents did most of the talking, while I went upstairs to throw a few things into a bag. I came down to find them sitting in the living room, a strange atmosphere shrouding the four of them like a heavy mist. As soon as I walked in, Mum and Dad stood up to leave, saying they would let them know how I was feeling in a day or two.

As we reversed out of the driveway one sensation managed to pierce the numbness: relief. I didn't care that it was only for a few days – I was going home. To Ane. My brothers. My grandmother. Everyone and everything that felt familiar. Safe.

But it didn't seem to help. In fact, my condition deteriorated. Over the next few days, the panic attacks became a frequent occurrence. I would have them multiple times a day. The first time it happened late at night, Ane got really scared and called an ambulance. I was in the back of it on the way to hospital when I woke up. The back of my hands were covered in red marks from the paramedics who had pinched me to try to wake me up. I hadn't felt a thing.

At the hospital, the doctor spoke to me about controlling the panic attacks. He told me that I didn't need to let them happen. That I could control them. I could hear his calming voice, but I wasn't able to stop them. They were too strong for me.

For the next few weeks, I was bedbound. I had no idea what was happening to me. All I knew about panic attacks was what I'd seen on TV, when they show people hyperventilating, taking deep breaths to try to calm themselves down. That's not how it was for me. Mine were almost like having a fit. I would completely collapse, then wake up and think: what just happened? To me it felt like it was all over in seconds, but, in reality, I could be passed out for thirty or even forty-five minutes sometimes.

My family quickly learned how to deal with it (it's amazing how quickly things become a 'new normal'). They tried not to get scared or panic; to remind themselves that I would be fine. In time, I would come around. They would sit with me while I was passed out. Say soothing things to me, like: 'Just relax, calm down. Don't worry, it's okay.' Sometimes my mum would read verses from the Quran; anything that they thought might provide me with a sense of comfort.

Tareq came to see me a few days after I moved back in with my parents. But we found out later on that Nazia and Atif weren't happy with him doing so. After that, he never came again. It seemed to me that he was controlled by his parents: always trying to please them first, while

I was secondary. Away from them, he and I might have had a chance.

But at the time, his absence barely registered. Mentally, I wasn't there. I didn't know what was going on in my life and I didn't care, either. Before, I used to worry about becoming a divorcee and weigh up the consequences it would have in our community; how I would be seen. But at that point, I was just a body.

A few weeks after moving in with my parents they took me back to the GP. I needed a note from the doctor so that I could be signed off from work. It only covered me for two weeks, though, so a fortnight later I was back there again to get another one. At that point, the doctor decided I needed medication. I was still getting frequent panic attacks and, despite spending all day in bed, I wasn't sleeping, which meant I was in a permanent state of exhaustion. I walked out of the surgery armed with a prescription for serotonin (for depression) and melatonin (for sleeping).

At that point, the days would just pass me by. I had no idea how long I'd been at home for. I was lost. Hardly even knew who I was any more. I remember trying to go to the kitchen for something one day and a panic attack just hit me. Mum was cooking, so she had to quickly grab me and put me in my grandmother's bed (which was in a room just next to the kitchen). It was Ramadan at the time, so after that my parents wouldn't allow me to fast.

I needed help with everything – Ane would bring food up to me, or help me get downstairs to eat with everyone else. Someone even had to hold on to me when I went to the loo, in case I fell down. It was so hard for my family. They hated seeing me so unwell, without knowing what they could really do to make it better. It was the first time I ever saw my father cry on the prayer mat.

But it was also a period that really pulled us all together. My family did everything they could to support me; I didn't have to worry about anything. Mum would cook for me, Ane would be there with me all the time. My brothers would put on funny films to try to lift my mood.

No one blamed me. In the culture I come from, it could easily have gone that way. They might have said: 'You could have done more.' Or: 'You could have done better.' But no one did that. I think they felt bad about what had occurred and didn't believe I deserved what was happening to me. They saw for themselves that I gave everything I could to make the marriage work. I never said to them: 'I want to move out'; never shouted or swore at anyone. Never said I was unhappy. I just did what I could.

After a couple of months of being off work, I was referred to see a psychologist. Actually, I was referred to two: one by my GP and one by my employers. I'd never seen a psychologist before so was a little apprehensive, but if it was something that might help me to get better, I was willing to give it a try. The first one I saw mostly focused on the panic attacks themselves; giving me a few tactics to try to deal with them. But she didn't seem interested in actually getting to the root of where they were coming from and why.

When Dad picked me up from that first session, he wanted to know what sort of things the psychologist had spoken to me about. I gave him a brief overview of the different approaches she'd suggested for dealing with the panic attacks and he nodded along, not saying much in return. As we got closer to home, I felt the urge to say something that had been circling around the back of my mind for weeks, but which I hadn't yet felt able to articulate. Now, with the antidepressants kicking in and things in my head starting to become a little clearer, I decided to just come out with it:

'I don't think I can see myself going back to that house.'

The car fell silent again. I looked over at Dad, wondering if he'd actually heard what I said, but his face gave nothing away. He was still looking straight ahead, concentrating on the road as if I'd not made a sound.

'Dad?'

'Yes, Tan, I heard. I don't know what you're talking about . . . you'll be fine.'

A sense of dread filled my insides. They wanted me to go back. To try to make the marriage work. But all I wanted was to be well again. I didn't care about being on my own. I didn't care how it would look to everyone else. If my reputation was affected by the breakup of my marriage then so be it – as long as I was healthy again, I could handle that.

A few days later, I was sitting on the sofa with Ane when the doorbell rang. I heard Mum's footsteps heading towards the front door, then a few moments later she appeared in the living room: 'It's someone for you,' she said with a shrug that told me it wasn't anyone she recognised.

I got up and made my way to the front door, where I found a smartly dressed man holding a letter.

'Ruqsana Lohani?'

'Yes . . .'

'You've been served.'

Tareq was divorcing me. *He* was divorcing *me*. I wouldn't have to end the marriage – he was doing it for me.

It was a wake-up call for my parents: a moment when they

finally pieced everything together. Nazia and Atif hadn't
come to the hospital to see me. They hadn't been to the house
once since I'd been at home. Mum and Dad felt Tareq's parents hadn't fostered any connection with me at all and now
their son was divorcing me when I had done nothing wrong.

Tareq hadn't been bad to me. At one point, I think I had
even loved him. But I didn't love him now. How could I,
when he'd given me so little support? From the first day I'd
moved into that house, he had been trying to please them
first. I was secondary. There was no balance. No compromise.
I felt I was always second best.

Now it was over. I'd never have to go back to that house
again. Except for the fact that most of my clothes were still
there (I'd been borrowing Ane's, which didn't really fit me),
as well as all the things Tareq and I had been given as wedding presents. There was no way they were going to bring
any of it to me, so I knew I'd have to pluck up the courage
and go back for it. It took me several days to build myself
up to it and decide whether it was best to turn up without
telling them we were coming (I still had a key), or if I should
warn Tareq first.

When the day arrived, I finally made up my mind and
called Tareq to let him know that we'd be over in a few hours'
time to collect my things. Naturally, he didn't answer his
phone but I left a message. Driving back there was strange. It
had only been a few months but everything looked different
somehow. Their street was prettier than I remembered. Even
the house looked nicer from the outside than it had before.

Uncle Surath and my brother Moynul had come with me
to help and the pair of them stood behind me as I opened the
front door. The house was quiet (as usual), but I could hear

124

the sound of the television coming from the living room. I took a deep breath and pushed the door open gently. It was only Atif. He told us Nazia was out with some friends so only he and Tareq's youngest sister Afsana were at home. That was fine by me.

Upstairs, I packed all of my clothes into one of the suitcases we'd been given as a wedding gift. I'd brought a smaller bag with me for things like books, perfume and jewellery. But when I opened up the drawer where I'd put away all the gold I'd worn on my wedding day, it was empty. Gone.

Part of me couldn't believe it. Part of me could. Traditionally, the groom's family buys all the wedding gold for the bride, so my guess was that they saw it as theirs. All £10,000 of it. Other things had gone missing too — all the nice gifts we'd received. All it did was reaffirm to me that I was better off without his family. Fine, I thought. I don't want the gifts — even the gold. He can keep it.

Just as we were about to leave, my phone buzzed. It was a text message from Tareq asking whether he could keep the television. I almost laughed.

We said a brief goodbye to Atif and left, hoping never to return.

At home, Mum was pretty upset about the whole thing. The way she saw it, the gold was mine — my dowry, basically. But I couldn't bring myself to care that much. All I wanted was for the whole thing to be over and done with. If that meant leaving them with all the wedding presents, then so be it.

With time, the panic attacks were becoming less frequent. Some days I could leave the house without fearing one would suddenly hit me. And I was learning how to deal with it if that did happen. A lot of that was down to Meera, the therapist in Romford who my employer had sent me to see. We had weekly sessions that were making a real difference to me; helping me to understand that although I couldn't control certain things, I could control how I reacted to them.

We talked a lot about my upbringing: who I am. What I'm doing now and what led to that moment in Nazia's kitchen where my body and mind finally reached breaking point. I remember her once asking me: 'Who is going to look after you?' At the time I answered without even thinking: 'Of course, it's going to be me.'

It was only much later that I fully understood what she meant by that: in every situation it is going to be you. You are the one who needs to put yourself first. You have to love yourself. Value yourself.

She taught me that the only way I could do that was by controlling my thoughts, because they are what govern my emotions. The panic attacks only took over when I allowed certain thoughts to come in and control my emotions. I'd heard the phrase: 'mind over matter' before, but Meera really helped me to understand what it meant and how closely aligned what happens in our minds is with what happens in our bodies. Her words took me back to a different place. A place where I was alone, but this time I felt okay with that. I was comfortable in my own skin. Confident.

I was in the ring.

And again, Bill's words were ringing in my ear: 'I don't worry about you ... You can't teach someone to fight.' So much of what Meera spoke about took me back to KO and the things I'd learned about myself inside the four walls of that sweat-infused gym. Even down to her advice about controlling your thoughts – which is something fighters have to do all the time.

Think about it: whenever you step into that ring, your aim is to win, which either means knocking out your opponent or at least hurting them more than they hurt you. That's something I've always struggled with. What if I hurt someone, or worse? How does it fit with my faith? With my values as a human being? But I can't allow my mind to go there when I'm in the ring, because it would have a big impact on my emotions and my ability to compete. I have to control my thoughts, just like every fighter tries to do. It's the only way.

Somewhere over the previous nine months, those lessons had become lost. I'd forgotten about that person inside the ring and everything she'd learned about the strength of her own mind, her own character. I had to find her again. But I knew I wasn't quite ready for that yet.

After a few months, I felt confident enough to speak to work about going back in. I was still having the attacks, but they were much less frequent and the antidepressants were helping with my general mood. I hated taking them, but they were the only thing that gave me the ability to get out of bed in the morning. The only thing that would lift the darkness.

The company knew about everything I had been going through and that I was still on antidepressants, so they said a gradual reintroduction would be the best solution for me. Instead of going straight back into full-time work, I only went in for half a day two times a week to start with. It didn't sound like much, but I really struggled. On mornings when I was due to go in, I'd feel overwhelmed and anxiety would grip me. On those days that I made it in, I often ended up having a panic attack and being sent home anyway.

I'd never had feelings like that before. Never suffered from anxiety or doubted myself. I was always the go-getter in my family and among my friends – the one who was confident enough to apply for jobs she wasn't 100 per cent qualified for. The one who was optimistic and always looking for opportunities. Out of all my friends from university, I'd been the only one who actually managed to get a job in architecture – the others all went into teaching or did something else. That wasn't because I was smarter than them; it was because I had that positive attitude. That willingness to just go for it.

Now, I was different. I was bruised. When I was getting ready for work in the mornings, I'd have to ask Ane three or four times if I looked all right. Was my hair okay? It had always been the other way around with us – I had always been the one to throw on an outfit and be out of the door five minutes later. But now I was the one unsure of myself. I didn't even know what food I liked, I was so numb. I went from being vibrant and happy to someone who had no idea who she even was any more.

It wasn't anything about my job or the people I worked with that was affecting me. I liked it there, had made some really nice friends and felt like I was finding my feet. But I just didn't want to be there any longer.

It was closely linked to the last year of my life. The journey from home to the office was the same one I'd made from my in-laws' house. The desk I sat at was the same one where I'd sit and watch the clock, wishing it to stop, so I didn't have to go home at the end of the day. The receptionist was the same one who called to let me know my husband had arrived with flowers for me on Valentine's Day. It was all the same pattern and I couldn't handle it. I needed to get away from it. To make a fresh start somewhere that had no ties to my past.

I applied for a new job at a different architectural firm in Tower Hill. It was only for a contract position but that was fine – I just needed to be somewhere different. Within a week of me applying they got in touch and invited me in for an interview. I'm not sure how I came across during that half an hour, but they must have seen something in me because the very next day they offered me the role.

There was a mixture of relief and guilt when I handed in my letter of resignation at BPTW. I felt bad because they had stuck by me over the last few months, but I also knew that I was no good to them any more. Not with the way that my body reacted every time I went in there.

The week that I was due to start at the new place, I got a phone call from them on the Monday morning. It wasn't good news: the project I was supposed to be working on had fallen through and they were very sorry but they had nothing else for me. There was no way I could go back to BPTW. They had already moved on; there wasn't even a job there for me now. So that was it. I was stuck at home, with no job, relying on antidepressants to get me through each day.

I needed them. It was only when the doctors tried to lower my dosage that I realised quite how badly; I was shaking like an addict going cold turkey.

I might not have known exactly who I was, but I knew that this wasn't me. This wasn't what I wanted for myself. I had to find a way out. A way back.

Chapter 9

'Was this you?'

Ane stood in front of me waving an empty shampoo bottle in my face.

'Er, yeah . . . but I swear I only used a little bit. It was practically finished anyway.'

Since moving back home, we'd fallen easily back into our old routines; having breakfast together (once I was well enough), talking late into the night about everything and nothing and 'sharing' Ane's precious Toni & Guy hair products.

It had hit her hard when I moved out. Maybe even harder than me in some ways, because at least I had Tareq to fill some of the gaps. Ane had lost me faster than either of us had expected. I wasn't there to meet her after work any more. In the evenings she had no one to sit and chat with as she drifted off to sleep. She had to go and buy herself a television for the bedroom, so that she could fall asleep listening to that (instead of listening to me, like she always used to).

When I came back home, there was no one I felt I could trust more than her. My friendship group had shrunk so much over the last twelve months because I simply hadn't been able to keep in touch with a lot of them. The connection we'd had was either gone completely or was going to take time to rebuild. But Ane was constantly there for me. She'd calm me down when I needed, bring me food if I was too weak to get it myself, reassure me when I lost my job. We weren't just sisters; we were best friends.

But it wasn't going to last. Marriage proposals had started coming in for her and my parents were already keen to begin moving forward with them. It was like déjà vu. The thought of Ane potentially having to go through the same experience that I'd had filled me with dread.

Initially, though, I did my best to stay out of it. Ane had always been more traditionally minded than me, so being a wife and starting a family was something that she had looked forward to. She felt ready for that process to begin. I had to respect that and remind myself that there was no reason to believe that the family Ane married into would be anything like the Lohanis.

And I was sure that, after my experiences, Mum and Dad would take things more slowly this time around.

But it didn't happen that way. Ane really liked one of the first guys to put himself forward and so within a few months of them getting to know each other, preparations for their wedding were already underway. It was too much. Too fast. I couldn't hold it in any longer; I had to say something.

I tried to speak to Mum: 'Are you sure you want to do this? She doesn't even know him ... why don't you slow things down? You don't want to rush the wedding and make the same mistake that you made with me.'

It didn't make any difference. Over the next few months I tried again and again, but my parents didn't want to hear it. I felt as though they thought I was jealous of her moving on, while I was going through a divorce and stuck at home trying to rebuild my life. But it wasn't jealousy; I was just being cautious and maybe a little bit selfish because, having only just got her back after my own failed marriage, I hated the idea of losing her again.

The day of the wedding was really tough for me. In the weeks leading up to it I forced myself to take a step back. To allow Ane to be happy. But, actually, being there and watching her formally step out of our family into her new one made me sink deeper into a darkness that I could see no way out of. Not without her there.

Her in-laws lived some 40 miles away from us in Kent. It was too far for any midweek catch-ups after she'd finished work or to pop over for a cup of tea. My best friend – the one person who had always been there for me – was gone. And I was so lonely without her.

I had never lived at Mum's house without Ane being there too. So everything – every room I went into, every time I took a shower – was a reminder that she was no longer there. Every morning, I got up and sat in the same seat as always at the kitchen table. Sipped my tea from the same mug. But Ane's seat was empty. I felt her absence like an ache, deep in the pit of my stomach.

At that point, I knew I needed to do something to help myself. I didn't want to be on antidepressants for the rest of my life, but I didn't know how else to get through the days. As soon as my last dose started to wear off, I felt myself sinking lower and lower and the only way I knew to stop it was to reach for another tablet. The effects of them could be so extreme it was almost comical. I'd go from being so low that

I could hardly get off the sofa to feeling like I was walking on air and laughing for no reason at all. My brothers would only have to say something like: 'Are you all right?' and I'd collapse into fits of giggles. I had no idea what I was laughing at. It was all so artificial. Mechanical. Outwardly, I looked like I was having the time of my life. But inside, there was nothing. Not a single shred of happiness.

When the lows took hold, the only way I could stop myself from taking another tablet was to go to sleep. It could be the middle of the day but I'd close my curtains, get under the duvet and try to fall asleep, hoping that when I woke up the feeling would have passed. Sometimes it worked. Often, it didn't.

I needed a distraction. Something that would take my mind off the way I was feeling and allow me to focus on something else. I also needed to learn about myself. Discover who I was – who I wanted to be now that I was free to be that person again.

I want to be a fighter.

Those were my own words on the day I'd first met Bill. Back when I'd known who I was and what I wanted to be. When that clarity had given me all the confidence I needed to walk into the unknown and say: I belong here.

Maybe what I needed was to go back there. Maybe the gym was the place where I would be able to find some semblance of that girl – the one who had been so sure of who she was and what she wanted to be. Months – and so much besides – had passed since I'd been there. But somehow, I still felt it was where I belonged.

Muay Thai itself was one thing that I knew made me happy. And more than that, I thought back to how it made me feel when I was competing or even just surviving a tough training session. How I would get out of the ring feeling like I could take on anything, because: if I can do this, then I can bloody well manage the rest of my life. And, on the most basic level, being at the gym would mean not being at home with only my own sadness and Ane's absence to focus on.

The very next Sunday, I told my parents I was going back to the gym. Mum couldn't keep the smile off her face. After seeing me so low for so long, it was a big relief for her and Dad to see me doing something that they knew I used to enjoy (even if it wasn't quite what they thought it was).

It felt strange to be making that journey again. Carrying the same kit that I always had. It was almost like nothing around me had changed, while everything inside me was almost unrecognisable from the Ruqsana who used to travel this route religiously every Sunday.

As I walked towards the gym, I saw a small black dog watching me from the doorway. My pace automatically slowed – I've never been particularly comfortable around dogs. As I got closer, I saw that he was tied up, but I still had to walk right by him to actually get into the gym.

I was a few paces away when he started barking loudly at me. I froze.

Shit. What do I do now?

I kept my eyes firmly fixed on the dog while I stood there deciding what to do. Maybe if I positioned my bag in between me and the dog I could get past him without being attacked . . .

'Rox? I see you've met Zeus, then.'

Bill had heard the barking and come to see what the fuss was about. It turned out that Zeus was his dog, and that, as soon as Bill was in sight, the vicious-sounding animal that had scared the crap out of me was replaced by a doe-eyed, tail-wagging pup.

As we stood in the doorway, Bill looked me up and down. I'd lost weight over the past few months and looked as physically drained as I felt emotionally.

'You coming in then?'

I nodded and followed him inside; the familiar stench of sweat and old boxing gloves hitting the back of my throat the moment I walked in, just like the first time. The feeling was instant. This was me. I was at home again.

We made our way over to a crumpled old sofa that occupied a small space near the doorway. It was covered in discarded hand wraps and headguards, which Bill swiped aside, motioning for me to sit down next to him. I'd been so fixated on simply getting myself out of the house and to the gym that I hadn't really given much thought to what I was going to say to Bill about the last year or so – how much I was going to tell him. Now, sitting beside him, I didn't quite know where or how to start.

'I'm ... I'm getting divorced. The marriage didn't work out. And, well, I'd like to start training again.'

Bill nodded. I could tell he had questions, but he stayed quiet, giving me the space and time to talk. It worked. I knew Bill well enough to know that he wouldn't judge me, or think me weak for what had happened. So, over the next half an hour or so I gave him a rundown of how things had been for me at my in-laws' house and how that period had affected me. How it had robbed me of everything I had built for myself during the many hours spent inside these four walls.

While I spoke, Bill's expression remained as inscrutable

as ever. After I finished by explaining what had led me back to the gym and how I hoped it might help me, he allowed himself to speak, keeping his voice low so that no one else could hear.

'Everyone has challenges in life, Rox – whether they're personal, financial or to do with health or relationships. You just have to work through them. Yes, at times they might take you to a dark place, but when you come out of it, you'll discover who you are, what you are and the strength you need to push forwards.

'Every fighter understands that life is problematic. That crap is going to happen. But when it does, you have a choice: you can either dig down and overcome it, or you succumb to it and let it overwhelm you. And every time you overcome, you learn. Every time you overcome, you get mentally and physically stronger. Every time you overcome, you are better prepared for the next battle.'

His words had always had an impact on me but, now, they felt more important than ever. I knew this was where I belonged. And where I would recover my health. It was going to be a long journey back – I had hardly done any exercise at all since getting married, so my fitness was probably worse than it had ever been. But I wasn't scared of the hard work it would take to get it back. I relished the thought of it. Having something to focus on lifted my spirits instantly. And any time spent in the gym was time that I wasn't spending at home, desperately trying to resist the urge to take another tablet.

The class had already started by the time Bill and I finished talking, but he said I should jump in for the rest of it anyway – 'Just take it slowly. Go with how you feel.'

It felt amazing. I mean, it felt terrible at first, because

everything was so much harder than I remembered it being. But the sensation of moving my body, of the sweat gathering on my forehead, was wonderful. I'd forgotten how it felt to ask questions of my body. To see what force my own limbs could produce and to feel the welcome burn of physical hard work.

The high I got from just those thirty minutes was so much more satisfying than anything the antidepressants had given me. It was real. This was my path to recovery.

But as I packed up my kit and ran for the train home – as I always used to do – I knew that I couldn't live the same life as I'd been living before getting married: the double life that Bill had always accused me of. Deceiving my parents wasn't something that I'd wanted to do in the first place, but now it was something that I felt I *couldn't* do. I didn't have it in me to keep fighting them in that way.

I spent the journey home feeling increasingly nervous about telling them the truth. What if they reacted badly? What if they told me I couldn't do it any more? Then what would I do?

By the time the train pulled into Seven Kings station, I realised that I had no choice. I couldn't lie to them any longer, so if I wanted to go back to Muay Thai then I had to tell them the truth. And I had to tell them straight away, while my thoughts were clear. At home, I herded Mum and Dad into the living room and asked them to sit down. They adopted their usual positions: Dad in his armchair nearest the TV, Mum on the end of the sofa closest to the door. I sat in between the two of them and took a long, deep breath.

I went right back to the start – telling them about the Muay Thai session after college with Zeeshan and how much I had loved it. Explained how that had led me to KO and to meeting Bill, a former world champion who was one of the most respected teachers of the sport in the country.

I paused, looking from Dad's face to Mum's and back again. Blank expressions. I went into a detailed description of the art of Muay Thai – explained why it's referred to as 'the art of eight limbs' and how it is a sport that's steeped in ancient traditions and Thai culture.

'What are you telling us, Tanni?' asked Dad. 'That you are fighting people? That you're a boxer?'

'Sort of . . . not really. Just that the gym is somewhere that makes me feel good. Where I can build myself back up again. It will give me something to do, instead of sitting around here all day . . .'

'But a boxing gym?' said Mum. 'Are there any other females there?'

'Why don't you come with me next weekend and see for yourself? You can meet Bill, too.'

It was a bit of a risky move. There was no guarantee that taking my parents into the gym would convince them of the positives of me doing the sport, any more than my little speech had done. But it had to be worth a try. If they could see for themselves what kind of place it was – that everyone was there for the same reason: to work hard and get better; and that no one was underdressed or shouting and swearing – then maybe it would help them to feel more comfortable with the idea.

'Okay,' said Dad.

'Okay, as in you will come?'

'Yes, okay.'

It felt like such a relief to tell them the truth. For a split second, I wondered if I should have done it earlier. But context is everything. It was unlikely I'd have got the same reaction from them a few years earlier. Now, I sensed that they felt an element of guilt over what I had been through. Seeing Dad crying on the prayer mat had shown me how their own world had been rocked by my situation. I felt like it was a wake-up call for them – a moment where they perhaps realised that some of the expectations they, and our culture, had of me were just too much.

The following Sunday I found myself in the back of Dad's car directing him into a parking space beneath the railway arches in Bethnal Green. The journey had been a silent one, neither Mum nor Dad quite knowing what the next few hours would hold. I don't think either of them had ever stepped foot into a normal gym before, let alone a boxing one. As we got out of the car, I tried to warn them about the smell, but I knew nothing could really prepare them for the assault on their nostrils that was about to take place.

The loud barking made all three of us jump: Zeus. I was much more confident around him now that I'd seen what a softie he really was behind the bark, so walked straight past him into the gym. Spotting Bill holding pads for a young boy in the centre of the ring, I turned around to point him out to Mum and Dad. Only, they weren't there.

I made my way back towards the doorway and saw them both standing frozen to the spot a few feet away from Zeus, just as I had been the previous week. Seconds later, they were saved by Bill – just as I had been – as he strolled past me to pick up Zeus and clear the way for my parents to enter the gym.

I'd sent Bill a text message that morning, warning him that

Mum and Dad were coming in with me, so he knew exactly who my guests were. After returning Zeus to his spot by the door, he came straight over to introduce himself and invited them both to take a seat on the same sofa where he and I had chatted a week earlier.

Mum was hesitant (as her English isn't as strong as Dad's she's sometimes shy of getting involved in conversations), so while Dad went to sit with Bill, I stayed with her a few feet away. The usual sounds of the gym – punchbags being pummelled, coaches shouting instructions, music blaring out of the old speaker sitting next to the ring – meant we couldn't hear much of what they were saying, but I kept a close eye on the two of them. I wanted Dad to like Bill; wanted him to see how respectful he was and how much I could learn from him. That way, maybe he would feel okay with me spending my time at the gym under his guidance.

For well over an hour, they were locked deep in serious conversation. Every so often, Dad's eyes flicked over to me, indicating that I was front and centre of what they were discussing. But I could also see Bill gesturing around to the rest of the gym, highlighting that the environment he had created was one of great discipline. That it was a place where I was free to observe the pillars of my faith and was fully respected for doing so.

When the two of them finally made their way back over to me and Mum, Bill gave it one final push: 'Look, she's in a safe place. She's training. And she's a good girl. She doesn't wear make-up or spend time chatting – she just comes in and trains.'

He and Dad shook hands before the three of us edged past Zeus and headed back to the car. Part of me was desperate to jump in straight away and ask Dad what he thought of the gym and Bill, but the fear that his answer might not be the one I wanted to hear held me back from doing so.

As we drove away from KO, Dad took the decision out of my hands. He started telling me some of the things that Bill had said about my situation – repeating what he'd told him: 'That family, they wore you down ... drained you.' He seemed angry. But not with me – with my in-laws. Hearing someone from outside of the family – someone impartial – talking about it had made him see things so much more clearly.

Bill had obviously left an impression. It didn't change the view that Mum and Dad had of the sport – they still didn't like the idea of me doing it – but their desire to see their daughter happy and healthy again was strong enough to overcome that. If Muay Thai was a way for me to get better, then Dad said they were willing to turn a blind eye. To let me get on with whatever I felt I needed to do.

I had my parents' blessing.

For the next few weeks, I threw myself into the gym, training six days a week. It gave me a routine: somewhere to be. Something to focus on. My fitness was shocking – I was out of breath before the warm-up was over. After five minutes of practising my kicks, I thought I might actually be sick. But I embraced the fatigue. It helped me. When the endorphins wore off after a session and I felt myself needing to take a tablet, the exhaustion meant I could put myself to sleep for a few hours and hope the craving went away.

I didn't want to take them any more and now that I was back in the gym, I told myself I didn't need to. Every day was a challenge, though. When your body and mind are so used to reaching for the 'fix' that stops the darkness from closing in, it's so hard to stop yourself going back for 'just one more'. I tried to turn the gym into my 'fix' instead. The physical exertion, the mental challenge, the feeling of making even the smallest improvements in my technique or fitness – inch by inch, it all helped to put those tablets further out of reach.

The panic attacks were a different matter, though. They weren't the same as they had been before; I wasn't collapsing in a heap and spending thirty minutes unconscious. Now, they were more like the panic attacks I had read about in magazines and seen on TV. There was the shortness of breath. A racing pulse. And a wave of complete fear washing over me. They could happen anywhere. All it took was for something to upset me or make me feel anxious or worried. I even got them in the gym.

When I first walked back into KO, it had felt like home. It looked (and smelled) very much like the same place where I had spent so many happy hours training. But once I was back training there regularly, I realised that while the physical aspects of it remained the same, something inside had changed.

There were so many more women there than before. And while the ones who'd come before had all been pretty 'alpha' – purely there to learn how to fight and compete – this was more of a mixed group. Some were still there to fight, but there were others who were there for different reasons – whether that was to work on fitness, or to look or feel a certain way. It seemed like the broad range of benefits Muay Thai has to offer were finally starting to be understood.

That didn't just go for the women, either. There were also more guys now who weren't just there to become a competitor. So there weren't only fighters in the gym, but 'normal' people too. It gave the gym a whole different energy and atmosphere compared to before. It felt like there was more of a team vibe. I liked it.

Even though I had four years of training behind me from before my marriage, I'd assumed Bill would start me off at the lower level - in the 'general' class – when it came to sparring. After all, I'd been away for over a year. And for the first few weeks, he did.

Then, one week, I arrived for the session as usual and one of the coaches turned to Bill and said: 'Should she be in this class or the fighters' class?'

'No,' said Bill. 'Take her to the fighters' class.'

The fighters' class was the group that everyone else in the gym looked up to. The elite. It was a big step for me, but I trusted Bill's judgement. If he thought I was ready then I *was* ready.

I could sense a few people in the gym looking at me, thinking: who's she? How does she get to move up to the fighters' class after just a few sessions? The few who knew me from before were less confused by it, but there were a lot of new people who had no idea of my history in that gym.

I wasn't the only girl in the fighters' group. While I'd been away, five or six other females had worked their way up into the fighters' class. Like I said, the sport was becoming more popular – and even those who might have come into it with the intention of doing it to keep fit, rather than to fight, could find themselves sucked deeper into it.

I was so happy to see more females there. I didn't mind sparring the guys but I felt much more comfortable training with a group of women. The girls were a really tight-knit group. They had obviously formed a bond inside the gym and had become really close – they'd talk about nights out they'd been on and gossip about other people they knew. To start with, I tried to fit in with them. Tried to start up conversations or get one of them to partner up with me for training. But I never really got much back. After a few attempts that went largely ignored, I started to think they weren't as pleased about my presence as I had been about theirs.

After a few sessions, it was clear that even though I was a lot smaller than any of the other girls in the fighters' class, I was more than capable of holding my own. Instead of helping me to earn their respect, though, it seemed to upset them even more. They would do whatever they could not to include me in their little group. They'd make sure that none of them partnered up with me. And whenever we were all in the changing room together at the same time, they'd move their stuff to the opposite side from where I was getting changed.

I didn't know what their issue with me was – whether it was a sense of injustice at seeing me get into the fighters' class without climbing the ladder like they had, or perhaps jealousy of the relationship I had with Bill and some of the coaches who I'd known from before. I even started to wonder if it was to do with the colour of my skin, or my religion . . .

Whatever the reasons, their actions brought back familiar feelings. Isolation. Loneliness. And now anxiety. Sometimes, they didn't even have to do anything; their mere presence would put me on edge.

In one session I remember seeing some guys near me giggling while we were doing an exercise. Something made me think they were laughing at me – taking the piss out of the way I was doing the exercise. I felt myself getting hot. My breathing getting heavier. In front of the whole gym, I started hyperventilating. The only thing I could do was to take myself away from the situation – go and sit in the changing room and try to calm myself down. Sometimes I was able to rejoin the session, but if it had taken too much out of me, I just went home.

I had moments like that all the time, though – in and out of the gym. It could be that a friend, without even knowing it, said something that really upset me or sent my thoughts running wild. In my head, I'd be thinking: my friends are all talking behind my back . . . they hate me. Then I'd start feeling anxious and panicky. The more I tried to hold it all in, the worse it got until it escalated into a full-blown panic attack.

I tried to remember what the therapist had told me about controlling those thoughts. Because it was only when I allowed them to spiral that I'd end up somewhere that I didn't want to be. Controlling them meant breaking them down. Stripping them back. Telling myself that, actually, those guys could just be laughing at a private joke that has nothing to do with me.

Every day I was trying to control my own thoughts, but I found it really difficult. I don't know if it was to do with the antidepressants, but sometimes my mind would just run wild with negative thoughts. And those negative thoughts made me feel like crap, so it became a vicious cycle. Half the time I didn't even know where those thoughts came from, I'd just suddenly realise that I was feeling anxious or upset.

Over time I learned a big lesson about how to take a step back and ask myself: why am I feeling like this? Then I could reason with myself – rewire my mind – so that even if I was upset over something that I knew could be true, I was able to remind myself that I didn't have to let it overwhelm me.

Friday night sparring sessions became a real test, not only of my ability to do that, but of my determination to keep practising the sport I loved. It was one of the few times the other girls couldn't avoid me. If Bill said we were sparring, then we were sparring. And then it became a battle of survival.

Those girls thought I had no right to be there. They thought that I had just strolled into the fighters' class without putting the work in like they had. Sparring sessions gave them an opportunity to prove their point. Physically, mentally, technically, they pushed me to give everything I had, just to hang in there. The most important part was in my head. I had to constantly remind myself: this is what I do. This is what I love and have always loved. I can't let them beat me.

The first time Bill put me in with one of them, it was Naomi – a girl about two weight divisions above me. She was seriously strong. And everyone knew she hit really hard. I steeled myself for a tough few rounds, pulled my headguard on tight and tried to shake the tension out of my shoulders.

Right from the first bell, she really went for me. Normally, sparring sessions are about practising skills. You will take hits and kicks here and there but, usually, both fighters recognise that they're in the ring trying to improve – not trying to pummel the other one into submission. This felt different, though. It felt personal.

But I fought back well. In fact, I was using my speed to land more shots than she was. As soon as the bell sounded, signalling the end of the round, Bill went straight over to Naomi, picking her up on the things she did wrong: 'Rox landed more shots than you, so you've got a weakness there that you need to work on . . .'

Naomi looked seriously pissed off. The smallest, lightest female in the group had shown her up and she clearly hated it. As we climbed out of the ring, she hardly looked at me, going straight over to join the other girls who had been watching the spar. They stood in a sort of huddle, talking in low voices so that no one else could hear. But I sensed that I was a hot topic of conversation. If I'd thought that showing my abilities as a fighter would help to win them over – maybe earn some respect – I was clearly wrong. If anything, it felt like I had just made things a whole lot worse for myself.

I went home that night feeling empty. And alone. I should have been on a high – I'd held my own in the ring against a bigger, stronger opponent who had been training more than me. But any positivity I'd taken out of the ring had been shattered by the way Naomi and the rest of the girls had made me feel.

The gym was a place where I'd felt at home. A place where, in many ways, I had grown up. Now it was starting to feel like somewhere that I wasn't welcome any more.

Chapter 10

I felt like I couldn't breathe. It was like all the air had been sucked right out of my lungs, but I was in too much agony to try to suck any back in. I hadn't even seen the shot coming.

I was sparring with a guy called Nas. He was a bit stockier than me but a similar height, so Bill paired us up for a few rounds. It was competitive, but I was holding my own until the moment I decided to step in with a jab. That was Nas's opening. As I leaned forward, he drove his left knee hard into my ribcage.

The spar was over. So was the session. I couldn't even finish off with any abdominal work. The pain was crippling.

On the way home, I stopped to buy some super-strength painkillers and went straight to bed when I got in, avoiding any form of conversation with my parents. It would be too hard to hide the pain from them and I was determined not to give them any cause to go back on their word and stop me from training.

Unfortunately, there was no way I could do the same with work the next day. A couple of months earlier I'd managed to get a new job, working for a project management company that had the contract to build a new hotel near Waterloo (which became the Park Plaza hotel). The building work had already started, but they still needed some on-site architects to oversee certain aspects of design while the building was going up. It was perfect. I loved being on-site as opposed to being sat in an office all day. And the hours and location allowed me to get to the gym one or two evenings a week, as well as at the weekend.

I was okay getting to work the day after Nas's knee had sunk into my chest, but as soon as I had to move around a bit, or someone made me laugh, I was in all sorts of trouble. It was my colleague Jo who noticed first and told me to go straight to A&E to have it x-rayed: 'If it's a broken rib it could puncture your lung!'

She scared me enough to make me follow her advice. I'd never had a broken rib before but it certainly felt as though some damage had been done. Even lying down and trying to sleep the previous night had been painful.

The x-ray confirmed it. A broken rib. That meant no sparring for months and very little training at all for at least a few weeks.

The job kept me occupied, though. It was a really enjoyable project to work on, but unfortunately it only lasted for six months. When the building work was finished, they let go of everyone, which meant I was back looking for work again. I didn't think it would be that difficult, now that I had the Park Plaza experience to go with the time I spent at BPTW, but when I started looking I realised there was hardly anything out there. The financial crisis hit the architecture world hard and, in 2009, it was still suffering the effects.

Nearly everything I'd earned from the Park Plaza job had gone towards paying lawyers to sort out my divorce from

Tareq, so I was left with almost nothing. I felt guilty living at my parents' and taking advantage of everything that came with. I'd eat my lunch or dinner and know that if it wasn't for them, my plate would be empty.

Getting to the gym became a worry, too. I started to think about swapping the train for the cheaper option of a two-hour bus journey just so that I could extend my savings for a little while longer.

I'd been out of work for about three months when the idea of signing on (for the dole) started to look more attractive. Initially, I'd sworn it was something I wouldn't do. To me, signing on seemed like failing. I felt like I needed to earn my money. And part of me was also a bit worried it might make me complacent. On the other hand, it would give me enough travel money for the gym.

I was still wrestling with the idea when an alternative option presented itself via the local newspaper. I hadn't read it for years, but picked it up while I was house-sitting for a friend one day (she was at work and had someone coming over to check her gas and boiler). As I flicked through the pages, I spotted an advert for a job at my old secondary school, Swanlea. They were looking for a science technician.

It wasn't exactly the kind of work I was looking for and it was only part-time, but given the fact that there didn't seem to be any architecture jobs around, I thought I might as well apply. I double-checked that there weren't any specific qualifications required, wrote down the details and decided to email over my CV as soon as I got home.

For the next two months, I heard nothing. It was soul-destroying – not because it was a job I particularly wanted but because, at that point, I just wanted a job . . . any job.

I had pretty much given up all hope of hearing back from Swanlea when, one day, I got a phone call from the school asking me to come in for an interview with Mr Martin, who was one of my ex-teachers. It was strange to be back there after so many years, walking the same corridors I had done as a young teenager. I wondered if the Prayer Room was still as I remembered it.

Mr Martin certainly was – he hadn't changed a bit, although he'd had an upgrade to head of technology since I'd left. We sat in his office, where he had my CV laid out on the desk in front of him and a confused look on his face.

'Well, you're definitely overqualified for this role, Ruqsana . . .'

I smiled.

'And there's no way we can offer you the same kind of money you've been earning in architecture . . .'

I told him that wasn't a problem. That I was happy with whatever they could afford to pay me.

'In that case, we'd like to offer you the job.'

It was only two days a week, but it was better than nothing. Especially considering I had been scraping the bottom of my piggy bank for the last few weeks. Two days would give me just about enough each month to cover my gym fees, travel and food.

On the other three days, I started volunteering for a small architectural firm. The guy who ran it said I could come and help him out and, in return, he would help me to develop my skills as an architect. That gave me a game-plan. By the time the job market picked up again I would be in a great position to get back into working in architecture.

The sport was a passion for me and I was improving all the

time. Since recovering from the broken rib I'd even started competing again, but I still didn't see how it could ever be much more than a hobby. I suppose I didn't really think I was good enough. Didn't believe that I was the fighter that I'd told Bill I wanted to be.

Part of that was the way I felt before getting into the ring. Before my marriage, I'd never really felt fearful of fighting. But ever since coming back to the sport, that had changed. Suddenly I was feeling a sense of fear and anxiety before competing. Sometimes even before sparring.

A few weeks before I started working at Swanlea, I had my first fight since returning to the sport, on one of Bill's own shows. He put them on throughout the year to give his fighters some fight-night experience. This one was in a leisure centre in Bayswater one Saturday night and there were loads of fighters from KO on the bill, including Naomi and a few of the other girls from her clique.

It would be my first fight as a professional. All that really meant was that we'd be fighting without the headguards or shin pads that we used in the amateurs. No one actually got paid because the show itself cost so much to put on that the ticket sales would all go towards reimbursing that money, as opposed to paying the fighters. We just felt we were lucky to get the opportunity to be part of the show.

An hour or so before the fights were due to start, we were all in the changing room getting ourselves ready – the girls gathered together on the opposite side to me, as always. I was sitting on my own, headphones on and trying to relax when Bill came in. He liked to have little chats with everyone, giving last-minute words of advice and encouragement. When he came round to me, I told him the truth: I was scared.

The moment I spoke, the room suddenly fell silent. Everyone heard.

And then they started laughing. First, the girls and then eventually even Bill was laughing at me. I could take it from Naomi and her mates – I almost expected it from them – but from Bill too? It was a blow I was not prepared for. And one that sent my mind into overdrive.

Maybe I'm weak. Maybe I'm not normal. Maybe I'm not a fighter.

Everyone else was so confident. It seemed like I was the only one who wasn't.

I was one of the first ones due to fight, so I busied myself with getting warmed up and tried to push those thoughts aside. I could stew over them later. For now, I had to focus on what was ahead of me – and try to channel the nerves into an energy I could use to positive effect in the ring. In twenty minutes or so, it would all be over.

Once I was inside the ring, it almost felt like the hardest part was done. Now it was just me and my opponent. I could forget about the other girls. Forget about Bill's reaction. All I had to do was focus on giving everything I could for the next four rounds.

It was a really close fight, so when the bell went at the end of the last round I couldn't be sure of which way the result would go. The judges clearly couldn't decide either – they called it a draw. As the referee stood in between us and raised both of our hands, I felt pretty satisfied. She was a tough opponent for what was my first fight as a professional and I hadn't competed in any amateur fights or inter-club events to build up to it. Bill had thrown me straight in. And I'd survived.

It was just like he'd told me on the day I first returned to the gym – when you're challenged you have a choice: 'You can either dig down and overcome it, or you succumb to it and let it overwhelm you. And every time you overcome, you learn.'

I was learning. Maybe the fear didn't matter as much as I'd thought. Maybe it didn't make me weak or a shit fighter. Maybe the fear was just something I had to accept for now and I'd have to learn how to deal with it along the way.

My performance must have made Bill think a bit too, because a few weeks later he entered me into a tournament in Cambridge that was part of a qualification process for the upcoming World Championships in Thailand. It was the weekend before I was due to start my new job at the school, so I was coming off the back of five months or so when I had been able to train for six days a week and it was paying off.

The idea of making it to Thailand never entered my head, though. I just wanted to keep adding to my experience in the ring – and if Bill thought I was good enough to enter, then I wanted to show that he was right to believe in me.

Together with Bill and a few other fighters from KO, we got an early train to Cambridge on the Saturday morning, making sure we were there in plenty of time to register. As soon as we arrived, I saw why Bill had wanted to leave so early – the queues were snaking all around the competition hall. I'd never seen so many fighters in one place before.

But it turned out that not very many of them were suitable opponents for me. In fact, there were only a handful of female fighters there at my weight. We were split into two groups of three, with the winners going straight through to a final.

So at least I would get a minimum of two fights, which just about made the journey worthwhile.

I ended up winning one and losing one, which meant I didn't get through to the final. It had been a decent day for me, though. I was pleased with the victory and knew the girl I'd lost to had lots more fights under her belt than I did.

Before we left to catch the train back to London, Bill was called over to talk to one of the selectors for the World Championships. They were chatting for five minutes or so, before Bill came over to me and said: 'Do you think you could make 48kg?'

I wasn't sure. I was around 52–52.5kg at the time and couldn't actually remember the last time I'd been that light – it certainly wasn't for a good few years.

Bill told me the selectors were struggling to find females to fill that weight category at the World Championships and had asked him if he thought I was at a good enough level to go. 'I told them I thought you were. That I believed in you. And that you could be really strong at that weight.'

'But I've never lost that much weight before. That's 4kg and it's only a month away.'

Bill told me not to worry; that once we got to Thailand the weight would drop off me. He'd been through so many weight cuts with his fighters before that I trusted his judgement. But I still wasn't sure I was ready to fight at that level. I'd only had a handful of fights so far. What if I got humiliated?

'Look, we're just going for the experience,' said Bill. 'No one's expecting you to come back with a medal, so anything you do out there will be a huge bonus. There's no pressure.'

He was right. It's notoriously tough to get a medal at

a World Championships in Muay Thai, because for some of the other countries it's their main sport. In places like Russia, Ukraine and Kazakhstan, the top fighters are all fully funded – so all they have to do is train and the government supports them. Some countries would offer their athletes incentives too, like cars or Rolex watches if they won a medal. They were hugely incentivised to win.

We didn't have the same level of support. We even had to pay for our own flights and accommodation. So, for all of us it was really just an opportunity to go and give it our best shot.

By this time, though, I was only a few weeks into my new job and wasn't entirely sure how they would feel about me asking for a month off to go to Thailand. I needed the wages from that first month to cover my costs of going, too, so was aware that upsetting them could make getting to Thailand difficult in more ways than one.

But I was fortunate that the headmistress at the time had also been my headmistress when I was a pupil there and remembered me fondly. She told me they had a rule in the handbook that actually said that if a member of staff (or pupil) was selected to represent the country in a sporting event, then they were able to take a certain number of days off to do so.

The next obstacle was my parents. I decided it was best to keep the detail to a minimum, so all I told them was that I was going to Thailand on a training camp for the GB team. I didn't reveal anything more than that and they didn't ask any questions. Did their silence mean I wasn't allowed to go? I didn't really know the answer to that. I decided that, until the moment they categorically said no, I would just continue planning for the trip. I had to live my life and I think, deep down, they were just happy to see me excited about something – whatever that might have been.

As the departure date neared, I started to accept it was actually happening. I was going to Thailand. Unfortunately, so were the other girls from KO.

Thankfully, we travelled out to Thailand on separate flights. But once we were there, it was difficult to avoid them. If there were just one or two of them, it wasn't so bad, but when they all got together they would basically act like I wasn't there. They would go for food together without telling me. Leave for training before I was ready. Unless I could find one of the guys to go with, I was basically on my own.

To give us time to acclimatise and drop weight if we needed to (which I definitely did), we flew out there two weeks before the competition was due to start. For that fortnight, the routine was basic, but brutal: training twice a day. Two meals a day. And that was about it. There were no shops nearby to sneak off to for chocolate if you wanted it (even if there had been, it would have melted in the hot weather before you got the chance).

Locked in the safety of that routine, I spent enough time around the rest of the group to manage the isolation from the girls. The atmosphere as a whole was pretty tense, though. Everyone there knows they're going to be competing, so there's a lot of stress and tension around.

Bill did what he could to keep us relaxed. We'd been out there for about a week when he gave us a day off and organised a motorbike ride out to a beach about an hour away. Halfway there, we all stopped at a café for lunch and, once again, I was left eating alone while the clique sat a few metres away. They were talking among themselves but kept looking over to where I was sitting. It made me nervous. Then they suddenly burst into fits of laughter.

I felt myself getting more and more anxious. Felt my breathing start to go. My vision blurring.

The next thing I knew, I was lying on the ground, with one of the guys propping my head up and holding smelling salts under my nose. They all assumed I had fainted from the heat. But I knew it was something else. It was the memory of not being accepted. Of feeling worthless. It was like some part of my brain hadn't fully accepted that we weren't in that situation any more and was ready to tell my body to shut down whenever those old feelings reappeared.

I didn't want to say anything to Bill. I thought it would make me look weak. And I wasn't sure how he'd react. He liked those girls and they were paying clients. There was no way he'd want to upset them.

So, I stayed quiet.

Day by day, the training-camp regime was taking weight off me, like Bill said it would. But it wasn't quite enough; as weigh-in day approached, I was still a few pounds over the 48kg limit. On our final day of training, Bill handed me a sweat suit to wear over my training kit (it's basically like wearing a bin bag). If the Thailand heat wasn't enough to squeeze those last few pounds out of me, then we would just have to force them out.

It did the trick. The next day I stood on the scales and was bang-on 48kg. It was a huge relief – for the first time in about twenty-four hours, I felt like I could breathe again. After Bill had given me his backing in front of the selectors, the last thing I wanted to do was let him down without even getting into the ring. It almost felt like I'd done the hardest part; now all that was left was to try to win a few fights.

I loved seeing world-class fighters from all over the world inside the venue – it was like being at the Olympics. There were even athletes from Muslim countries like Iran and Iraq – and most of them had more female fighters than the GB team did. It was amazing for me to see. I had always felt so conflicted between my faith and the sport, but seeing other Muslim females there showed me that you could compete without compromising your beliefs or your faith. They fought in leggings (as did I). Some even fought in hijabs – whatever they felt they needed to do to respect their religion.

My first opponent was a Malaysian girl who came to fight. By that I mean that as soon as the bell went, she came for me in a big way. And, after two rounds, I was definitely feeling it. But midway through the third I landed a hard body shot that I could see straight away had hurt her. Instead of coming back at me she was covering up. Struggling to get her breath back.

I saw the referee taking a good look at her and started walking towards the neutral corner, anticipating a stoppage. Suddenly I heard Bill yelling: 'Why are you stopping? Get back in there!' I shouted back: 'The ref is stopping it!' Just as the words came out of my mouth, the referee waved it off.

I'd won! A third-round TKO (technical knockout) against a top-level fighter in my first-ever World Championships. I hadn't expected it at all. But it proved, not only to myself but to Bill and to my peers at the gym, that I did belong. That I was deserving of my place on this trip. I had demonstrated my worth.

The best part was that I had a bye in the next round so went straight through to the semi-finals, which guaranteed me a bronze medal (similarly to the tournament in Cambridge, there weren't a huge number of females at my weight).

Next up was a Swedish fighter. I took her to the fourth round, but her movement and power were just a level above mine and it was her hand that was raised after the final bell. Still, coming home with a bronze medal was far more than I ever imagined would happen and I felt like the whole experience of being somewhere new had really given me a lift.

It was the first time I'd been away from home for such a long time – away from family and friends. I'd also been eating foods that I wasn't accustomed to, experiencing a new culture and been a part of a huge sporting event. Yes, there had been moments when I'd felt lonely and isolated because of the girls, but the confidence that I took from everything else was enough to help me see past that.

I came back with a real desire to push forward in the sport. To see what I could really do. If I could get a bronze medal with minimal experience and a mindset that was telling me I wasn't really good enough, what could I do if I was able to remedy both of those things? Maybe next time, I could go to the World Championships as a real contender, instead of someone who'd just turned up to give it a good go.

At that point, I realised that I didn't want to go back to architecture – I loved the sport too much. I started finding it harder and harder to make the time for my volunteering work. Three days at the firm went down to two days. Two days to one day. Eventually, I couldn't even turn up one day a week – I was constantly making excuses. In the end I had to be honest with them. For now, the sport had to be my main focus.

The experience in Thailand had shown me that Muay Thai

was the right path for me. And that if I put everything into it, I had a chance of really doing something with it. But none of that was enough to stop the girls at KO from treating me like dirt. However much I loved Muay Thai, the bullying was beginning to wear me down.

These weren't even girls, they were grown women – accountants, lawyers, managers. But for some reason, when they got together, they turned into a pack of bullies who thought it was funny to do juvenile things, like throwing my bag onto the floor in the changing room so that my stuff ended up all over the place.

That time, I actually told Bill and he addressed it in front of everyone in the class: 'Who chucked Rox's bag on the floor?' I heard one of the girls whisper to her friend, 'It was me', but Bill either didn't hear it or chose not to. He knew what was going on. Since coming back from Thailand I'd talked to him about the bullying a few times and was honest about how it was making me feel. But he didn't get it. He'd just come back at me with stuff like: 'They never said a bad word about you,' and tell me to ignore them; if I focused on my own training, they would soon tire of it.

I'd been trying that since the start.

Now, simply walking into the gym had become an exercise in mental fortitude. On days that I knew they were going to be there, I'd stand by the gym entrance with Zeus, taking a few deep breaths to steel myself before going in. Some days, I would go in, put my stuff down and go straight back out for a run, just to clear my head and refocus before taking them on.

During the sessions I was mostly able to stay strong and hold myself together, but as soon as I got on the train home it would all come out. I'd sit and cry all the way back to

Seven Kings. The next day, it would be the same story all over again.

On one occasion I decided I'd had enough and confronted them. It was Bill's birthday and they were organising a 'surprise' dinner for him at a restaurant near the gym. For weeks, everyone knew about it and everyone was invited, except for me. I knew Bill would want me there, so I decided to go anyway. When I walked into the restaurant, there was a look of surprise on their faces. We had a big, long table, so I went straight up the opposite end from them and sat with Bill and a few others. After ten minutes or so, I got up and walked down to where they were sitting.

'Guys, it would have been nice if you'd invited me. Why wasn't I told?'

Silence.

They didn't even acknowledge me. I could feel tears welling up but refused to cry in front of them, so I turned around and walked out of the restaurant to get myself together. One of the instructors came after me, but acted like it was my fault: 'Why are you doing this? Why are you being like this?'

These girls ruled the gym and it was clear that anyone who tried to stand up to them was automatically seen as being in the wrong. I blew my nose, took a few deep breaths and went back in to finish my meal.

It was a horrible time. And there wasn't anyone I could go home and share it with because I knew their solution would just be to tell me to leave the gym. But there was no way I was going to let them win. I felt like I had already been bullied out of my marriage; I wasn't about to let the same thing happen again.

Looking back now, I am proud of the way I handled

it. I did what I thought was best at the time and told Bill. Normally, he had all the right answers but in this case I don't think he did. That meant it was up to me to handle it on my own and that's what I did. The way I framed it was to make sure that I separated those girls from the sport. Because if you don't do that, you can start thinking that maybe this sport, or this gym, isn't for me. Muay Thai and KO had saved me in so many ways – I refused to let them take either away from me.

I was resilient. I confronted them. And I showed up in every session, making it clear that I was going nowhere.

Winning bronze in Thailand not only gave me the determination to carry on fighting, it opened up opportunities for me to keep moving forward in the sport. Around six months after we got back from the World Championships, I found myself sitting in the passenger seat of Bill's car on the way to Wales for my first-ever title fight.

The idea of me becoming a British champion seemed crazy at first, with so few fights still behind me, but Bill made it sound like a no-brainer: 'We can either get you ten fights to lead you up to this fight. Or, we can get you this girl and you can fight her and become a British champion overnight.'

I didn't need to go through ten battles to get there. And I believed I already had the technical ability to do it, so why waste time with warm-up fights? By the end of the weekend, I had my answer to that question.

I started the fight really cautiously – holding myself back to make sure I saved enough energy and power for the later rounds. But in the third round, I landed a hard right hand that knocked her to the canvas. I stepped back, waiting for the referee to begin his count (every time a boxer is knocked over, the referee gives them until the count of eight to get back up), but, instead, he started helping her back to her feet. I watched, stunned, as he took her over to her corner and waited, while her coach gave her a sip of water before bringing her back to the centre of the ring.

Bill was going crazy, shouting: 'It's an eight-count! What are you doing?'

But the referee just let the fight continue, as though it had never happened. After that, my head was all over the place. I was so angry and confused by what had occurred that I blew the rest of the fight and she ended up winning on points.

I was heartbroken. I knew that if I had kept my head, I would have won the fight.

But it was also the kind of experience I needed. Because it taught me that technical ability is only one small part of what you need to win in the ring. You can be the most skilled fighter in the world, but without the mental strength to keep your emotions in check – to be able to pick yourself back up when things go wrong – you won't have what it takes to get through the toughest fights.

But the only way to build that mental toughness and mature as a fighter is to go through those kinds of challenges and experience those emotions inside the ring. I might not have recognised it then, but failing that day was probably the best thing that could have happened to me as a fighter. At the time, though, I came back from Wales feeling really rough – like I was coming down with the flu. Physically, I had actually been suffering a bit since getting back from Thailand. Every so often, I'd notice that my recovery from training sessions wasn't as good as it had been – that I was walking into the gym still feeling fatigued from the previous session.

It wasn't all the time – on a good day I'd be on fire, but

on a bad one I couldn't even keep my guard up. Or I'd be breaking out in a cold sweat before we'd even started and I'd have to tell Bill I wasn't sure if I could even train that day. I had no idea what was wrong with me.

I'd been to my GP a few times thinking that maybe I had some sort of extended flu bug. I had come back from Thailand with a bad cough that didn't seem to be budging and there was a weird strain of flu called swine flu going around at that time, so I was worried I'd caught that. But the doctor sent me for a few blood tests and everything came back clear. There was nothing wrong with me.

As the months went on, I became used to training through the bad days. On really bad ones, I'd simply take an extra rest day and hope I'd recover in time for my next session. But, gradually, things got worse. Bill kept telling me to go back to my GP, but every time I did, the doctor would just tell me that feeling fatigued was normal for 'someone like me' (an athlete who spends so much time training). But I knew my body. And I'd been training for enough years to know the difference between post-training tiredness and something else altogether.

Eventually, the bad days got so bad that even walking and talking to people felt like too much effort. If I could, I'd struggle through a session, but then go home and bury myself beneath the duvet for a few hours before dragging myself up to make some dinner. It was starting to affect my work, too, even though I was only doing two days a week at the school.

Bill was adamant the doctor was missing something: 'You're not lazy and you know what tiredness feels like. This seems like something else – like you're not recovering from whatever is going on in your body. Like you don't have an immune system.'

This time, the doctor decided to take me seriously and referred me to Queen's Hospital in Romford to see a specialist. More tests were done, questions asked, examinations carried out. Eventually he sat me down and said: 'You have all the classic symptoms of ME.'

I had no idea what that even was. He talked at me for a while, explaining that it was a chronic neurological condition that can cause all sorts of symptoms like pain and fatigue and often affects the brain and body's ability to recover, even after expending only small amounts of energy. Then I was sent away with a booklet that offered some advice on how to manage it and a prescription for a load of vitamins.

I'd never really heard of ME before. And when I told other people about the diagnosis their response suggested they hadn't either. Someone at work even suggested the specialist was probably just trying to sell his own batch of vitamins or something. I stuffed the booklet away in a drawer and told myself it was fine. I'm a fighter. I can push through this. Besides, I didn't have time to be ill. After almost a year of waiting, I had another shot at winning the British title in a couple of months' time.

This time, it was against a girl called Paige Farrington, who I knew was going to be good. She was far more experienced than me and had already fought for a European title (losing it on points). I could tell that Bill was nervous about it too, just from the way he'd been during my training sessions in the build-up to the contest – I lost count of the number of times I heard: 'She's going to have a really strong jab, Rox . . .'

The fight was part of a show called 'Duel at the Dome' in Doncaster, which had something like ten fights in total on the bill. One of the guys from the gym, Greg, was also on it, fighting for a European title.

The three of us, plus one of my oldest friends, Thahera, who I'd known since I was eleven years old, piled into Bill's car to drive up to Doncaster the day before the fight. What should have been a four-hour journey turned into a six-hour one when Bill got lost. I was exhausted and starving. I hadn't eaten and was so worried about making weight that even when we stopped at a service station, I stayed in the car with Thahera while the guys went in to get food.

Thahera suggested that we say a prayer while we waited – I think she could tell how tense I was getting. And I found it really helpful. By the time Bill and Greg came back to the car, I felt a sense of calm in place of the stress that had built up over the last few hours of driving.

When we finally made it to Doncaster, Greg and I had to go straight to the venue to get weighed in. I made it with a pound to spare, while Paige was right on the borderline. Another few ounces and she'd have been spending the evening trying to sweat it out.

The four of us grabbed a quick dinner at the hotel before heading to our rooms to try to get an early night. Thahera and I shared a room, which was really nice – the night before a fight you can feel really alone and trapped inside your own head. Having someone else there to chat to about 'normal' things helped to keep me relaxed.

The next morning we got up and had breakfast, then went for a walk around town with Bill and Greg. It's a good way to keep moving and stop yourself from overthinking what's to come. But nothing can stop the nerves altogether. Once we got to the venue later in the afternoon, I suddenly started feeling really nervous and a bit sick. I walked to the toilets at precisely the same moment as Paige was arriving. As our paths crossed, she gave me a little smile.

I took a deep breath, ran back to Thahera and said: 'Oh my God, I just saw her and she doesn't look nervous!'

She said: 'All right, let's take a walk. Let's fix your head.'

It was a good idea. I couldn't just sit and wait around in the changing room. When you're in there you feel like you have to get ready for the fight straight away, but it could be hours before you're actually in the ring. I followed Thahera outside and, as we started walking around the building, she talked.

'Okay, so you're nervous. Let's put things in perspective: so is she. If you're going to go that way, then let's balance the arguments out. You've got fears. Well, so has she.'

Everything she said helped me to clear my head and I started to feel a bit better. Rather than let my own fear consume me, I was balancing it out. Understanding that Thahera was right: we both feel like this.

We stayed outside for ten minutes or so, before deciding it was too cold to hang around out there any longer. I also needed to head back to the changing room for a pre-fight massage before I could start getting warmed up with Bill.

Thahera sat and watched as Bill held pads for me. The nerves were making my shoulders so tense I could barely throw a punch at first, but as I started moving around I felt them relax enough to satisfy Bill that I was ready.

I sat back down next to Thahera who was looking at me and smiling: 'You're actually not bad, you know? When I saw you looking so nervous, I thought: Oh my God, this girl's going to kill you . . . Why did you put me through that?'

Thahera had never seen me fight or even train before, so

she'd actually been just as nervous as I was. She just knew she had to be strong for me because, if I saw her looking anxious, that would make me even worse. 'You made me go through all that for the last few hours – being nervous for what? You're really good!'

Once the fights started, time seemed to speed up. It felt like I blinked and suddenly I was being called for the ring walk. As we made our way to the curtains one of the organisers said that Bill couldn't walk out with me. I had to do it on my own. At that point I got really scared. I was so used to having Bill with me. I didn't want to walk out there on my own. I just wanted someone to hold my hand.

'Rox, I can't. I'll meet you at the other end. I'll be right by the ring.'

I stood there staring at the curtains in front of me trying to shut out the voice in my head saying: it's not too late! You can still run.

I hated the ring walk. For me, it was the worst part. Once you're in the ring, you're already in the zone, but those moments before you get there are when the nerves really kick in. Some fighters thrive on the attention but I didn't like it. I wasn't used to it yet. Nor was I used to the thoughts and feelings that came with it.

As Bill made his way to the ring, Thahera appeared by my side. She said a short prayer, squeezed me in a tight embrace and kissed me on the cheek before going out to find her seat in the hall. I felt lifted by her prayer. It shifted my whole aura. Gave me the confidence I needed.

The music had started. I could hear the guys behind me saying: 'Time to go . . . remember, don't rush it!'

I took a big breath in. And let it out . . . okay. Let's do it.

Chapter 11

I knew that if I didn't go right away, I might not go at all.

Pushing aside the curtain, I stepped out into the hall and started walking. One foot in front of the other, that was all I had to do. If there was cheering or booing to accompany my entrance, I didn't hear any of it. All I was focused on was the small white-haired figure waiting for me at the corner of the ring. As I reached him, Bill whispered in my ear: 'Well done.' He knew how tough that part was for me.

While Paige did her own ring walk, I concentrated on stretching out, trying to rid my muscles of the tension they'd been clinging on to for the last few hours. As she climbed into the ring, I allowed myself a quick glance at her across the canvas: the smile I'd seen a few hours earlier was gone but there was still no hint of nervousness in her face. Just a steely focus and a solid glare in my direction.

Final words from Bill absorbed ('The jab, remember – watch out for the jab'), I said my own brief ones to God and stepped into the centre of the ring.

In the first round Paige came on strong. Halfway through, I felt a kick right to my neck: shit, if she lands another one of them, I'm going to get knocked out.

I tried to put pressure on her. Be the aggressor. I've got nothing to lose. Even if it kills me, I have to get through this fight. That was my mentality: even if I have to die, even if I have to lose an arm, I am going to give it my all because I don't want any regrets.

At the end of the first round Bill said things were going well: 'You're doing good. You're winning.'

That gave me a boost going into the second round, which again saw me taking the fight to Paige. But when I went back to my corner at the end of it, Bill had gone and Vinnie – another coach from KO – stood in his place. I looked around for Bill but couldn't see him anywhere. I told myself it didn't matter. I had to stay focused. There were two rounds to go; I just had to keep on going.

At that point I knew I was outsmarting Paige. I was smaller and she was stronger but I was faster. I was trying to use my mobility to hit and move and not let her counter me. And it was working really well. I knew I was winning every round.

At the final bell I threw my arms in the air in celebration. I had to have won. I was sure of it. Vinnie towelled the sweat off my face and shoulders while we waited for the official result to be announced. I looked again for Bill. I wanted him to run into the ring and lift me up in celebration, like he always did when one of his fighters won a big fight. But there was still no sign of him.

The referee called Paige and me into the centre of the ring, holding each of us by the hand. I looked down at the canvas, praying it was my name that was about to ring around the hall.

'Your winner . . . in the red corner . . . Ruqsana Begum!'

Oh my God. I was a British champion. I couldn't quite

take it in. I finally had a moment – a winning moment. But the high was tinged with disappointment because I had so wanted Bill there to enjoy it with me. When I went back to the changing room, I found him in there with Greg.

'Bill, are you proud of me?' That was all I really wanted – for him to be proud.

'Yes, Rox, I'm proud of you.'

Words like that don't come easy to Bill. Sometimes you just have to make it as easy as possible for him to get them out.

Sitting in the back of his car on the way home I couldn't take the grin off my face. I had a belt. It was right there, on my lap. It was the most incredible moment of my life.

When we got back to the gym, I started talking to Bill about what was next. I was excited; couldn't wait to get back to training and start working towards our next goal. I even thought we could have a gym night out to celebrate. But Bill told me it wasn't a good idea. That I should stay away from the gym for a few weeks, to 'let the emotions die down'.

It stung me more than any of the blows Paige had thrown at me a few hours earlier. I knew exactly whose emotions he was talking about and they weren't mine. The girls in the gym had already been pissed off with the fact I had the fight. They thought it should have been one of the other female fighters at KO who got the opportunity, despite the fact that none of them would ever have made the weight (below 51kg). So he knew how jealous they were going to be now that I'd come back with the belt.

My presence in the gym would be rubbing salt into the wound and Bill would do almost anything to avoid upsetting them. I asked him: 'Why does it always have to be about them? I've worked so hard yet I'm not allowed to celebrate?

When they win something, the whole gym goes out and I'm not included. Now, I finally want to throw a party or something to celebrate and I'm not allowed to.'

I felt like I was being punished twice: once by the girls and once by Bill, because he was refusing to deal with the problem. All he would say was that the gym was his business and he wasn't prepared to take sides. And that if it was such a problem, then maybe I should just give up now that I had my British title.

I'd heard enough. I was upset but I knew Bill well enough to know that he didn't really think I should give up. Over the years I'd heard him tell so many fighters to 'just leave the gym' for one reason or another and he always changed his mind later – whether that was in a matter of hours or days.

It was past midnight by the time I got home. No one was awake, so I went straight up to bed, laying the belt out on Ane's old bed so it would be the first thing I saw when I woke up in the morning.

When I showed it to Mum and Dad the next day, I don't think they could quite believe it. They're not the most expressive, so there were no hugs or kisses of congratulation, but they showed me in their own way how happy they were. After telling me: 'They should have you in the local paper,' Dad spent the morning calling all his friends to tell them his daughter was a British champion. I knew that he was proud.

I didn't want to disobey Bill, so I did what he asked and took a couple of weeks off to let things settle. The whole build-up and fight itself had taken a lot out of me anyway, so I thought the time off would help. It also gave me the space to think things through. To reaffirm that I wasn't going to walk away from the sport I loved. Or the gym that had given me my identity back. In my mind I drew a thick line between Muay Thai and the bullies. They were just a matter of circumstance – nothing to do with the sport itself.

When I tried to get back into training, it was obvious I still hadn't recovered from the fight. I was constantly sluggish. Exhausted. And no matter how much sleep I got, how much I ate or how many days – or even weeks – off I took, I still felt exactly the same way. It wasn't like any tiredness I'd ever felt before. My whole body was aching. I felt it in my bones, in my joints, in my muscles. It was as though I'd been in the ring getting beaten up for round after round.

I couldn't bury my head in the sand any longer. I had to do something about it. But I needed more information. More guidance. I called the specialist who had initially diagnosed me to see if I could make an appointment, but his secretary told me he was only working in a private clinic now and it would cost a few hundred pounds for a consultation. There was no way I could afford that.

So I started to read up on it myself. On the training side of things, Bill was able to guide me. We made changes to my regime – keeping my sessions shorter and focusing them on skill and technique instead of fitness. When we did that, I found I was able to recover better. It was only when I was pushing my body to its limits that I would crash and struggle to recover.

Bill also got the gym to sponsor me in terms of my nutrition. That meant I could see a proper nutritionist who did some more tests and provided me with supplements designed to help my body with recovery from training. He gave me advice on my diet, too, helping to make sure I was getting the right amount of protein and carbohydrates and staying away from sugar as much as possible.

On top of the training and nutrition, I prioritised getting nine to ten hours of sleep every night and did whatever I could to stay away from stress.

If I could get all of those things right at the same time, then it made a huge difference to the way I felt. But it has taken time – years, really – for me to learn the best way to manage it. One of the hardest things has been having the confidence to hold back in training. Only working at 40 or 50 per cent of what I'm capable of means that, unlike my opponents, I don't have the mental reassurance that I've done 'everything I can' in training when the time comes to step into the ring.

It's a dangerous strategy because, come fight day, I don't know if I can or can't do it. But I just have to keep what I can in reserve, apply it on the day and hope that it's enough to get me through. If I crash after that, it doesn't matter.

The 'staying away from stress' aspect of managing my ME led Bill to suggest he would train me separately from the rest of the group – or specifically, from Naomi and the other girls: 'You'll have your days and they'll have theirs.' I didn't like the idea of being isolated like that and now I look back and think it only served to create a bigger divide. But Bill had decided that it was the best thing for everyone.

On Tuesdays and Thursdays Bill held pads just for me. But it backfired. It only produced more jealousy – now I was the 'teacher's pet'. The girls hated the fact that Bill was giving me one-to-one attention. So, once again, he bowed to their feelings and tramped all over mine. 'Why don't you go and train at the other gym in Clapton?' he said, referring to another KO venue that would have added twenty minutes to my journey.

'Why am I going to go out of my way to go to another gym? These girls have only been here a year or two. I was here throughout my whole university life. I don't want to be bullied out of it.'

I also didn't want to lose Bill as a coach. He was one of the best Muay Thai trainers out there and someone who knew me better than almost anyone. Another coach wouldn't understand the limitations I had when it came to training. They'd push me too hard and then I'd be back to square one.

I suggested an alternative solution. I'd been doing some bits of coaching with kids at a charity called Fight for Peace in east London and asked them if I could train there a couple of times a week with Bill. It wasn't ideal – it meant I was being pushed out of the gym literally as well as figuratively – but it was the only way I could keep Bill as my coach. Sundays were my one day back at KO – when the other girls had their rest day.

Three short sessions a week (two with Bill) weren't really enough. Not when Naomi and the other girls were training six days a week. I had to try to learn everything they were in half the time.

Sometimes, one or two of the girls would come to the fighters' sparring class on a Sunday for an extra session. In isolation they were never as bad as when they were all together, so they'd even let me spar with them. Every time they did, I held my own. And so, every time, my self-belief grew a little more. 'Bill, can you see this? Can you see that I'm holding my own with your fighters – the ones who you give undivided attention to six times a week, while I'm training with you only twice a week? Imagine what I *could* do given the same attention.'

I wouldn't describe myself as a stubborn person, but I will always fight for what I believe in. For justice. If I believe I'm right about something then I will fight for it. In this case, I knew I was right. I knew that if I was given the same resources, I could be better than them. So there was no way I was going to stop harassing Bill until I felt I was being treated fairly.

For the time being, though, it made little difference. He was too concerned about losing the business of many, versus losing just me. And he still didn't seem to take me seriously. He even suggested I should take what I'd won and call it a day: 'Rox, you wanted a British title, and you've got it . . .'

But if I could get the British, why couldn't I get a European title? For me to retire when I knew my potential was for so much more – I couldn't live with that and I told him so: 'If I was getting my arse kicked by those girls and it was just about winning the British title, then I would take what I've got and retire, but I know that I'm more than that.'

My chance to prove that to him came in the summer of 2011. I was selected to compete for Great Britain at the European Club Cup Amateur Muay Thai Championships in Latvia. It would be my first time competing since I won the British title and I'd be going alone. Bill wasn't able to travel out with us, so it was just me and one other competitor for GB – a guy called Ash, who I knew from KO. He was actually a similar build to me so we trained together a fair bit around that time.

Bill made clear what he thought of my chances of coming back with anything: 'The girls you'll be competing against are fighting every weekend, remember. They're professionally based fighters – some of them state-sponsored. They're eating and breathing fighting.'

I knew all that. But I didn't care. It just meant I had nothing to lose.

Almost as soon as we arrived, though, I started to wonder if I'd made a mistake. At the airport, Ash and I collected our luggage and walked out into the arrivals hall, looking for a board with our names on – someone from the organising committee was supposed to be meeting us there to take us to the hotel. We waited. And waited. But pretty soon we were the only ones left in arrivals.

We sorted ourselves out with a taxi to the hotel, where things took another step in the wrong direction when the girl behind the check-in desk said there weren't enough rooms for the two of us. We'd have to share. I could just imagine Mum and Dad's faces . . . but there was nothing I could do about it. And it would only be for a few nights.

The moment we walked into our room, I knew we wouldn't be spending much time in there anyway. It reeked of stale cigarettes. Everything from the towels to the bed linen smelled as if it had been soaked in tobacco then hung to dry in an airport smoking lounge.

The next morning, we were up and out early to get to the venue for the weigh-in, which we'd been told started at 11am. The earlier we got there, the quicker we'd get weighed in and be able to go and eat – I was competing in the under 48kg category again, so had barely eaten since we'd arrived.

But when Ash and I got to the hall, there were no other fighters to be seen. Only a collection of officials, running around making last-minute preparations, none of whom seemed the slightest bit interested in the presence of two confused athletes wearing GB tracksuits. Maybe we were in the wrong place. As we wandered back towards the entrance, Ash spotted a sign on the wall: 'Weigh-in from 3 p.m'.

Shit. I was starving. The tiny chicken salad I'd eaten for dinner the night before was barely enough to see me through to lunchtime, let alone to three o'clock in the afternoon. Neither of us particularly wanted to go back to the hotel and sit in that room for hours, so we found a quiet corner to hunker down in and tried to nap there.

A few hours later, other athletes started arriving. There were some big groups, with loads of fighters and three or four coaches looking after them. Ash and I had already moved into position at the front of the queue, so we could get registered and weighed in as early as possible. But as we were standing there, I started to feel really light-headed. Like I was about to pass out.

Ash grabbed one of the officials to tell her I was feeling unwell and she pulled us out of the queue, taking us to sit in her room until the weigh-in process actually started. We assumed she would put us back at the front of the line when it came to the right time, but once she'd sat us down, she disappeared. We'd been in there for around twenty minutes when we saw the queue starting to move.

'We've got to get out there now or we're going to be waiting for hours,' said Ash, looking at the queue that was now around a hundred athletes long. We picked up our stuff and headed back towards the front of the line, hoping the official who'd pulled us out of it would be there to help us reclaim our place. But she was nowhere to be seen. And the Russian athletes, who were now at the front, weren't having any of it when we tried to explain what had happened.

Just when we thought we were going to have to admit defeat and retreat to the back of the queue, the coach of Denmark's team, who were just behind the Russians, stepped in: 'Before us, these two are first.' If I'd had the energy, I would have hugged him.

Ash and I both made weight and went straight out to find something to eat. You have to weigh in every day during the tournament, so it's not like you can relax and eat what you like. But, generally, once you've made the weight it's not too hard to maintain, as long as you're careful with your food.

That night, the draw was being made to decide who would be fighting on the first day. Normally, it's the coaches who stay up to check, while the fighters get their rest. For Ash and me, that wasn't an option. So, we sat downstairs with the coaches, watching them drinking beer and eating while we sipped on our water, waiting to see if either of us was scheduled to fight the next day.

It was getting late and we were still waiting, so Ash told me to go to bed. He'd stay up for the draw and let me know if I was fighting. About an hour later, he came up to the room and said that neither of us had been drawn to fight the next day, so we could have a bit of a lie-in.

The next morning we got up around nine, had some breakfast and decided to wander over to the venue to watch some of the fights and see what the atmosphere was like. It was about midday by the time we got there and the buzz of competition was already filling the hall, along with the sights and sounds of fighters getting warmed up and taking on board last-minute words of advice from their coaches.

Just inside the entrance was a whiteboard with the day's schedule on it, so you could see who was fighting when. We stopped to take a look (not that either of us knew anyone competing, aside from each other). Suddenly, I saw Ash's name. And, shit, there was mine, too.

Ash's face fell. He'd messed up. He was scheduled to be the fourth fight on, while I was the last fight of the night. We ran out of the building and jumped in a taxi back to the hotel to get our stuff. There was just about enough time for Ash to get back and warmed up before he was due in the ring.

As we didn't have a coach with us, Ash and I had agreed to corner for each other (meaning we'd be there in between rounds to hand over water, towel down and offer any tactical advice if we'd seen an area we thought the other one could exploit). I'd never cornered for anyone before in an actual competition, but Ash was pretty experienced, so I knew he wouldn't need much from me, besides a few sips of water.

He was up against a guy from Ukraine who, after the first thirty seconds, I could tell was a top fighter. But Ash did okay. He came back to the corner after the first round unscathed and feeling good. He was going well in the second, too, until about thirty seconds before the end of the round when he got caught with a head kick that knocked him down. I screamed at him to get up while the referee was counting: 'One, two, three, four . . .'

Ash got back to his feet, but I wasn't sure he was going to make it to the end of the round. He looked unsteady on his feet and was breathing heavily through his mouth, suggesting his nose had been broken. Somehow, he made it to the bell and stumbled back to the corner where I poured some water into his mouth and asked how he was feeling. He didn't say anything, just shook his head and kept his gaze fixed across the ring at his opponent. Before I could ask him again, it was too late and he was back into the centre of the ring for the third round. I felt sick. Should I have stopped it? If Bill was here, he'd have known what to do.

They weren't far into the round when the referee made that decision for himself and stopped the fight. Ash was clearly hurt – there was blood coming from his nose – and there was no way he was going to win it, so the referee made the right decision to prevent him from suffering any further damage. It was a relief for me because I didn't want to see him take any more punishment, but Ash was gutted. He thought he could have fought on.

As soon as the fight was over, I felt really sleepy. The lack of food and emotional stress of seeing Ash get hurt had wiped me out. All I wanted to do was lie down and close my eyes for a while, so we went back to the changing room, which was quieter than the main hall and, while Ash sorted himself out, I stretched out on one of the benches.

A while later I was woken by a series of loud bangs coming from behind me. I sat up and looked sleepily over at Ash, who was sitting on the bench opposite me. 'I think that's your opponent,' he said, looking over my shoulder at the source of the noise.

'You're kidding me . . .'

Ash was staring at her: 'She's strong.'

I could hear the noise of her slamming a series of powerful kicks into her coach's pads: *Bang, bang, bang, bang.* One after the other. Each landing with as much force as the last.

I stood up, grabbed my bag and walked out without looking at her. I didn't want to hear Ash telling me how strong she

looked. I'd deal with that when we got into the ring. I had
to start getting warmed up anyway. With Ash being injured,
I had no one to hold the pads for me, so I put my gloves on,
did a bit of shadow boxing and then jogged around the hall
for a couple of laps until I heard my name being called.

In my head, I'd been telling myself it didn't matter how I
did. That I was far away from home, in a place where no one
cared if I won or lost. All I had to do was walk into the ring
and then the hardest bit was done. I was there for experience
and to get the rust off after so long away from competing.

In ten minutes it would all be over.

My opponent was a powerfully built Finnish girl. I knew
from what I'd heard in the changing room that she didn't
only *look* powerful either – she could transfer that into some
solid shots. But in the first round I realised that technically I
was much better than her. I was beating her to the punch or
kick almost every time she tried to engage.

At the end of the first round I went back to my corner and
tried to block out the fact that, while she had someone there
to look for my weaknesses and give her advice on how to take
advantage of them, I had no one. Ash wasn't well enough
to be out there standing in my corner, so I was on my own.
As I was struggling to pick up my bottle of water (not easy
when you're wearing boxing gloves), I saw the Denmark
coach who'd saved me in the weigh-in queue running over
to help me. He picked up my bottle, poured some water into
my mouth and told me to take some deep breaths.

As I went back to the centre of the ring for the next round
I heard people shouting my name. We had no GB supporters
there so I had no idea who it was until later in the round
when I was able to see that the whole Denmark team had

followed their coach over and were supporting me. It was like a miracle. It felt amazing to have that support when I'd thought I had no one.

They stayed for the whole fight, giving me words of advice after every round. When the referee raised my hand at the end, I ran straight over to the Denmark coach and hugged him. I was so grateful to have someone in my corner and amazed that I'd done something no one at home thought I was capable of.

Before the fight I hadn't even looked at who I'd be fighting next, so it was only afterwards that I discovered I had a bye in the next round. That meant my next fight, against a Turkish girl, was for the gold medal. That night, Ash and I ended up in the same restaurant for dinner as the coaches from the Turkish team, who spent half their evening trying to stare me out. It was just a little glimpse of what they had in store for me the following day.

Before bed, I sat on my prayer mat. It gave me a sense of peace to speak to God. And a confidence from feeling that I wasn't completely on my own.

The next day, Ash and I got to the venue just after lunch-time. We were due on around three o'clock, so that gave me an hour or so to settle in and get warmed up (thankfully, Ash was now able to hold pads for me). There was no sign of my opponent, which was fine by me. It meant I could focus on myself and the mantra that had got me through the first fight: I have nothing to lose. I don't have a coach. No one expects anything from me. All I have to do is get myself into the ring.

When my name was called, I said another quick prayer and walked out, with Ash following behind me and some polite applause accompanying me into the ring. Moments later, my opponent's name was called out and there was an eruption of noise. Only then did I look out and see how many people there were in Turkey tracksuits surrounding the ring. They had a huge team and were clearly set on making the noise to match. It's an intimidation tactic – not only for me but for the judges. If you show the judges that you're the bigger, stronger team, it can sometimes influence them to think your fighter is the stronger one too.

I looked across the ring at her and thought: it doesn't even matter if she has her coach and all these supporters. Inside the ring she's the same as me – two arms, two legs. I'm just going to give it my best shot. Put everything into the first round and see what happens.

I dominated the first two minutes. As I walked back to Ash in my corner, I smiled at him: I was better than her. Now I had to change my mindset, because looking for a mediocre outcome would be cheating myself. It was within my power to win this fight. I just had to keep going. Even if it meant I'd be exhausted in the third and fourth rounds. As the end of the fight neared, I was running seriously low on energy. But I knew I'd done enough if I could just hang on until the final bell.

When it finally came, I threw my arms in the air, as did she. But I was sure I'd won it. And Ash was sure, too. A few moments later, the referee had the scorecards and it was my hand that she raised in victory. A gold medal. I couldn't believe it. I'd done it with no coach and against fighters with more experience and more resources than I'd had. And I'd done it when no one else believed I could. When I'd had nothing to lose and absolutely everything to prove.

During the medal ceremony, one of the organisers got

talking to Ash about inviting me back to compete again the following year. He said how impressed he'd been with me and said I must have had 'about eighty amateur fights'. Ash laughed: 'She hasn't even had eight!'

That evening, when we were back in our room, I sat on my prayer mat and prayed again. Ash watched me, then, as I stood up, he said: 'If you're praying and winning these fights, maybe I need to start praying.'

I also called Bill to let him know. I think it's one of the only times I've experienced him being lost for words. Dad's reaction was probably the one that shocked me the most, though. When I got home and showed him the gold medal, he took it out of my hand without saying a word. For a few seconds he stood there, silently examining it, then turned away from me and walked over to my grandmother's room, waving it at her and saying: 'She's come back with the gold!'

It was one of the few moments when my family allowed me to see that they were proud of me. That despite the day-to-day moans of 'you're going to that gym again', they were actually supporting me, in their own special way.

After that trip, something clicked in my head. I realised that these girls, who were among the best in the world, were not miles ahead of me. Despite the fact that they were training almost every day, with the full support and resources of their country behind them, the gap between us was small enough for me to believe that I was capable of closing it.

And maybe now, others would start to believe it too.

Chapter 12

'Push me hard, Rox. You need to push me so hard that I feel sick.'

Ash and I had been back from Latvia for a few weeks and he was feeling recovered enough to start taking his training back up a notch. Whenever I was able to train at KO, I was normally paired up with one of the guys and Ash was one of the best for me. We were a similar build and he was a really talented fighter.

Ash had already held the pads for me that morning, so now it was my turn to return the favour and make sure he got a good session in. For twenty minutes he went for it almost non-stop. Aiming power shot after power shot at the pads until he was dripping in sweat and every single muscle in my upper body was screaming at me to stop.

As soon as I let my arms drop, I felt a sharp pain in the front of my right shoulder. It was radiating right down into my upper arm. I told Ash that it was probably just a muscle strain from holding the pads, but over the next few hours I started to fear it could be something more serious. Every time I tried to lift my arm up above my head, it felt like someone was stabbing me in the shoulder. It was so bad I couldn't even wash my hair properly.

When I went to see my GP the next day, he just told me to rest it: 'It's probably a bit of tension. Go and get a massage.'

Bill knew it was more serious than that – I couldn't do any upper-body work in the gym. No punching. No weights. No pulling or pushing. He took me to a physiotherapist he knew in Liverpool Street, where my shoulder was put through a full assessment: manoeuvred in various ways, prodded, poked. Finally, the physio sat back down in his chair and said: 'You've torn your rotator cuff.'

'What does that mean? Surgery?'

Thankfully, he thought it was a relatively small tear that could be treated without resorting to surgery. But it would take months of rehab work to build up the muscles in the back of my shoulder and allow the tear to heal. I left his office with a sheet of paper detailing (via some terrible drawings) a range of exercises he wanted me to start doing, and a couple of strips of bright-blue Kinesio tape plastered over my shoulder, to help alleviate the pain and give it some extra support.

For the next few months I stuck rigidly to the exercise plan and went back to my physio every week for rehab and more taping (once I had a proper diagnosis, my GP referred me to an NHS physiotherapist). In the gym, I had to find ways to work around the injury. Focus on improving anything that didn't involve my upper body. Thai boxing without using your hands is pretty limiting, though. I could run or spend half an hour on the exercise bike to keep my fitness up, but when it came to actually landing some blows, all I could do was kick.

The upside of that was that my kicking improved massively over those few months. The downside was that it was insanely boring (and incredibly tiring), spending my sessions just kicking. Fortunately, I did have some distractions. Winning the gold medal in Latvia had caught the attention of the media back home. I'd had a bit of interest from the local press and the BBC Asian Network after winning the British title, but now things stepped up a notch. More people were getting in touch wanting to speak to me – to find out more about this Asian girl who knew how to fight.

The rise in profile also meant getting invited to more events and meeting more people. One that sticks in my mind is the Canary Wharf Sports Awards, which took place in February 2012. I'd been nominated for a Special Achievement award, which meant I got to sit on a table with executives from the sponsors, local MPs and even the mayor of Tower Hamlets. I loved having the opportunity to get dressed up for once but I was nervous. What did I have to talk about with people like that?

I needn't have worried. All night, everyone was asking me so many questions: what I did, how I got into it, what I'd won . . . and every time I spoke, I realised that everyone else went silent. It was as though they were captivated by what I was saying. I had no idea I could do that. All I kept thinking was: am I really that interesting?

That night, coupled with the interviews I was doing for magazines, websites and newspapers, made me start to think about the opportunity I was being given to reach so many people. Because of my background and the fact that I was the first British Muslim female to become a national champion in her sport, people were starting to talk about me as a role model. Saying that I could have a positive impact on other Muslim women.

I wasn't so sure. I found it hard to embrace the idea of being a role model. I certainly didn't feel like one, or that I was doing anything inspirational. I was just doing a sport that I loved. It was only after having a few conversations with friends and my sister that I started to come round to the idea. The sport had taught me so much – eventually, I realised that these were really useful skills that I could pass on.

The more I thought about what I'd achieved in Latvia, the more I felt confident of having useful insight that other people could benefit from. Being there on my own, without a coach to guide me, had taught me so much about myself. It was me who found a way to win. It was the thought process going on in my head. It was me being in the moment and figuring out solutions to every single one of my problems. I didn't have Bill there; I didn't look for people to support me. I became my best friend.

It was only afterwards that I realised: what I'm doing is actually something quite unique – something that a lot of people don't know how to do. And something I could help them to understand as they navigate their own obstacles in life.

It took about nine months for me to get back to full training after my shoulder injury, by which time the 2012 World Championships in Russia were looming. I'd never been to Russia before so wasn't entirely sure what to expect. And, to be honest, after my first day of competition I wasn't a huge fan.

I had a bye in the first round so my first fight was in the second round, against Ranini Cundasawmy, a girl from

Mauritius. She was very confident. The day before the fight we were both at the venue watching our teammates fight and she gave me a good look, up and down. I was slumped in my chair, feeling tired and I could see her thinking: little Asian girl from England. I'll have her for breakfast.

I often felt that opponents judged me on how I looked. My build is naturally small. Although I was chubby as a kid, as an adult, the way I'm built makes it harder for me to carry as much muscle as some others. So, even if I'm in the right weight division, my opponent will generally look bigger than me. I was always the smallest female at the gym and in fights I was always the small one. People tended to look at me as though I was fragile. And because I'm generally a happy, smiley person, it made people think, *Oh, she's going to be weak.*

But I knew what I had inside. And I actually loved having that feeling of being the underdog. No one expected me to win. Often, no one even expected me to be able to fight. When I showed them how wrong they were, they didn't know how to deal with it. It would take them a few rounds to come to terms with it and by then it was too late. My hope was that the same scenario was about to play out against Ranini.

The day of the fight, I arrived at the venue, got warmed up and was standing at ringside waiting for my name to be called when I saw one of the officials go over to speak to the GB coaches. I noticed him look over at me a few times, as if I'd done something wrong. A few moments later the coaches came over to me and said: 'Rox, they've said you're not allowed to fight in leggings. You're going to have to take them off.'

The other times I'd fought abroad there had been some

understanding. They knew they had to accommodate fighters from countries like Iran and Morocco, so they'd done the same for me, too. But here, for some reason it wasn't the case.

At that time, I wasn't comfortable with wearing shorts in the ring. I felt like it went against my upbringing and the values that my parents had ingrained in me and I didn't want to do that. These days, I don't have an issue with it. Your boundaries change over the years. Now I know that it's not about me looking sexy – it's about practicality.

But then, it wasn't something I felt ready to do. The tournament was televised in Russia and a few other countries, so I worried about what my parents would think if they ever got to see it. I felt grateful enough to them that I was able to go on these trips, so I didn't want to let them down by then going against their values. But my coaches said it was either change or be disqualified and I didn't want to go all that way only to come home without even competing.

I stood there, trying to decide what I should do, when the official came back to speak to the coaches: 'In thirty seconds she's disqualified.'

There was a fire exit on the opposite side of the hall, so we ran over to it and opened the door into an empty stairwell. I already had my gloves on and hands wrapped.

'Rox, I'm going to have to do this.'

I had shorts on over my leggings, so my coach pulled them down, took my leggings off and then pulled my shorts back up. It was excruciatingly embarrassing. But it had to be done.

As we ran back to the ring my coach told me that Iran had a female fighter due to fight the next day and the whole team was threatening to go home if the organisers didn't change the rules. So, the likelihood was that if I did make it through to the next round, I would be able to wear my leggings for that bout. Sure enough, later that night the tournament organisers held an emergency meeting and decided that, from then on, female fighters would be allowed to compete in leggings if they wished.

In the meantime, I had to block out my mortification at what had just happened and try to focus on winning my first bout. But my heart was still racing as I climbed into the ring. Fortunately, I had time to compose myself.

Both Ranini and I still had to carry out the traditional Thai ritual that every fighter has to perform before a bout at the World Championships. It's called *wai khru*: '*wai*' being the traditional Thai greeting, where the palms are placed together as a sign of respect and '*khru*' the Thai version of guru, or teacher. So the ritual is a way for fighters to show respect to their teachers before a fight.

The short version of the ritual takes about a minute. It's the one that most fighters do and basically involves each fighter completing one walk around the ring, stopping at each corner to bow their head three times. That was the one I did, but Ranini chose to perform the extended version, which takes twice as long and ends with a traditional Thai dance in the centre of the ring (a bit like the New Zealand haka). It was an intimidation tactic. She was trying to psych me out by making me wait. All it really did was give me more time to compose myself.

From the first few exchanges in the opening round, I could tell I was stronger. Almost every time we came together, I was overpowering her. The only thing bothering me was my shorts. Every time I kicked, they were riding higher up my leg. I kept trying to push them back down, but it's tricky when your hands are enclosed in a pair of boxing gloves. It's also not a great idea to keep dropping your hands right down to your waist in the middle of a fight . . .

The first three rounds were all mine, I was almost certain of that. But in the fourth and final one, I kicked her hard on the shin and felt a sharp pain shoot through my foot. I recoiled and cautiously put it down on the canvas. I could stand on it. Phew.

Seconds later, the bell rang, signalling the end of the fight and I went back to my corner where the GB coaches started taking off my headguard and gloves. Looking down at my foot I saw my little toe wasn't sitting straight.

'Is it broken?'

'Nah, you'd be crying if you broke it.'

As I walked back to the centre of the ring for the referee to raise my hand, my little toe was flopping around at the edge of my foot. It was definitely broken.

But the next fight gave me the chance to get through to the final. No way was I going to give that up for the sake of a broken toe. The next morning, I taped it up tightly, using the toe next to it as a sort of splint. I'd sort it out properly once I got home.

I was up against the European champion (while I'd won a European title in an amateur event in Latvia, she'd won a professional version of the title), Chyslova Liudmila, in the semi-final. She was from Belarus where Thai boxers have the funding to train full-time and get help with things like strength and conditioning and nutrition. Even if I'd had ten working toes, I would have been a huge underdog.

For the first time, I wished Bill was there with me. The

GB coaches were good but I didn't trust them in the same way that I trusted Bill.

That was my mistake.

Now, I look back at the fight and I know that the advice the coaches in my corner were giving me was right. They were the ones standing there watching how things were unfolding against Chyslova. But, despite the fact that he'd prepped me on a general level and not for a specific opponent like the GB coaches were doing that day, I was still trying to follow the advice Bill had given me before I'd left for Russia.

Nevertheless, I started the fight really well. In the first round, I caught Chyslova with a short left hook that caused her legs to buckle and sent her crashing to the canvas. But in the second, I got my strategy wrong: I was trying to kick (because the kicks score more points), but every time I did, she was making me miss and countering with a punch of her own. The third round was pretty even but in the fourth, I was sure I was the one on top. At the final bell I went back to my corner thinking I'd done enough to get the win. Sadly, the judges didn't agree.

It was gutting. I was so close to the final. So close to a gold or silver medal on the world stage. It showed me how little there was between me and these girls who were at the very top. On another day, I would have won against a girl who was not only an amateur national champion but who fought as a professional too. In Muay Thai there are not the same barriers to competing at both an amateur and professional level as there have traditionally been in boxing, so fighters are able to switch between the two.

It was time to reassess. To start testing myself on the professional stage as well as the amateur one. As soon as I got back to the gym, I told Bill exactly what I was thinking: I need a belt.

He set the wheels in motion. Now that I had two bronze medals from the World Championships, as well as a gold from the European Cup, it was more likely that we'd be able to convince one of the sport's professional governing bodies that I was deserving of a shot at a title.

It was about six months later that my phone rang late one night, just as I was getting ready for bed. I saw it was Bill and picked up: 'Rox, I've got some good news . . .'

I thought it was a European title fight, but he said: 'No, they want you to fight Silvia La Notte, who's a multiple world champion from Italy.'

Her people wanted it to be a normal bout with nothing on the line, but Bill pressed them hard. He was adamant that, if I beat her, then I should win a world title. And they agreed. I guess they saw my record and compared it to Silvia's – a proven, renowned world champion with many more fights than me – and thought she'd walk right through me. They even agreed to have the fight in the UK as opposed to Italy. That's how confident they were.

The fight date was named as 13 April 2013. We had six weeks to prepare.

I was still splitting my time between KO and Fight for Peace, where it was becoming increasingly difficult to train. They'd started running a lot of classes during the day, which meant the gym was often booked up when I wanted to use it. Whitechapel Sports Centre was my third option but, even there, space was limited. One time we ended up training in a corridor, with people walking past us thinking we were crazy. But it was the only area we could find.

All I wanted was a place that I was familiar with. Somewhere I could train whenever I needed to. But I didn't have that. I felt like I didn't belong anywhere.

Running around from place to place meant that six weeks flew by. The schedule was tough. I was training six days a week. Most of the time, that meant doing two sessions per day. In the morning, it was a technical session with Bill where we'd work on different drills, focusing on things like footwork, defence, striking, kicking – and, of course, those brutal knees. Sparring was on Friday nights and Sunday mornings.

Bill's sessions were smart, in that they were tailored around my ME – so while he pushed me hard, he seemed to know when to pull things back and give my body a break – and afterwards I'd head home to rest and get some food. I was typically eating two meals a day at that time, normally one after that morning session and one later in the evening. So, in the morning, I'd generally skip breakfast and head straight to the gym. It's not something that works for everyone, but it was fine for me. I've never been a big breakfast person anyway, so I preferred to be able to eat more later in the day.

Lunch would typically be something like grilled fish or chicken with some rice or couscous. Then for dinner I'd often have a really watery, low-calorie, low-carb soup (with a load of spices thrown in to make it taste of something) with a bit of grilled chicken. It was really limited, but I was just focused on keeping my diet as simple and low-calorie as possible (when you fight at a low weight, you *have* to keep an eye on what you're eating).

These days, I'm more creative with my food. I learned how to add more ingredients into my diet without necessarily adding a load of calories – things like egg whites and vegetable 'pasta' or 'rice' are great for that. I still eat very healthy meals, but there's more variety. That means it doesn't feel like I'm on a diet as much any more and I can be more flexible about eating out.

My afternoons would usually be spent resting, before an evening run of around 5km, which I'd finish off with some bodyweight stuff like push-ups and sit-ups. But despite the watery soup and daily runs, the day before the weigh-in for the fight against Silvia I was still half a kilo over the 48kg weight limit. I'd never really had any issues making weight since that first time in Thailand, but for some reason now it just stuck.

Bill told me to have a salt bath before I went to bed that night. I'd never tried one before, but he said it was something that models do if they need to lose weight fast: 'Make sure the bath is steaming hot, fill it with Epsom salts, then go to bed with your bathrobe on. You'll lose a kilo overnight.' He was right. The next morning, I was a kilo lighter but I felt dreadful. The salt drains all the water out of your body so I was completely dehydrated. I was basically a zombie.

The fight was taking place in Birmingham the next day, so that afternoon, one of the guys from the gym – Christian – drove Bill and me up there. They sat in the front chatting all the way, while I lay down in the back, drifting in and out of sleep. I was dehydrated and really hungry – engaging in conversation was the last thing I felt like doing.

Once we arrived in Birmingham we went straight to the venue for the weigh-in. I was desperate to get it over with so that I could start rehydrating and go and get some food in me. Luckily, as my fight was a world title bout, the promoters prioritised our weigh-in, pushing Silvia and me ahead of the guys who were all fighting on the same card. They weren't too happy about it but Bill just smiled at them and said: 'When you fight for a world title, then you can weigh in first.'

Silvia arrived shortly after we did. As she walked into the hall, I had a good look at her. Similar height. Strong body. But I thought I looked stronger. She looked like she'd really had to lose a bit of weight – her cheeks were sunken and she was a lot thinner than she was in the picture on the posters advertising our fight.

With the weigh-in ticked off, we could finally go and eat. There was no second weigh-in on the day of the fight so I could eat whatever I wanted, but you do have to be a bit careful after you've cut weight. Your stomach has gone through a bit of a detox, so if you eat the wrong type of food, or too much food, it can lead to some unpleasant consequences. My nutritionist had told me to have some grilled chicken and carbohydrates that night, so we found the one place in Birmingham that I knew I could trust: Nando's, for a chicken and rice platter before we headed to our hotel.

The promoters had booked us into a dingy little place. It was basically a pub with a few bedrooms upstairs. I walked into my room to find the window wide open. It was freezing. I switched on the small electric heater beneath the windowsill and started looking for some extra blankets to throw on the bed. It wasn't exactly a room that made me feel at home.

Christian came and sat with me for a couple of hours while we watched a film, which helped me relax a bit, but once he left I struggled to fall asleep. The bed was all spongy and the floorboards outside were so creaky that every time someone walked past my room it sounded like they were actually inside it.

In the morning I met Bill and Christian for breakfast but I couldn't eat. I was still worried about upsetting my stomach (either from nerves or just the fact I was giving it more food than it had been used to in recent days), so while they sat there shovelling down a cooked breakfast, all I had was a cup of tea before going back to my room for a mid-morning nap. It was stupid of me, really, because by the time we got to the venue, I was starving. And all I had to eat were a few protein bars stashed away in my bag.

The first job at the venue was to see the doctor and get the medical out of the way. After that, it was a waiting game. The doors opened at five, the fights started at six, but Silvia and I were one of the last bouts on, so there were at least three hours to go until we would actually be getting in the ring. All I could do was sit in the changing room and wait. It was purgatory.

The worst thing about it was watching all the other fighters build themselves up to go out there, only to return battered and bruised twenty minutes later; their nervous excitement replaced by a dark mist of negativity. One guy came in with blood dripping from a deep cut just above his eye. A second cut on the bridge of his nose was on the verge of contributing to the bloody mess on his face. I lay down on the bench, put my jacket over my head and closed my eyes, trying to sleep. I didn't want my head filled with negativity. I needed to see positive results. If I couldn't, then I'd have to close my eyes and imagine them.

I zoned out, trying to think about the people who had come to see me fight. My sister Ane was out there. She'd become a mum about a year ago and had left my little 1-year-old niece at home with Mum and Dad just so that she could come and support me. My cousin Sarina was there too. Even Moynul, my oldest brother, had come. It would be the first time he'd ever seen me fight.

Bill had also organised a little minibus to bring some of the KO crew up to Birmingham. It was nice to know there would be some familiar faces in the crowd when I walked out. This time, I was actually a bit excited about getting out there. I'd even arranged for a friend of mine, Viraj, to play the dhol (a big Indian drum that looks a bit like a barrel) for me to walk out to. If I'm gonna do this thing, I might as well do it in style.

I was still hiding under my jacket when I heard someone come over and tell Bill it was time for me to start getting ready. I sat up and saw Bill already holding my hand wraps. I nodded at him. I was ready.

I sat back and held my hands out for Bill to start carefully wrapping them. Before any fight, that's the moment you really start to mentally prepare yourself for what's about to happen. The armour is being applied, ready for battle. I warmed up lightly on the pads. Just enough to get the blood pumping; to feel the sweat start to gather on my forehead.

Just as I was about to walk out, Bill said: 'Let's make a prayer.' He put his hands on my gloves and together we asked for God to protect us. To give us strength. Just as it had before the British title fight, praying helped me to feel at ease. To feel calm. To feel ready.

Silvia was already in the ring. She looked different to how she had the previous day. Bigger. Much bigger. This was not the skinny girl I'd seen at the weigh-in. She had ballooned.

I had to walk halfway around the hall to reach the catwalk that would lead me down to the ring. As I made my way around, I could see Silvia jumping around the ring out of the corner of my eye. Shadow boxing. Getting herself loosened up. I couldn't panic. Even if I couldn't knock her out, all I had to do was keep the intensity really high. If I did that I could still win on points.

As I walked, I went through a checklist in my head, trying to reassure myself mentally: I've been in the ring with the boys in the gym and they hit really hard, so if she's got power, then fine, I can handle that. If she's stronger than me, then fine, I can handle that too. How am I going to win this fight? Once that bell goes, I'm just going to give it my all.

From the moment the bell sounded, that's what I did. I had the speed, which meant I was able to land a few extra shots after every combination, without getting caught. That meant I was outscoring her. She was strong and tenacious, but she wasn't as intelligent a fighter.

Soon, she realised that too. When a fighter's back is against the wall, that's when they are at their most dangerous. In the third round Silvia landed a combination that knocked me down. Before the referee could start the count, she drove her knee into my chest while I was still on the floor, which is illegal. I could hear Bill shouting at the referee from my corner, but it had no impact. He simply started the count and I had to get back to my feet before he stopped the fight.

At the end of the round Bill was furious with me: 'You're too nice. You don't let anyone do that to you.' And he was right. She could have broken my ribs.

As the bell summoned us for the fourth round, Bill put his mouth next to my ear: 'You need to get nasty in there.' I nodded but I didn't have it in me to do anything like that. I wanted to win, but I wanted to do it fair and square. And I knew I was ahead on points anyway. Despite what Bill had said, I didn't think there was any need for me to resort to dirty tactics.

We were more than halfway through the fourth round when I took the punch that ended the fight. Silvia threw a hard jab at my forehead at the same moment I went to kick her. Being off balance meant I wasn't able to steel myself for the shot as I normally would have and it jerked my head right back. I wasn't knocked out, but I was dazed. I looked across at Bill for a few seconds, trying to figure out what had just happened and what to do next. I looked back across the ring and saw Silvia walking towards me. I was still trying to process what had happened.

This wasn't something I'd ever experienced before. I'd been tagged with shots that had left me seeing stars for a few seconds, but this was different. It was weird. Instead of lifting my hands up to protect myself, I looked back across the ring at Bill. It was only for a second or two but it was enough to convince him I was done. As my eyes refocused on the ring, I saw a white towel come flying in from my own corner.

That was it. Bill had ended the fight.

I was devastated. Furious – with myself, with Bill, with everything. I was ready to carry on. There was only one more round to go. One more round to become a world champion.

Bill tried to explain his decision; told me that my safety had to come first: 'When you watch the video you'll see – you were dazed for a few seconds too many. Nothing is worth risking your life.'

It felt so strange to have the fight ended like that – prematurely. I didn't get the result I wanted but I also didn't get the release that I wanted – the feeling that comes from knowing you've given something your all, no matter what the result might be. That outcome was never an option in my head. I thought maybe I would lose, or I'd win, but never about the fight being stopped like that. It haunted me for a few years. Mentally, I struggled to get over it.

After Silvia was awarded the belt, the referee came over to our corner and handed Bill the scorecards. He nodded his head at me and said: 'Your girl was ahead.'

Part of me understood Bill's decision. It was difficult for him with me being who I am. Female. Muslim. My parents knowing what I'm doing but still not being entirely happy with it. If I got really hurt, Bill is the one who would have to answer to them. He'd have to live with it. He'd have to take responsibility and accept that he could have stopped that fight.

He didn't know how hurt I was, or if I could carry on. He had never seen me dazed like that before in my whole career. So, as heartbroken as I was, I had to respect him for his decision.

After the fight, my brother wanted to go out somewhere to get food. But I didn't want to do anything. I just wanted to sit and gather my thoughts on my own. But no one was giving me the space to do that.

Bill had already left. He was disappointed too. It wasn't the result either of us had hoped for.

The next morning, I went out shopping with a friend. He was trying to take my mind off the night before, but I couldn't interact with the world around me. While he bought new trainers and tried on clothes, I sat in the shops in a complete haze. I couldn't gather my thoughts. Couldn't get on with normal life.

I saw myself as a world champion. It was my journey. This should have been my day: the day I was sitting there with my belt, knowing I had reached my goal. Yet, instead, I was sitting there as just another Sunday shopper. Not a world champion.

At the time I found it so hard to deal with, but mentally, emotionally, physically, it was such a great lesson for me. It was there to humble me and to teach me about failure. About success. About hard work and being resilient.

When the next opportunity came, I would have so much more respect for it. And there would be a next opportunity. I was sure of that. How could I stop pushing for it when I had been one round away from winning?

Bill felt differently. He'd put so much of his time and energy into preparing me for that fight. More than with any other fighter, he had to take notice of every little thing, because of everything I'd been through with my health. It was his responsibility to make sure my mental and physical well-being were always the priority ahead of anything else. If I wanted to push harder, it was his job to tell me if it was worth the risk. If I was worried about not doing enough in training, it was his job to build up my confidence so that I still believed I could win.

It had exhausted him. When he told me that he didn't have it in him to lead me to another title fight, I knew him well enough to realise there was little point in arguing. Not yet, anyway. I couldn't wait too long, though. What happened that night was like an itch that I couldn't scratch until I knew I was getting a second chance.

A couple of weeks later I was sat having a coffee with Bill in the gym. He was in a good mood. The gym was busy, just as he liked it and there was a plate of food in front of him. There would be no better time.

'Bill, I know what you said but I'm not ready to give up yet ... I was winning that fight. Let's go for a rematch.'

Just as I knew Bill well enough not to press him a few weeks earlier, he knew me well enough to realise that, once I've got something in my mind, I will find a way of doing it. It's never about the obstacles or the difficulties in the way; it's just about the solution. If I have a clear goal or destination in mind, then my only focus is on how I'm going to get there.

Bill was back in. When he spoke to the ISKA (the governing body) to submit our request for a rematch, they told us to hold tight – that Silvia would have to fight me again in a year's time because at that point her title would become vacant.

So that was our plan. In the meantime, Bill didn't want me to take any risks: 'Just keep active. Keep training. You already know you can beat this girl and a year will go by really fast. We can do a few fights abroad, below the radar, if we need to and then that's it – we go for Silvia again.'

While we waited for the rematch, Bill tried to line up those fights to keep me sharp and focused. But every time we got close to the fight date, my ME would kick in. The training was vigorous and I knew that was how I had to train to get to the level I needed to be at for a fight, but I didn't yet know how to manage it with regard to my ME. So, every time I got close to the optimum level – every time I reached that threshold – my body would completely give up on me.

I could push and push and then in the week before the fight, I was done. Game over. Bill knew there was no point in waiting until the day before the fight to pull me out because he already knew what my body was like and how long it would take me to recover: 'We can't put you into a fight knowing you're already 50 per cent low in battery.'

We had to think about the bigger picture: any fight I lost would damage my ranking and put the rematch in danger.

So, that year was about trying to stay healthy more than anything. That meant keeping my life as simple as possible. I learned that if I wanted to train hard, I *had* to make sure I was recovering fully between sessions and not doing anything else that would stress my body out. I thought of it as being like a set of old-fashioned scales: if I overloaded them on one side with training, I had to make sure the other side (which would normally be filled with stuff like work stress, social-ising, etc.) was as light as possible to keep myself balanced. If I could do that, I'd give myself the best chance of staying healthy, energised and able to make it into the ring with the best possible chance of beating my opponent.

The minute I pushed too hard, or skimped on my rest and recovery, the tell-tale signs would start to appear – the lethargy, the breathlessness, the weak and aching muscles. My mantra had to be: train, eat, rest. Keep life as simple as possible.

As the twelve-month mark since the first fight approached, Bill got back in touch with the ISKA to arrange the rematch with Silvia. But he was told we would have to wait another six months for them to put everything in place – contracts, a date and a venue. Fine, I thought. I've waited this long, what's another six months?

As it turned out, another six months was everything.

The next conversation Bill had with the ISKA was for them to tell him that Silvia was now out of action for one year. Why? They wouldn't tell him. All we knew was that she couldn't fight. It felt like she'd punched me in the face all over again. I'd waited a year and a half for this opportunity. A year and a half of being eaten alive by what had happened last time. A year and a half of putting everything else on hold to make sure I was in the best possible position to win.

As unprepared as I had been for losing the first fight the way I had, I was even less prepared for this. Silvia had dropped off the radar and I was stuck in limbo. All we could do was wait and hope the ISKA were quick to find another opponent for me.

She ended up being the French national champion, Ludivine Lasnier.

The fight would take place in six months' time, in London's Earl's Court – the fact that she was getting a shot at a world title was enough for her team to accept that she would be fighting on my home turf. I didn't know much about her and neither did Bill. A few weeks before the fight, when we sat down and tried to find some footage online that might give us some idea of the best strategy to employ, there was hardly anything there – just a few rounds of a fight from a few years ago that had been filmed on someone's phone and uploaded to YouTube.

By the time of the fight, almost two years had passed since my defeat to Silvia.

Outside of the handful of fights Bill had lined up for me that I'd been forced to pull out of, I'd found other things to occupy my time. Things that were equally important to me. One of them was the women-only class at the gym. When I'd got married, Bill had passed the responsibility for running it on to someone else. But it never really kicked on in terms of numbers and when the new person running it left the gym, they never replaced her, so the class just stopped.

I'd wanted to take it on again since going back, but I still didn't feel the demand was really there. Yes, there were more women in the gym now, but they were all happy to take part in the main sessions so I never felt it would be worth my while. But then something changed. I was invited to speak one evening as part of a panel discussion about diversity and inclusion in sport, alongside the former footballer Paul Elliott, an Asian rugby player whose name I forget (sorry!) and Rimla Akhtar, the chair of the Muslim Women's Sport Foundation. I was a bit nervous about it, as I'd not done much public speaking before, so Bill came with me for moral support.

We each spoke a bit about our experiences of being a BAME (black, Asian and minority ethnic) athlete within our respective sports. Rimla, for example, had captained the British Muslim women's futsal team and I – the final one to speak – told the audience about my own experiences growing up and hiding the sport from my family. After the discussion, there was a period set aside for questions from the floor.

I automatically breathed a sigh of relief and relaxed back into my chair, thinking that my speaking part was surely over – with an established football player alongside me, I was certain most of the questions would be directed at him. But when the first question came, it was for me. Then the second one was, too. Thankfully, the next few went elsewhere but, by the time of the final question, I must have answered more than half of them. It was phenomenal – everyone was intrigued by my story.

I think it was the moment that I first realised how

important my role as a female and a Muslim was in what I was doing. That I could make a difference to others.

On the way home, Bill and I were talking about it; both of us amazed that so many people wanted to speak to me. He went quiet for a few minutes, seemingly lost in thought, then said: 'Rox, do you want to start up the class again?'

I think he realised that, with my profile rising and my story apparently generating so much interest, there was an opportunity to bring more people into the gym – people who might not feel a Muay Thai gym is a safe space for them because of their background or beliefs. People like me.

I was excited about it. There were many women who either weren't confident enough to join a gym like KO because they felt intimidated by the atmosphere or the fighters, or who thought that joining meant they'd *have* to fight and were scared of getting hurt. But I hoped that the opportunity to train as part of a women-only class would take away some of those fears.

There was also much more awareness now of the fitness benefits that fight sports can offer (even without the need to spar or get hit), as well as the mental boost. It just felt like the right time to try to start it up again. We scheduled it for 12.30 p.m. on a Sunday, so I could go straight into it after finishing my own training at midday. The first week I think we only had about three women show up, but, gradually, word spread and each week would see new women walking nervously into the gym, until eventually we had a solid core of around eight to ten women coming to train every Sunday.

There were even a few Muslim females among that group, which made me feel amazing. But regardless of whether they were Muslim or not, I felt good because, week by week, I could see the impact that the training was having on them. They were growing in confidence; coming into the gym with the air of someone who believed they had every right to take up space in that arena. Those women who'd first walked in with their shoulders slumped and a look of constant anxiety on their face were fast becoming a distant memory.

And I knew exactly how they felt, because I remembered how it was for me. I remembered how I used to look forward to my session the whole week. How I saw it as my little bit of 'me-time'. I related to that.

I still run that class now, because there's no better feeling than seeing the impact that it has on the women who come. And over the years I've noticed that it gives them so much more than just sport. As well as the sense of empowerment that comes from pushing their bodies and minds to do things they never thought possible, it also gives women from different backgrounds, age groups and cultures a place to connect. Somewhere they can unite with a common goal. It's beautiful.

It's something I wished I'd had when I started out; when I walked into the gym as the only Asian girl. The only Muslim girl. And one of the very few females in an altogether male-dominated sport. But, just like Michelle Obama would later talk about doing, I learned how to survive – and thrive – in that environment.

I learned that I don't need to fit in with everyone else. That I can just be me. And that the more I am myself, the happier I will be. As long as I stay aligned with who I am and my beliefs and values, I am free. So, I never try to fit in. I just let the world fit around me.

Aside from teaching the classes, I was also trying to start

a business. In 2012 I'd been glued to the Olympics, taking place in my home town, when one scene at the athletics caught my eye. It came during the early heats of the women's 800m, when the camera panned across the track, pausing for a second on each individual athlete. When it reached lane eight, I took a sharp intake of breath. The athlete standing there, smiling nervously down the camera, was wearing a hijab. I'd never seen an athlete competing at such a high level wearing one. I hadn't even thought it would be allowed.

I later found out the athlete was Sarah Attar, one of the first two women to compete for Saudi Arabia at the Olympic Games, the other being Wojdan Shaherkani, who was taking part in the judo competition. I was captivated as I watched Sarah run, dressed in a long-sleeved top, black leggings and a plain white hijab that wrapped tightly around her head and tucked into her top. She finished last, forty-three seconds behind the winner, but the crowd roared as she crossed the finish line. As she did so, a small shiver went down my spine.

The next day, I read everything I could about her and how she'd come to compete. In one of the newspapers, they told the story of how she and her mother had made the hijab themselves. From my own experiences during those years I'd spent wearing one at school, I knew how incompatible they could be with playing sport. And now, a few years later, I saw first-hand how conscious the girls at Swanlea school were about wearing them for PE, getting them sweaty and having to keep them on for the rest of the day. They also had safety pins holding them together, which isn't the safest when you're playing sport.

I wondered why no one had designed one specifically for everyday people to play sport in? Something made of the right fabric and with the right kind of fit. Once I started thinking about it, I couldn't stop. If Muslim women had access to a hijab that they could comfortably wear while playing sport, it would remove a really big barrier for a lot of them. We don't expect women to get hot and sweaty while wearing a regular bra, instead of one that's specifically designed for sport. Why should it be any different for women who wear a hijab?

Now, I felt I had the time to really do something about it. In my spare time after training sessions, I'd come home and do research – looking into factories and fabrics and getting samples made up. I even took part in a two-week course that the Prince's Trust organised to teach you some of the skills needed to set up your own business.

It took time, but, after a year or so, I got to the stage where I had a website set up that I could sell the hijabs from and a factory in Pakistan making them. Because I was only putting in small orders of sixty or seventy at a time, the factory wasn't exactly quick in turning my orders around – I guess they prioritised the bigger jobs. So, after I put in my first order, I had to wait about six months for it to arrive.

When it finally did come, I was so excited. I ran to get some scissors and carefully sliced down the centre, making sure I didn't cause any damage to the fabric inside. I pulled one out of the box, held it up in front of me and burst into tears.

It was a complete mess. The stitching was all wrong.

When I spoke to the factory, they told me it would take another six months for the order to be replaced. I was devastated.

But now that I had my design and fabric, I decided to try to find another factory that might be able to deliver something quicker. I was put in touch with a different one in Pakistan by the boxing brand RDX, who had kindly been supplying some kit for my women's class, and this time the order came within a few weeks. It was perfect.

From that box and the replacement one, which eventually arrived, I must have sold about 100 hijabs. It was hard work, though – I was the one posting orders, dealing with queries and chasing factories. I knew that, ideally, I should have made visits to the factories and be looking at new fabrics to keep improving the product, but I was too focused on my other job – winning a world title.

Given the long gap between fights, I think my parents had started to hope that was it for me in terms of competing. And it wasn't just them hoping that. At family weddings I'd be surrounded by aunties and uncles asking me: 'Are you going to get married soon? You don't want to get out of date . . .'

It was all anyone talked about. Well, that and having children. I loved going to visit my sister but the topic of conversation at her in-laws was always about babies – whether you were in the process of having one, or you were struggling with the one you had, or looking forward to having another one. It was what their world seemed to revolve around. My world was so different. In the gym I would mix with people from all walks of life – some were directors of their own companies, some worked in McDonald's. The conversations I joined in with there seemed a million miles away from the ones I'd have outside of KO's four walls.

It seemed crazy that the two things that had been part of my life for so long were still as far apart from each other now as they had been the very first time I'd put on a pair of boxing gloves. I had aged. Married. Divorced. But the two worlds I straddled hadn't changed a bit.

Two years is an incredibly long time to be out of the ring and, as the fight with Ludivine neared, I couldn't help but worry about how it would impact on my performance – 'ring rust' is a well-known phrase in boxing for a reason.

I'd been nervous going into the fight against Silvia, but my excitement at being in a world title fight for the first time was on a par with those nerves. This time was different. The two-year gap had left me doubting myself. I wasn't sure what I was capable of any more. And that was making me scared.

Fear is something that most fighters deny – especially the guys. They don't admit to it. Don't talk about it, because they see it as a sign of weakness. By now, Bill was used to me telling him I was scared, but it had taken him years. At first, he'd panic and think: *Shit, is she going to be okay?* But with experience he realised that my admitting to feeling afraid doesn't mean I'm not capable. It's just me being completely honest. And saying it out loud helps me to deal with it. A lot of the time, I don't even need Bill to say anything back or reassure me – I'm just letting him know that I am really scared and that's it. Once I say it, it's released. The fear might still be there but it isn't consuming me any more.

It took me some time to learn how to manage it, though. To understand that the fear is just a feeling I'm experiencing at that moment and that the only way of overcoming it is to go through it and come out the other side. There's nothing else you can do.

To some degree, fear is a good thing to have going into a fight – it heightens your responses. Sends adrenaline coursing through your veins. But too much of it can be overwhelming and that's when it becomes dangerous. It can paralyse you. Suddenly, you're in the ring and you can't feel your hands or legs any more. You're numb.

It's about controlling the fear and finding the right balance to make sure I don't get to that point.

With every fight, I learned more about how to do that. I found different ways to reassure myself. Sometimes that was through prayer, because if I'm afraid that something's going to happen, I believe that God will protect me. With some fights – like my previous one against Silvia – I was excited because I knew I was fighting for a world title. Other times I told myself the pressure wasn't on me; that no one cares if I win or lose, so it doesn't matter. Every fight was different.

This time I just had to keep telling myself that I was the kind of fighter who always rose to the challenge. That once I was in the ring, I could trust myself to perform well under pressure, no matter how long it had been since my last fight.

I had no issues making the weight this time and neither did Ludivine – both of us hitting the 48kg mark with ease the day before the fight. It was all much more relaxed than my trip to Birmingham had been. And, thanks to the fight taking place in London, I could even spend the night before relaxing at home instead of in a dingy hotel room.

The following afternoon I met Bill at the gym so that we could take the tube together to Earl's Court. He was really quiet on the train and that suited me just fine. All I wanted to do was zone out and take my mind forward twenty-four hours, to when it would all be over.

Over the next few hours I felt like I was in a battle with myself. This wasn't about Ludivine, this was about overcoming the nerves, the doubts and the fear inside my own head. One by one I tried to push the negative thoughts away, but as I walked out to the ring they still occupied more of my mind than they should have done.

The crowd was shouting for me but I kept my eyes straight ahead – now was not the time to lose focus. I knew my sister was out there with my niece Aleena (now a 3-year-old who my sister tried to protect from seeing me get hit by putting a hand over her eyes, only to watch Aleena turn her face up towards the big screen so she could still watch the fight), my cousin Sarina and my younger brother Eklim, but I didn't need to see them to feel their support. Just knowing they were there was enough.

My parents have never been to see me fight (although I think my brother once showed Dad a video of one of my fights on YouTube) and I understand that. I never really expect my brothers to be there either. As long as I know they are supportive from a distance, that's enough for me. My sister is the one person who I do always like to be there. Probably because she always has been, right from the start.

Once I got in the ring, I was desperate for that first bell to go. Moments after it did, my doubts dissolved. I was stronger than her. I was hurting her. And I knew I could win this fight.

After every round, Bill told me what I already knew. I was pipping her to each one. It was a close fight but we both believed I was doing enough to win each round. All I had to do was avoid taking any big hits like last time and the title would be mine.

I couldn't keep the smile off my face when the final bell rang. Even Bill was convinced. After taking off my gloves, his face broke into a half-grin as he said: 'Now go and collect your belt.'

Bill doesn't bullshit. So, the moment he said that I started picturing myself holding aloft the shiny white ISKA belt that was about to belong to me. By contrast, Ludivine's head was down. She knew.

We stood in the centre of the ring, either side of the referee who was holding my left arm and Ludivine's right. I was ready to have mine raised in victory.

But in the seconds before it happened, I heard or felt something. It was almost like a whisper coming from the back of my mind. And it was saying: 'It's not your time. Not your moment.'

I watched, almost expectant now, as Ludivine's hand was raised instead of mine. Her face dropped. She was in shock. In my home town she was the one who'd got the decision.

No one else could believe it either. Yeah, the fight was close but everyone thought I had done enough to win it. I walked back to my corner, feeling sick with disappointment. It seemed so unjust. After two years of stewing over what had happened in my first world title fight – two years of waiting for my second chance – the belt had been ripped out of my hands all over again. And all because someone on the judging panel looked away at the wrong moment or missed a few shots.

Bill could hardly speak. I could see the pain in his face – he was as devastated as I was. He was convinced I'd done it. Before leaving that night, he said just one thing to me: 'You can never leave it in the judges' hands, Rox.'

There was an afterparty booked for me at a local hotel. I asked my brother to call and tell them it was cancelled while

I grabbed my stuff. All I wanted to do was go straight home with my sister and Sarina.

I was heartbroken. But at the same time, I knew that I'd won that fight. And so did she. Everyone knew who the real champion was.

Chapter 13

When a ball hits the back of the net during a game of football, no one can deny that a goal has been scored. But scoring fights isn't like that. Unless there's a knockout, everything is down to the judges. So, there's more room for error. For subjectivity. For doubt.

And that doubt inevitably leads to questions. Did I lose that fight because of who I am? Because of the colour of my skin?

It was something I was always wary of saying, because it's so hard to back up. And you don't want to sound like you're making excuses or being a 'bad loser'. But in the days and weeks that followed the fight, I kept coming back to those questions. When I first spoke to Bill about it, he was dismissive, which only made me angrier: 'You don't understand, because you're white. That decision should have been mine and you know that I won that fight.'

Bill took a deep breath. 'Possibly. But we'll never know for certain, Rox. Yeah, I thought you won that fight, but I told you – you can never leave it to the judges.'

He was still annoyed enough to go to the ISKA and ask them to overturn the decision, though. That's when I understood how deeply he believed that belt should have been mine. Otherwise, he would have just told me to my face: it wasn't good enough. Retire. Go do something else with your life.

The ISKA were unmoved: there was no way they could overturn the decision. The only thing they could do was to offer us a rematch.

I was heartbroken. It felt like the dream was over. How much longer could I go on for? I was getting older. Still managing my ME. I didn't know how my health was going to be in a year or two. Or even whether I would get another opportunity to fight for a world title – I had already been blessed to get two.

I was even less sure about Bill wanting to go through it all again. He'd been dealing with some health problems of his own of late and I knew it would be asking a lot of him to go through another camp with me. Getting me ready for a world title fight puts a lot of strain on Bill. He's the one who has to build me up mentally and physically – putting me through my paces in a training camp and dealing with my mental state throughout the whole journey.

You get so many thoughts and feelings in the lead-up to a fight and I relied on Bill to help me manage those thoughts. To challenge them and make sure that I was in the best possible frame of mind. Whenever anything negative got into my head, it had to be rectified quickly. I've learned to do it on my own now, but back then I needed Bill's help and guidance.

For a few weeks after the fight I didn't know what my future held. Everyone was asking if I was going to carry on and I couldn't give them an answer. I knew I'd lost heart at the game – that the game had broken my heart – but I still couldn't bring myself to say that it was definitely over.

Because I wasn't ready for it to be.

The fighter in me couldn't admit defeat. I knew that I was good enough – that my name should be up there, among all the other world champions. All I had to do was convince Bill to stay with me for one more shot. But I had to let him calm down first. Give him time to get that last fight out of his system and allow his mojo and excitement for the sport to return.

He'd been there so many times before, dedicating months of his life to building a fighter up for a bout, only to see their hopes and dreams shattered into a million pieces by a decision that's gone against them. My defeat was just another kick in the teeth – but one that, in some ways, he found harder to take because of all the obstacles we had overcome to even get that far.

I bit my tongue for a few months, giving Bill the time and space I knew he needed. In the meantime, I tried to keep a training routine of some sort. Not long after the fight I met a sprint coach called Chris Zah at an event and he invited me down to train with him at the athletics track in Mile End. He'd coached the likes of Olympic athlete Perri Shakes-Drayton and told me how beneficial sprinting would be to my speed and power. It was something I'd always enjoyed doing at school, so one evening the following week I took him up on his invitation.

Luckily, the group I joined in with wasn't an Olympic-level one, but the standard was still pretty high. We started the session with a thorough warm-up and some drills designed to develop strength in various muscles of the legs and hone our sprinting technique before moving on to the main part of the session. After twenty minutes, I felt as though all the life had been sucked out of my legs. The intensity was so different from what I was used to in my usual half-hour run – we didn't run as far, but the running we did do was much, much harder.

The session finished inside the gym situated next to the track. 'You've done weights before, right?' Chris asked. I had used dumbbells and done a lot of bodyweight stuff before, but nothing like the barbell work that Chris was referring to. I watched as the others went through their drills, moving the weights with real intent and speed. It was obvious how the work they did inside that gym would translate into faster times on the track.

Before I left, Chris took me through some beginners' drills using something that looked like a broomstick. He told me to come back the following week so we could work on them and I was more than happy to do that. After training the same way for so long, it was nice to add some new things into my routine.

From then on, I introduced more weight training and sprinting into my week, replacing two of my evening runs with sessions down at Mile End. I could feel it having an impact on my work at KO – my kicks were faster and more explosive, and my recovery between rounds was improving.

Every time I saw Bill at the gym, I'd examine his face, looking for a flicker of enthusiasm, and listen to his words for clues that the passion was coming back – anything that told me he might be ready to go again. Gradually I saw the spark returning. He was back on the gym floor more often. Holding pads for fighters and staying with them after their session to break down the good and bad of what he'd just seen.

One Thursday afternoon, I sat down next to him on KO's saggy old sofa, took a deep breath and went for it: 'Bill, I can do this. I can go for a world title again.'

He looked at me, grimacing as if he was in pain: 'Oh my God, Rox, you're like a dog with a bone. When are you going to give up and call it a day? I haven't got it in me to go through all that again.'

But he knew that once I had that idea in my head, there was no going back. With or without his support, I was getting back in the ring – though I would have hated doing it without him. Thankfully, Bill hated the idea of that too. He wanted to retire, but if there was a chance to take me all the way to the top first and make me his final world champion, he was willing to give it a shot. I think that's what kept him going. It gave him a purpose. A goal. Deep down, he wanted it just as badly as me and I knew that. I was his legacy.

There were two governing bodies we could go to: the ISKA (who my previous fight was with and who we hoped would offer us a rematch with Ludivine) and the WKA (World Kickboxing Association). I was happy to go with whichever one came up trumps first, fully aware that, either way, it would probably take months for anything to happen.

When the phone call did come a few months later, it was from the WKA, offering an opportunity for me to fight the Swedish champion Susanna Salmijärvi in Hackney, east London. And there would be a world title on the line. It felt like a miracle.

The fight was set for 23 April 2016, giving us just under two months to get ready for it. But in reality, the training time was a lot less than that. Every day was a challenge – if Bill wasn't ill, then it was me who was struggling. On the days when we were both feeling good, the temptation was to make the most of it – to push hard in the gym, knowing that tomorrow might not be such a good day. But, if we did that, we knew it would only leave me in a deep hole for days afterwards. So, we held back, only doing what we knew my body could handle.

But, mentally, that was so hard. Especially because one of the other girls in the gym knew Susanna from a training camp she'd been on with her in Thailand. She told me Susanna was mega-fit. That she basically lived out in Thailand and spent every day smashing herself in training. That meant she'd be more than a match for me when it came to intensity, fitness and speed.

Those words haunted me throughout the camp. I knew that every session I missed was an extra one for Susanna. Another opportunity for her to improve while I was standing still.

On the Sunday before the fight, I turned up at the gym for what was supposed to be our final tough session before tapering things down for the following Saturday. I did some skipping and movement drills to get warmed up before Bill walked in and asked how I was feeling.

I told him I felt good. And I did. As the session got going, Bill pushed me harder and harder. More punches. More kicks. Faster footwork. I was leaving a trail of sweat all over the ring canvas. But it felt good to be working hard. Mentally, it was what I needed to give me the belief I would be able to keep pace with Susanna. Maybe it was what Bill needed too.

As Bill took off my gloves and hand wraps after the session, I downed a bottle of water, hoping it would help to stave off the hunger pangs I knew would hit me as soon as my body cooled down. Making the 48kg limit wasn't getting any easier as I got older – with a week to go, I had to watch every little thing I put into my mouth. After a hard training session, although my body was craving the energy I'd just burned off to refuel, I could only give it lean protein like chicken or fish, with some vegetables or a salad.

We agreed that I would have the next day off and come in on the Tuesday for some light recovery work. But as Monday went on, I started to feel a sense of extreme tiredness taking over my body. I got into bed around nine o'clock that night and set my alarm for eight the next morning. But when I opened my eyes it was still dark. Why was I awake? As I shifted in my bed, I could feel the sheets sticking to my skin. They were cold. And soaking wet.

I threw the covers off and got up to go to the bathroom. My head was pounding. Looking in the mirror I saw a girl with hair matted to her forehead and a face like death. I needed to get back into bed – to try to sleep off whatever virus it was that had taken hold of me. But I was freezing and my bed was soaked in my own cold sweat. I opened my wardrobe and took out an old winter coat, wrapping it around me before getting back into bed.

Over the next few hours, sleep came and went. I was exhausted, but every time I closed my eyes the pounding in my head got even louder. By sunrise I knew this was something I wasn't going to shake off within a day or two. My body was in meltdown. Every muscle ached. My arms and legs felt so heavy I didn't even dare try to move them. I just lay in bed, drifting in and out of sleep until my alarm went off. Slowly, I moved my arm out towards it, desperate to stop the noise from adding to the pain in my head.

I sent Bill a message, telling him what was going on and that I probably wouldn't be in the gym for the next few days. He told me not to come in all week. To stay in bed and rest as much as possible. We still had almost four days until the weigh-in on Friday night, so we just had to hope and pray that would be enough time for me to be able to fight off whatever bug had knocked me sideways.

I called the school where I worked on Wednesdays and Fridays and told them I wouldn't be able to make it in. I cancelled an interview with Sky Sports, too, which I was gutted about. I'd been approached by a PR agent after the fight with Ludivine and she'd been gradually getting me more publicity. I'd even signed up to W Model Management to see if I could get some work modelling sportswear. But Sky Sports was seriously mainstream and I'd been desperate to do it.

I was in bits. I basically spent the next two days in bed, with Mum bringing me up hot drinks, water and little bits of food.

I didn't think of anything beyond getting the weigh-in done. Once that was over, I would be able to eat properly and that could make a really big difference to how I felt. But by Friday, my body was still weak. It was using all of its resources to fight off the virus. Whatever was left over was barely enough to get me into the taxi I'd booked to take me to the weigh-in.

As we pulled up to the venue, Bill was waiting for me outside. He helped me out of the cab and kept a tight grip on my arm all the way up the stairs. The single flight of steps left me out of breath. I was scared I might not even have the energy to get up on the podium where the scales were.

'Let's just get through this,' Bill whispered in my ear as we walked into a room filled with people who had come to see the weigh-ins for the 'Blood and Glory' show that my fight was due to be a part of.

My first sight of Susanna was when we were both called up

to the scales. She was taller than me and had a bigger frame, so I knew she would have had to strip off more weight than I'd had to, to make 48kg. Maybe she would feel that in the ring ... at that point I was clinging on to any small bit of hope I could find.

As we stood opposite each other for the face-off, I looked into her eyes and saw what I believed was a hint of nervousness. But when I told Bill that later on, he shut me down completely. He didn't want to hear it. And I certainly didn't have the energy to argue with him as I usually would have done. I headed straight home to eat and get to bed, hopeful that food and a good night's rest would make all the difference.

But it wasn't the case this time. I woke up in the morning with my body still in the grip of exhaustion. Even talking felt like an extreme effort. I got up to say a quick prayer and went straight back to bed. The next time I woke up, I felt the familiar sensation of chilling dampness. My body was drenched in sweat again.

It was also two o'clock in the afternoon. I'd slept for about fifteen hours. That's when I panicked. How the hell could I fight for a world title when I could barely lift myself out of bed?

I called Bill. He could hear the note of panic in my voice and told me just to get a cab to the gym and we'd take one from there to the venue together: 'We'll make a decision once we're there. If you need to be pulled out, let the medics pull you out.' Bill was thinking of the financial side. I'd sold tickets, so if I pulled out, I would have to reimburse all the people who had paid to come and see me. But if the medics pulled me out, I wouldn't have to.

Before I began to get ready, I read a sura (verse) in the

Quran called Ya Sin, which is known as the 'Heart of the Quran'. If you recite it on a day before the sun sets, you will be protected during the whole day.

That was the start of me trying to get my mind ready. My body might not be in the right place but if I could get myself there mentally, maybe I could push my body through whatever was to come. But even as I packed my bag, in the back of my mind I knew that I might not even get the chance to try – that the medics were sure to take one look at me and say: no chance.

There was a weird feeling in the house. Mum and Dad knew about the fight but both of them were keeping their distance from me. I don't think Dad said a single word to me before I left. I felt like I'd disappointed him. In the moments before I left, I saw Mum sitting on the prayer mat. She was praying for me.

I took a cab to KO where Bill was waiting for me. He'd already been on the phone to the promoter, Paul (who happened to be one of his students at KO), to tell him I was unwell. He asked Paul if they could bring my fight to the beginning of the schedule so that I wouldn't have to hang around all night. But Paul wasn't having it: 'She's fighting for a title, there's no way she can be on first!' He did agree to move me up to the middle of the show, though, which was something at least.

Normally, the medical check you have done before a fight has to be carried out before the show even kicks off. But, so that I didn't have to get there quite so early, Paul saw to it that mine wouldn't be done until around six o'clock, when the fights had already started. We even had to go down to ringside for it – something that's almost unheard of.

Bill and I were certain they were going to pull me out.

I wasn't sweating any more but I felt exhausted – like I'd had about five hours' sleep as opposed to the fifteen-plus I'd actually had.

I stayed quiet as the doctor checked me over: eyes, ears, blood pressure, heart rate, temperature . . . He took a step away from me and let out a sigh. I waited for the inevitable.

'You're good to go.'

I stood there looking at the doc, my feet frozen to the floor. He thought I hadn't heard him over the crowd, so he said it again: 'You're good to go, Ruqsana.'

Bill's face had lost all its colour. He looked terrified.

If I'd been any of his other fighters, Bill would have pulled me out before we'd even reached this point. He'd told me he'd had sleepless nights that week, wrestling with himself over what to do.

He'd trained countless other fighters for world title bouts. In their training camps, he'd been able to push all of them ten times as hard as me. He'd have them doing two sessions a day, would push them until they were sick and then the next day they'd be back in doing it all over again. With me, he hadn't been able to do any of that and it scared him. I was going into the ring against a strong, fit opponent and I'd done barely anything in training compared to her.

He had a duty as a coach to look after the welfare of all his fighters. But he also knew that if he pulled me out, the opportunity might never come again. More than anything else, he wanted me to have my day. He told himself he'd just get me into the ring and if he saw me take even one shot that he knew a healthy Rox wouldn't get caught with, he'd stop it. No risks. That would be it. All over.

After the medical we went back to the changing room,

where Bill told me to rest. It was a massive space with huge windows that flooded the room with light. The building had been a church originally. I'd felt it from the moment we walked in. For me, there was something spiritual about it. It doesn't matter whether it's a mosque or a church, it's still God's house and being there gave me a sense that, whatever happened, I was being looked after.

There were a few other fighters in the changing room but I found a quiet corner and lay down, propping my head up on my bag. My mind was all over the place. I'd been so convinced that the fight wouldn't actually take place that I'd barely given any thought to what would happen if it did. Now, I couldn't stop thinking about what the next few hours might hold.

I was more nervous about how long my energy would last than about the actual fight. This wasn't about Susanna – or whoever my opponent might have been that day – it wasn't even about my desire to win, or my willpower or skill set. It all came down to the question of: will I last? I'd learned so much about controlling my mind but I had no control over my physical condition. And that was such a hard thing for me to accept – that I couldn't control my own body.

I decided that my only option was to do everything I could to try to knock her out in the first round. That was the thought that kept me going. The thought that made me go through with it – why pull out if there was even the smallest chance I might knock her out within the first two minutes of the fight?

If that didn't work, then it would be about surviving. For ten minutes of my life (five two-minute rounds), I just had to give it everything. And if things got too tough in there – if

I got hurt or was too unwell – I knew that Bill would throw in the towel.

Knowing that I was ill and that if I lost nobody could really blame me, took some of the pressure off me. But at the same time, I knew that this was my last chance. I had to go for it.

I told myself: I can't pull out. I've had too many bad decisions and bad outcomes. This time it's all or nothing.

When the time came, Bill made his way over to me and told me to start getting warmed up. He wrapped my hands, put on my gloves and held up the pads for me to start throwing some light shots. I raised my hands up to my face and threw a jab at the pad.

'One-two.'

When Bill started calling out combinations, I dropped my hands down to my waist and took a step back from him. Hitting pads was draining my energy. The little that I had was precious – I wanted to save every ounce of it for the fight.

We agreed that was the smartest option. No pad work. No shadow boxing. No warm-up.

Around ten minutes later, it was go-time. That's when the nerves took hold of Bill and he ran off to the loo while I made my way to the doorway leading into the main hall. As I stood there waiting, I closed my eyes and said a quick prayer. This was it. No going back.

I could hear the ring announcer hyping up the crowd. Showing them the belt. Telling them to give both fighters equal support. Then it was time.

'In the blue corner, from Gothenburg Muay Thai, Susanna Salmijärvi ...'

Bill rushed past me, tapping me on the shoulder as he headed out to take his place by my corner of the ring.

'And in the red corner, coming from KO gym, Ruqsana Beguuuuuum.'

I took a deep breath and walked out, pausing in front of a sponsors' board that was positioned in between two plumes of smoke shooting up from a fog machine. The room was illuminated by flashing strips of red light. It was as good an atmosphere as I'd ever felt walking out for a fight. As I made my way towards the ring, I tried to quicken my steps. Flung out my arms to loosen my shoulders.

There was a block of three steps leading up to the ring. I put my right foot on the bottom step and pushed through my leg. Two more, Rox. Left foot. Right foot. A dull ache flooded through the muscles in my lower body as I reached the top and climbed through the ropes and into the ring.

I could feel the atmosphere in the room lifting me, but I kept my focus inside the ring. Susanna was in her corner, her eyes fixed on me while her coach mouthed final instructions into her ear. I made the traditional bow in the centre of the ring and went to my corner where Bill unzipped my jacket and gave me a few sips of water. I reminded him what we'd agreed about the time: 'Make sure you tell me when there's thirty seconds left of the round and I'll give it everything.'

Even if it meant I collapsed after the round, I didn't care. That last thirty seconds of each round is when you can really leave an impression on the judges – when they're scoring you, those last thirty seconds are what they remember, much more than the first thirty.

Susanna and I touched gloves in the centre of the ring. I had two minutes to get the job done.

'Round one.'

From the second the bell went, I unloaded. The complete

rest I'd had over the past week had allowed me to save enough for this one last energy surge. You know when you need to make an emergency phone call on your mobile and you turn it off for a minute or two, to give you enough juice to make that one life-saving call? That's what I did. I went for it.

I threw flurries of five or six punches followed up with hard kicks. More punches. More kicks. I must have thrown around twenty shots before she got enough time and space to throw back one of her own. But as she went to kick, I caught her leg and threw her to the canvas. That gave me valuable seconds to try to catch my breath.

As the round went on, I slowed down, which gave her more time to put combinations together. But with fifty seconds left, I had her on the canvas for a second time.

'Last thirty!'

I didn't have enough energy left for the flurries of five or six shots I was throwing at the start of the round, but I did what I could. Single shots. Sometimes two or three. As the seconds ticked away my hands were dropping lower and lower. My feet were slowing down.

Where was the bloody bell? The second it rang, I dropped my arms to my sides and walked heavily to my corner. I was done. Bill stood in front of me: 'How do you feel?'

'I feel dead.'

His face didn't even flicker. 'This is a world title fight, Rox. That's how it's going to feel.'

If I felt like this after one round, how was I going to feel after two? Or three? I had to think more strategically. Pick my shots more carefully and pace myself. Realistically, I wasn't going to have enough energy to knock her out now. But I knew I'd won the first round, so it was about doing enough to win at least two more, while conserving as much energy as I could to make sure I survived to the end.

One round at a time. That became my mantra.

In the second round I landed three or four accurate, hard punches. One more, I told myself and she was surely going down.

But she wasn't going anywhere. Susanna was one tough fighter.

As the round came to an end, I could hear Bill shouting: 'Score again. Score again. Score again.'

When the bell went, I raised my arms to show the judges I was confident I was winning the rounds. A lot of it is about body language, especially in professional bouts. In the amateurs, they tend to view it as showing off, but in the pros it's about showing them you're in control of the fight.

As I walked back to my corner after the third round, I couldn't help thinking: if this was an amateur fight, I'd only have one more round to go. As it was, I knew this was the point in the fight that was the most dangerous for me. Susanna and I both knew that I was ahead, which meant she was going to have to come on strong and try to knock me out. I didn't have the energy left to go up another gear – if she did, I could be in trouble.

All the hard work I'd dug so deep to put in for the first three rounds would go to waste if I couldn't keep it going.

'Go again, Rox. Go again. Strong. Dig deep.'

I could hear Bill's words but my body wasn't able to respond to them. As soon as the fourth round started, Susanna was on me. At times, all I could do was try to push her away. But she was strong and she was aggressive. As the round went on, my shots became looser. Wilder. I was just doing whatever I could to disrupt her.

There were moments where I wished I had the energy to move and I just didn't. All I could do was take one or two of her shots while I recovered the energy to move, then I lifted my guard up and let shots go in small bursts. All the while, I could hear Bill: 'Strike again! One, two, three! Hands legs, hands legs.'

At one point she caught me with a knee to the head and I just let her do it. I didn't have the strength to struggle with her and change my position. I just took it and used the moment to try to catch my breath. I was so zoned out, I don't think I even felt the pain.

'Fifth and final round.'

Two more minutes. One hundred and twenty seconds. I just had to survive one more round.

Susanna changed her strategy – started coming at me with more kicks than she had previously, forcing me backwards.

'Dig deep, Rox. Catch her kicks.'

Thirty seconds into the round she knocked my head back with a hard jab. My body turned to jelly. I felt my legs wobble. I was completely gone. For a few seconds, I just stood there watching her loading up as she came towards me.

Move! I told myself. Make it difficult for her. Make her miss. That's all I need to do.

'Thirty seconds, Rox! Thirty seconds.'

I tried to pick it up. To finish strong, because I knew that could make all the difference. But she kept on walking me down. Kept on coming.

As soon as the bell rang, I raised my arms high, walked to my corner and fell to my knees. I put my head into my gloved hands and prayed. I thanked God for his protection. For giving me the strength to survive.

Bill helped me to my feet and raised my arm in the air. 'I don't know how you did that, Rox. Now go get your belt.' I didn't have the words to respond. And I didn't want to tempt fate. I'd been there before.

But moments later, it happened.

'Your winner . . .

'In the red corner . . . Ruqsana!'

I fell to my knees for a second time. I couldn't believe it. The moment had finally come. I was a world champion.

I wanted to cry but it was like my body didn't even have the resources for that. All I could do was smile as the belt was placed around my waist. I looked out into the crowd and saw my sister jumping up and down with my cousin and brother Eklim. A rush of sheer joy went through me. I was in ecstasy.

As Ane drove us home I was still trying to take it all in. It was remarkable. I'd had everything against me this time and yet this was the time I'd won it. I was overjoyed. It was one of the most memorable moments of my life.

We went straight to my favourite restaurant in Seven Kings. I'd been dreaming about a chicken biryani for weeks and now I could finally enjoy one. I ordered so much food – all the things I'd been wanting to eat while I was making weight – but I couldn't finish half of it. When you go through that process of dieting, your stomach gets used to eating less; it takes a while to get back to normal.

I wanted a cookie dough ice cream from the Creams dessert lounge around the corner too, but by the time we got there it was past midnight and they'd already closed. I just wanted everything that night.

I knew we should go and see my parents, simply so that

they knew I was okay. We walked into a house in darkness. They'd already gone to bed. I went upstairs, still carrying the belt and knocked on my parents' door. As I pushed it open, my dad switched on the light next to his bed. He took one look at me with the belt and jumped out of bed, grabbing it out of my hands.

He ran downstairs with it and started calling all his friends. I think he was happier with me in that moment than when I got my degree. It was a complete contradiction. All morning he'd been moody with me, thinking: off she goes for another fight. I don't think he'd even known it was for a world title. It was just: there she goes again. But now, he was so excited.

My parents have their own ways of showing they're proud. There were no hugs or any physical expressions of emotion that night, but seeing my dad's reaction was enough to show me that he was proud of what I'd achieved. And that was all I needed.

The whole thing felt miraculous. For days afterwards, I struggled to get my head around it: the fact that I'd won a world title against someone who was fully fit, fully trained, while I was struck down with ME. It was a miracle – a blessing from God.

All those times when I'd been disappointed and heartbroken – suddenly, that all went away.

There were so many people who I owed so much to for making it that far – Bill, my sparring partners, nutritionist, my sister. I wanted to say thank you to them, to show them how much I appreciated their support and everything they'd done for me. So, I organised a party in a restaurant near the gym and booked out the whole place, so that everyone could come. We made up posters telling everyone when and where the party was and stuck them up all over the gym. Bill had never let me celebrate my wins before – but after working for it for so long, this one was different.

Now I was a world champion, lots of things were different.

In the weeks and months that followed, there were appearances (finally on Sky Sports), interviews and photo shoots. It was amazing, getting the opportunity to have my hair and make-up done by a professional and dressing up in some of the most expensive clothes I'd ever laid my hands on.

And there were awards. Early the following year I won the Inspirational Performance of the Year award at the British Ethnic Diversity Sports Awards. There were even advertising campaigns. When my agent got in touch to say that adidas wanted to speak to me about being part of their new global campaign, I could hardly believe it. Adidas! Apparently, they'd read about me on CNN's website and loved that I'd designed a sports hijab to help Muslim women take part in sport. It fitted right in with their Creativity advert, which would go around the world. I was also asked to take part in a campaign for Selfridges, called Incredible Machines. It was all so surreal.

But the best moments – the ones that will live with me for ever – are the ones that take place away from the brightest spotlight.

As more people heard or read about my story, I was being asked to give talks as a motivational or inspirational speaker. It sometimes took me by surprise that people thought of me like that, but I just tried to see it as my opportunity to help others.

One talk that will always stick in my mind was at the offices of a financial company, who wanted me to come and speak about my experiences in the sport and the barriers

I'd overcome to become a world champion. The talk itself went well and, as usual, there were lots of questions from the audience afterwards.

When it was over and people started to file out of the room, a young Pakistani girl came up to speak to me. She had been quiet throughout the whole thing – hadn't put up her hand to ask any questions – but she obviously had something she wanted to say to me. And I'll never forget her words. She told me that I'd given her the strength to cope with what she was going through at that moment, because she could relate to me and I'd given her courage. She was going through some family problems and an arranged marriage as well and said that she no longer felt that she was alone.

She thanked me and my own eyes filled with tears. I felt her pain. The fact that she shared so much with me made me realise that was what it was all about. I could be a voice for people like her. Give them hope. If sharing my story could help, then I would continue to do it for as long as people wanted me to.

The guys from my community would all say they were proud of me, that I was one of them and it was amazing to see me do so well. But with the women, it was different. They knew I'd had some of the same experiences as them. Some of the same struggles. And seeing someone come through those things not only to be a success in their chosen field, but to have the strength to be who they really are, was inspiring to them.

I've lost count of the occasions when people have come up to me after I've told my story to say they identified with the bullying that I faced or the challenges from growing up pulled between two cultures. Every time I'd hear things like:

'Ruqsana, you've given me the courage to face . . .' Or: 'Now I can take a deep breath and handle the situation.'

It still amazes me that I can have that impact. It's something I will never tire of and it's the reason I'm determined to continue on my journey.

Chapter 14

It was around six months before I could take a step back from everything and try to figure out what was next for me.

Since winning the title, I'd been going to the gym as often as I could and just ticking over really – keeping myself fit. My plan had always been to win a world title and then retire. I'd dedicated ten years of my life to the sport; I thought that would be enough.

But the way that I'd won it left me wondering: if I can win a world title with ME, what can I do when I'm fit and well?

Two thousand and sixteen – the year I'd become a world champion – was coming to an end when Bill and I sat down to talk about the future. 'What motivates you?' he asked. 'Is it another world title? Because we could always go for another one . . .'

I knew what he was thinking. When women's boxing was introduced into the Olympic programme for 2012, we'd spoken about the possibility of me giving up Muay Thai for it. Bill was convinced that it was a sport I would do well in. And the fact that it was going to be an Olympic sport meant there would be more opportunity to actually build a career out of it.

At the time, though, my heart was in Muay Thai. I was too deeply into it, too close to achieving something in it, to simply walk away. I couldn't give it up.

Now, he brought it up again: 'Boxing is the one, Rox.'

I thought about his question: what did motivate me? At that point it wasn't getting another world title in Muay Thai. I felt like that would be staying in my comfort zone some-how. So, I needed a new challenge. And I wanted it to be something that was going to continue to make a difference to others.

Every time I gave an interview or did a talk, the reaction to my story blew me away. It seemed to have such a positive impact on people. And particularly on Muslim women, who had always seen sport (not just boxing, but *any* sport) as being something that wasn't for them. Something that existed behind seemingly insurmountable barriers: reli-gion, values, family traditions. The idea that it was possible for them to take part in sport while still respecting all of these things opened up a whole new world of opportunity for them.

Since winning the world title, the gym had started to feel like it was changing a little. The group of bullies had lost a key member over the last few months – she was pregnant and decided the time was right to retire – and her absence proved to be the beginning of the end for their clique. Over the next year or so, they appeared less and less regularly, until the point when there was just one of them remaining. And, on her own, she was powerless.

At the same time, the number of women coming to my women-only class at KO every Sunday had shot up. Some girls came in saying they'd read about me in the paper and wanted to give Muay Thai a go. Others came in saying they weren't really interested in the sport at all, but had heard my story and wanted to meet me. Either way, they usually ended up coming back for more the following weekend.

Lots of these women were from a Muslim background. They saw my class as a safe space, but one that also allowed them to step out of their home life and do something positive for themselves – whether that was to get fit, de-stress or simply build their confidence.

Soon, my class was busier than the normal one on a Sunday. There were girls from all backgrounds, races and faiths. All shapes and sizes. All ages. It made me realise that I could reach out to people from all walks of life and show them that no obstacle is too high for them to climb. Show them that you can be female, Muslim, traditional – all of these things – and still take part in sport. Even one as male-dominated as Muay Thai.

I loved the fact that I could do something that made a change for them; something that brought joy to their faces and made them feel good about themselves. So, when Bill asked me that question about what motivated me, I knew it was this: making a difference. But being able to do it on a bigger scale than KO gym on a Sunday morning, so that I could reach even more people.

Boxing was the obvious way to do it. The rising profile of women's boxing meant it could give me the kind of platform that Muay Thai couldn't. It would allow me to make a bigger difference. And I knew the time was right to move into boxing. To kick off 2017, I'd start a new challenge.

But it wasn't easy. My heart was still with Muay Thai, too. I'd spent so many years working at it. Using it to help strengthen my mind as well as my body. It felt like a part of me. I wasn't sure how I would be able to give that up.

I didn't know if boxing would make me happy. And I needed to be happy and passionate, just like I was in Thai boxing, because however brutal a training session might be, I have to be able to go back in the next day feeling that it's something I want to do. And I didn't quite have that feeling with boxing at first.

For a while, I thought I could do both – that I could keep Muay Thai as a hobby while pursuing boxing as a career. KO had a boxing gym right next to the Muay Thai area so, logistically, it wouldn't be too difficult. I tried it for a while, but whenever I was working on my boxing, I was always looking over my shoulder to see what the Thai boxers were doing.

I was more inspired by watching them than by what was going on in the boxing gym. I'd always felt that Thai boxing was the harder sport of the two. And the more exciting – it gives you so many more weapons to play with. Gets your adrenaline pumping in a way boxing just didn't for me.

Bill could see what I was trying to do and he knew it was taking me nowhere. 'You can't have one foot in this door and one foot in the other door,' he kept telling me. And deep down I knew he was right. If you want to be the best at something you have to put everything you've got into it.

I decided to give it a year. For twelve months, I'd commit to boxing and give it my all. I wasn't in love with it, but I had to give it a chance to win me over. Maybe it was the change that I didn't like. Maybe it was the fear or the fact I wasn't at the top of the tree any more. There were so many elements.

But something told me that I could do it. In my core, I believed that I had what it took. I'd already reached the top in one sport, so if I applied the same principles to the new sport, I saw no reason why I wouldn't be able to achieve the same.

I hadn't mentioned anything to my parents about it yet. I wanted to wait until I was absolutely sure it was the right decision. It had been such a stretch for them to accept me doing Thai boxing in the first place; now here I was at the age of thirty-three about to tell them that my journey in that world hadn't ended.

But before I could reach the point where I felt ready to tell them, in the summer of 2017 our family was forced to come to terms with the devastating loss of my grandmother. I'd grown up sharing my home with her. She'd been a constant presence in my life. And now she was gone. She'd been our connection to my grandfather, too, so losing her felt almost like losing him all over again.

Mum had devoted her life to looking after my grand-mother, especially in the last few years when she'd been bedbound. If Mum went shopping she'd make sure she was never out for longer than an hour and one of us always had to be in the house with my grandmother, in case she needed to go to the loo or felt hungry. So, when she passed away, it gave my parents the opportunity to do something they had been wanting to do for a long time – something that would allow them to pray for my grandmother while reinforcing their faith.

Umrah is an Islamic pilgrimage to Mecca and something that holds huge reward and value in our religion. It's not compulsory for every Muslim to do it, but it is highly rec-ommended for those who can afford to and it was something my parents had always talked about doing.

When I first heard that they were going, I didn't really

think too much about it. I knew it was something I might want to do one day, but I hadn't given much thought to doing it just yet. The more I thought about Mum and Dad going, the more I started to feel I should go with them. The pilgrimage is pretty tough physically and I wasn't sure if Mum would be able to manage it, or even if Dad realised how hard it was going to be for her.

I felt I needed to be there to look after her. But I was also scared about the potential consequences of going – what my parents might expect of me when we came back. They might want me to start wearing the hijab again, or expect me to give up the boxing (or Muay Thai, as they believed I was still doing). I needed to make sure I was doing it for the right reasons.

I realised, though, that the pilgrimage is about your connection with God. I may not be the finished article as a Muslim – not where I want to be – but this was part of me taking the steps to get there. Part of learning and being enlightened.

Deciding I wanted to go was one thing, but actually being able to get there was something else entirely. Pilgrimages are normally fully booked well in advance and I'd left it to the very last minute to apply, with the trip due to start in just two weeks. So, when I applied for my visa, I was half expecting it to be declined.

But a few days after applying I was in the gym when my phone rang. It was Ane (who was now separated from her husband and living back at home with my parents). As soon as I picked up, she started talking: 'I'm just going to tell you this: your visa's been accepted and Mum and Dad are thrilled . . . so you're definitely going.'

I didn't know whether to laugh or cry.

Mostly, I was petrified. I wasn't sure if I was ready for it. I knew I was still doing things that weren't fully Islamic and this was such a big, religious step. If I went, I wanted to come back a changed person. I wanted to live up to the experiences I'd have gone through in Mecca. The ones that were going to help me to be a good person.

A couple of weeks later I was in Medina, Saudi Arabia, sharing a single hotel room with my mum and dad. A few months earlier, I'd moved into my own place about ten minutes away from my parents' house – it was only a small one-bedroom flat but it gave me my own space, which I found really helped me to relax and recover after training. Now, I was confined to one room with both of my parents. There was nowhere to breathe. No space. Mentally and emotionally, I found it really tough. As it was Ramadan, we were all fasting too, which made it even more challenging.

We'd wake up, go to the mosque together, come home and rest and then go back to the mosque again. Going to mosque made me realise I was one of the lucky ones, though. I sat next to one girl there who told me she was sharing a room with her in-laws. I really felt for her. You can't have a go at your in-laws. At least I could shout at my dad and say, 'Get off the loo!' if I needed to have a wash or something. Both of us had rooms though, and for that we counted our-selves fortunate. We met a lot of people in the mosque who couldn't afford one and were sleeping right there.

The initial plan was to spend a week in Medina before travelling to Mecca for the Umrah. But after a few days in Medina, Dad decided we should drive to Mecca for the day. We were into the last ten days of Ramadan and, if you can do Umrah twice in those last ten days, you are well rewarded.

So, we hired a car and drove seven hours overnight, arriving in Mecca in time to carry out our first Umrah. It starts with a ritual called *Tawaf*, which involves circling the *Ka'bah* (a building that's considered to be the house of God) seven times. I felt so blessed to be there. And even more blessed to be able to touch the Black Stone – a rock that's set into the eastern corner of the *Ka'bah*.

If you touch it, it's said that all your sins are forgiven. But touching it has become an almost impossible thing to do in modern times because of the huge crowds of people all trying to get their hands on the stone. All three of us – Mum, Dad and I – tried to work our way into the mass of people surrounding it, but I was the only one who managed to penetrate it. Mum and Dad simply weren't strong enough.

I found myself crushed in among a heaving mass of bodies, everyone pushing and fighting to get to the stone.

It was suffocating. I couldn't breathe.

Suddenly, I felt a shove from behind. A guy who was about three times my size pushed right past me and was working his way forwards. I quickly got in behind him and tried to follow him, step for step. As we got closer to the part of the *Ka'bah* where the stone is encased in a silver frame and attached to the wall, I looked for an opening, using my boxing brain to spot the right moment to make a move.

When the opportunity came, I grabbed it, throwing myself into the gap. Placing my hands firmly on the Black Stone, I quickly recited the words: '*Bismillahi Allahu akbar wa lillahil-hamd*' (In the name of God, God is great, all praise to God), before planting a precious kiss.

Making my way out of the throng was equally as difficult as getting in – like trying to fight your way through a crowd of football fans. I craned my neck, looking everywhere for my parents, having lost all sense of direction long ago. Finally, I spotted the top of Dad's head and screamed at him to help me get out. He pushed his way closer and reached an arm out towards me. I grabbed onto it and, together, we had the strength to pull me free from the crush.

'Where's your scarf?' Dad asked, pointing at my head.

I reached up to feel for it, only succeeding in grabbing a handful of hair. It must have been ripped off in the crowd. No chance I was getting it back now.

The Umrah continued with a ritual called *Sa'i*, which involves running in between the hills of Safa and Marwa seven times. It's a re-enactment of the story of Prophet Ibrahim's wife Hajar, who was in the desert alone with her baby son and needed water. She ran back and forth between the hills seven times in search of help. For me it was okay, but for my parents it was quite challenging.

We did it all while fasting and then drove the seven hours back to Medina. It was one of the most exhausting days I've ever experienced.

A few days later, we were back on the road to Mecca to do it all again. This time, though, we were staying in a hotel close to God's house. Thankfully, our room was bigger than the one in Medina. I was sleeping in the living room – my own little bit of space, at last. I hadn't realised quite how important that was to me; how much I needed it mentally and physically.

I had taken a few resistance bands away with me, so every night I spent twenty minutes or so doing a little series of exercises. That bit of movement was all I needed. It was a way for me to reset at the end of each day. To tune out all my anxieties and find a sense of calm.

I loved Mecca. There was a beauty and peace about it. And a warming feeling that people from diverse backgrounds, of all ages, those with nothing who were living on the streets, were all able to come together and be united inside the mosque. And it was inside God's house that I felt able to speak to Him in a way I never had before.

There was one day of the trip when Mum was feeling unwell, so I went to the mosque on my own. As I sat in God's house, there was something I knew I had to do. For so long, my life had been filled with doubt and fear. I had pursued success in Thai boxing without really knowing if it was some-thing I was allowed to do. I loved it but I had to be honest with myself – there was a chance I should not be doing it.

Before I started another new journey inside the ring, I had to know. I said to God: 'If the boxing is good for me, then bless me in it. And if it's not good for me, then take it away from me, take my heart away from it and give me the courage to walk away. I'm here for you to guide me to the right things.' I had faith that from that moment on, whatever happened, it was God's will.

When I look back over those two and a half weeks, I'm so thankful for the time I got to spend with my parents. It was beautiful to be able to connect with them. At home there's always so much going on that I rarely spend a whole day with them, but while we were away I was with them almost every minute of every day. I was having breakfast with my mum in the mornings (after Ramadan was over) and going to prayers with her – things that we just never do together at home.

I got to know both of them in a different way. Bonded with them in a way that I never had before. It taught me so much patience and care for my family. After all my fears and anxieties about going on the trip, I felt incredibly fortunate to have been able to do it with my parents.

It was overwhelming. Life-changing. Special.

I came home feeling that I could handle whatever life threw at me so much better than before. I felt cleansed and happy. Like the dark cloud that I had always felt hanging over me was now gone.

Doing Umrah gave me perspective. Humbled me. Brought me peace.

Everything that I was holding on to – the fears, the doubts – all of it had gone away. Now, I don't feel fearful of anything apart from God. It has helped me become so much better at managing my anxiety, because, whatever happens in life, I know that God has a plan.

If I look at the difficult moments in my past, I see that things have always worked out. There are hard experiences and hard times you go through, but it has always been temporary and I've always learned something from it.

I've realised that when I learn the lesson, God takes me out of that situation. So now I know that if I'm in a challenging moment, it's because I need to grow. Because I need to learn something. And as soon as I do that, God can move me on to the next challenge. Seeing things that way gives me so much more peace. I don't get drained by problems any more, because I don't see them in a negative way. I see them as experiences that are elevating me as a person.

So, there's no longer any need for me to be afraid. God has led me to this path for a reason, so I should just embrace it and be confident that whatever obstacle I come across I can overcome it. All is possible if you have faith and never give up.

Doing Umrah was the most memorable and greatest experience of my life, because after spending so long trying to be everything to everyone – while also trying to do what made me happy – it allowed me to find peace. It taught me that even when things seem bleak, there is always hope. That's what gets me through most of my day-to-day challenges. What keeps me optimistic. Even when I feel like giving up I remind myself that God has a plan. And that I don't have to fear it, because I'm on the same page.

A few months after I came back from Mecca, in November 2017, I got a phone call that confirmed that belief.

After winning the world title, I'd been signed up by an agency who were helping me with media requests. But they also had connections in the world of professional boxing, which I knew would be really important if I was going to make a proper go of the sport. It's such a difficult arena to navigate without someone who really knows it to guide you.

The phone call was from my agent, Adam, who told me that the former world champion boxer David Haye was interested in signing me to his new promotional company, Hayemaker Promotions. It seemed like a miracle. This was a major promoter, and they wanted me – someone with no amateur experience and who was the wrong side of thirty. I could hardly believe it.

The next piece of news blew me away even more. David and his team were out in Las Vegas on a training camp with one of his heavyweight fighters, Joe Joyce, and I was invited over there to meet everyone. There were just ten days before

I was due to fly to Vegas. So ten days for me to tell my parents that I was moving on to a new career. And to hopefully have their blessing.

I was petrified. They'd been so reasonable and under-standing about me doing Thai boxing for so long. And I was sure that when I became a world champion they felt hugely relieved, thinking: finally, she's done. Now she can retire and we can find her another husband.

They were going to be devastated when they heard that I was starting the journey all over again in a different sport. How was I even going to bring it up?

I put it off and put it off until there were just two days left before I was due to leave. I couldn't leave it any longer.

We were driving back from a visit to my grandmother's grave when I went for it. I was in the back, with Dad driving and my youngest brother Eklim next to him in the front. I was chatting to Eklim and tried to casually drop it in: 'I'm thinking about going into boxing. I'm not in love with it so far, but it's something that I want to try . . . I just think it will give me a bigger platform to inspire more people.'

Dad stayed silent.

After a few seconds, Eklim started speaking. He said: 'You know what? You should continue boxing, because we need a female, Asian role model for the community. They really look up to you.'

Finally, Dad spoke: 'Yeah, we have this house, but we want another house. The dream keeps getting bigger and bigger. Nothing is ever enough.'

I told him I understood what he was saying, because I'd said to myself that when I became a world champion, I would retire. But now, I was hungry to see what I could do in the boxing arena. Whether I pursued it at a high level or not, I wanted to give it a go.

Before Dad could respond, Eklim jumped in: 'Can you imagine when you're sitting there on Sky Sports talking about inspiring people from all backgrounds – especially those from our community? Do you know what that would do for those girls? It would give them so much hope – so many aspirations for what they can do.'

Dad said nothing. But from the back seat I saw him nod gently when Eklim spoke. To me, that was enough.

It lifted me immediately. Whereas before I had been asking myself whether I really wanted to spend the next two or three years in the ring getting hit, now I was picturing myself talking on Sky Sports, telling everyone that I was going to become a world champion again, in boxing. All of a sudden, I believed it was possible.

And when Eklim said: 'There's no one else like you. No one else who has won a world title and can make that kind of impact in our community', I thought: *I have to do this. I have to go for this.*

It's not about me loving the sport. I've got a bigger purpose. I've got the ability and the mindset of a fighter. I've got what it takes. And hopefully, with David Haye's backing, I've also got the support system to go for it. I'll be selling myself short if I don't give it a go.

I felt a responsibility to try to make a difference. Because I believed I could do so much more for my community by challenging myself – by coming out of my fear and all those emotions I was feeling and trying to suppress. Whether I become a world champion or not, it doesn't really matter. Just stepping into that boxing arena is going to have a huge impact.

When Eklim said those things about me being a role model to these girls, that's what truly motivated me.

Some forty-eight hours later I was on my way to the airport.

Las Vegas. Wow. I was so nervous, and excited. I had no idea what to expect. I spent the entire flight over trying to get some sleep but failing miserably. There were so many questions firing around my mind. Why me? Was I good enough? What if my ME stopped me from training?

Adam told me he'd arranged for a car to meet me at the airport, so as I walked through into the arrivals hall I tried to look for someone holding a board with my name on it. But the place was packed. There were so many people trying to get you to take their taxis or go to their casinos. I was starting to feel a bit panicked, when I finally spotted a man dressed in a black suit and wearing a chauffeur's hat who was holding a board with RUQSANA BEGUM spelled out in big black capital letters.

He took my bags and led me outside, where a shiny black Mercedes-Benz with tinted windows was waiting for us. 'I'm Walter,' he said as he strapped himself into the driver's seat. 'Sit back, relax and make sure you help yourself to a cold one . . . inside the arm rest.'

I lifted up the arm rest in between the back seats to find a selection of soft drinks and snacks. I was starving but my stomach felt like it was tied into a million knots; it had felt that way from the moment I'd woken up that morning. I picked out a bottle of water and sipped it slowly as we made our way towards the Platinum Hotel, where Adam promised he'd be waiting for me in the lobby.

It was positioned just off the Las Vegas Strip; a place I'd heard so much about. But nothing quite prepared me for what it was really like – the lights, the shows, girls wearing hardly any clothes – it was fascinating. Everything looked larger-than-life.

The Platinum wasn't one of the flashiest hotels but it was nice enough. And it was convenient. Adam had arranged for me to have a room with a kitchen so I could make my own meals. And, most importantly, it was just a ten-minute drive from City Athletic Boxing, where I'd be training for the next couple of weeks.

By the time I'd settled into my room and showered away the plane feeling, it was late afternoon. Adam had left me to get on with it and gone to meet up with his business partner, Sam. I knew if I stayed inside I'd end up nodding off and that would not be a good idea if I wanted to get any sleep later that night. So, I headed out to try to find a supermarket where I could stock up on some healthy snacks to keep in the room.

The moment I stepped outside, the heat hit me. I glanced up at the sky. It was an endless expanse of bright blue, without a single cloud to take the edge off the burning-hot sun. I felt the knots in my stomach tighten as I realised that, this time tomorrow, I'd be training in these temperatures.

That wasn't the only thing making me nervous. I was also going to meet Ismael Salas for the first time – the legendary Cuban trainer who worked with all of David Haye's fighters and who would now be training me, too, if all went to plan.

It was scary for me, because I'd spent my whole life training with Bill. I grew up in his gym. Became a woman through the sport and his teachings. He knows me inside out; he knows my strengths and weaknesses. Knows all my flaws and has seen all my tantrums. He's like my best friend. He is my coach but he's also someone who I can turn to for advice. I rely on him.

The thought of working with somebody who I'd never even met before was daunting enough. But to know that he was also someone who worked at the very highest level of the sport – with countless Olympic and world champions – made it even more so. I was a novice in this sport. My Muay Thai world title would mean nothing once I was inside the boxing ring.

I wouldn't have anyone's respect in that gym tomorrow. If I wanted it, I'd have to earn it.

After ten minutes of walking, my t-shirt was heavy with sweat. But I had found a 'mini-market' (which was actually huge) and filled a basket with some fruit, crackers and herbal tea to take back to my room.

I met up with Adam again for dinner in the hotel that evening so we could make our plans for the following day. We arranged to meet in the hotel lobby at 10 a.m., so we could go together to City Athletic Boxing where I'd meet Salas and the rest of the team – including David Haye and heavyweight prospect Joe Joyce, who'd won silver at the 2016 Olympics and was now starting his career as a professional boxer.

As we ate, I could feel my eyelids getting heavier and heavier. By the time I got back to my room, I just about managed to get washed and brush my teeth before falling into bed and surrendering to the tiredness that I'd been fighting off ever since the plane had touched down hours earlier. But by 5 a.m. I was wide awake. I lay in bed thinking; all my fears about the day ahead becoming bigger with every passing minute. I had to get up. Get out of the room.

I threw on some shorts and a t-shirt and went out for

a jog – not too far, as I didn't want to get lost and end up exhausted before I'd even got to the gym. But far enough to get the blood flowing through my body and flush out some of the nerves that were threatening to take over my body and mind. At 6 a.m., Vegas is actually pretty quiet. Almost peaceful. It feels like a completely different place to the one it becomes as day turns into night.

I refuelled on fruit and a few crackers and packed my kit for the gym. This was it. The next few hours would show me whether I was doing the right thing, or whether the boxing business wasn't meant for me.

When I got down to the lobby for 10 a.m., Adam was already there waiting for me and had an Uber outside, ready to take us to the gym. Within a matter of minutes we pulled into a car park outside a low-rise white building that stretched across the entire width of the car park. It was about five times the size of KO. But when we walked inside, it felt much the same. It had that same smell – the smell of hard work. And the universal sounds that fill every boxing gym all over the world: the pop of gloves on pads, the metronomic tap, tap, tap of skipping ropes lightly touching the floor beneath a boxer's floating feet and the inevitable beep of a timer marking the end of one round or the start of the next.

It was almost comforting. Almost like being at home.

Almost. There were differences.

The first one that hit me was the heat. Despite the stifling temperature outside, there were big heaters positioned above the boxing rings, pumping warm air out over fighters wearing sweat suits beneath them. They must have been cutting weight for a bout, but it was making the whole gym about 10 degrees hotter than it was outside.

After the heat, came the music. And the atmosphere it created.

It was like being in Cuba. Salas's team of coaches were all Cuban or Latino and the gym was filled with the happy beat of Cuban music. There was so much life in there. I could see everyone was there to do serious work, but there was no shouting, just people having a laugh and joking around while also getting down to business.

The gym was split into two areas: the main part was open to anyone who wanted to go and train, whether that was just to get in shape or to actually learn to box. There was a real mixture of people in there – all ages, shapes and sizes, and even a few women. Then there was a smaller side area, which was reserved for 'fighters only'. That was where Salas and his coaches worked with the pros.

There were no other women in that part, just a small group of exceptionally talented male fighters. And standing on the far side: David Haye and Joe Joyce, who were deep in conversation with the diminutive, baseball cap-wearing figure of Ismael Salas.

I followed Adam over to them and he introduced me to the guys. David flashed me a big smile and shook me warmly by the hand, as did Joe, before Salas grabbed me by the shoulders and said: 'Champion! Welcome!' He was so welcoming and had such a great energy about him. I automatically felt at ease in his presence.

With the introductions done, Salas invited me into the ring to hit pads with him. I took a series of deep breaths as I wrapped my hands, trying to stay relaxed and not think about the talent that was all around me.

David watched on as Salas got me moving around the ring,

calling out some basic combinations to see what my punches and footwork were like. I must have been such a beginner compared to the fighters he was used to working with, but he never made me feel that way at all. Every word he uttered was positive. He was like the opposite of the voice in my head that was trying to tell me I wasn't good enough to be there.

After three rounds, I was soaked in sweat and my head felt like it was full of cotton wool.

I told Salas: 'I feel really light-headed,' and he just smiled at me: 'Okay, we're stopping!'

'No, no, I can do one more . . .'

'No, you are still jet-lagged. You should rest and come back tomorrow.'

That afternoon was my first glimpse of what the professional boxing world could be like. And I loved it. I loved the vibe. The energy. And I could see that Salas was more than a great coach – he was a great person. After we finished our session I sat and watched him with the other fighters. Saw the way that he worked with them and communicated with them. There was a real presence about him that I felt drawn to. A light.

A light that I felt had the power to put every little doubt and fear about my new path into the darkness.

Chapter 15

Why was I getting hit so much? I couldn't understand it. I'd never taken that many punches in Thai boxing – not to the head, anyhow. But now, I was getting caught all the time. I felt like a novice again, but this time I didn't have years ahead of me to learn – I had months.

A few weeks after we got back from Las Vegas, David lined up my first pro fight. It was set for March at York Hall in Bethnal Green – just a short walk from the tiny flat where I grew up. Where I'd first fallen in love with martial arts, watching Bruce Lee over my uncle's shoulder.

It was also going to be shown on terrestrial television, on Channel 5. That was the kind of platform Muay Thai had never been able to give me. I'd be fighting live in people's living rooms. Showing everyone that a fighter is a fighter, no matter what gender, ethnicity, religion, shape or size they are.

I had two months to get ready, which was no time at all considering how early into my transition to boxing it was. I hadn't even started sparring yet, because I'd wanted to make sure that my heart was 100 per cent in the sport first. I needed to be happy and passionate, just like I had been in Thai boxing, because, whatever obstacles I came up against (and I knew there would be many in boxing), I had to be able to go back into the gym the next day and feel: I want to do this. As I've said, initially, I didn't quite have that feeling with boxing.

But those two weeks in Vegas had changed everything. I felt stimulated. The change of environment lifted me so much and working with Salas – a guy who's so spiritual and has such a positive energy – put me on a real high. I hadn't realised just how much I'd needed a completely fresh start.

As soon as we were back in London, though, everything was flipped into fast-forward mode. Salas and David tried hard to line up sparring partners for me, but it was really difficult to find any who were suitable, in terms of weight and experience. The three they did manage to locate were all a lot bigger than me (around 60kg) and already in the GB boxing squad, so the challenge for me was massive.

It was too big, really. There's a sweet spot with sparring where you are being tested enough to help you learn and improve, but not so much that you're going to get hurt. In my case, the challenge in front of me simply didn't match my skill level at the time. As soon as the sparring started, I realised just how much work I had to do. And how, in so many intricate ways, boxing was more different to the sport I'd dedicated so many years of my life to than I'd expected.

Footwork, balance, range, rhythm – all of it required a shift in the habits that had been programmed into my body and brain over the course of thousands and thousands of hours of training. These were habits that I no longer had to think about in Muay Thai – my body just did what it knew it had to do. Block the kick? Done. Counter with a punch? Easy. Catch them coming in with an elbow? Got it.

But boxing was a different kind of rhythm entirely. I had to learn the nuances of how to attack and when. I had to learn to play the game: enticing an opponent in, setting traps for them and creating an opportunity to land your punches while also planning an escape route.

If it had been the other way around and I was moving into Muay Thai from boxing, then I'm sure I'd have found it just as difficult – if not more so, because there are so many more weapons to learn about in Thai boxing. But the timescale added an extra layer of difficulty to everything. Most people dedicated years of their lives to learning the same things I was trying to squeeze into a matter of months.

Part of me couldn't wait to get started with the sparring, because I knew how important it was in terms of my prep-aration for my first professional bout. But I was also incredibly nervous. What if I looked like a complete amateur? I didn't want to embarrass myself in front of everyone at David's gym in Vauxhall. Salas and David were used to working with guys at the very top end of the sport. I was operating in a different stratosphere compared to them.

The morning of my first spar, I woke up with the same nervous feeling in the pit of my stomach that I get before a fight – created by a mixture of adrenaline and anxiety. It was still there by the time I walked into the gym. The whole team was around – Salas, David, strength and conditioning coach Ruben and heavyweight fighter Joe Joyce. And, as there was only one ring in the gym, I knew all eyes would soon be on me.

Lauren was the girl I'd be sparring first. I was warming up with some shadow boxing when she arrived with her trainer, Steve. David had told me she was a 60kg fighter, but she was a tall 60kg – a good head taller than me. We said a brief hello and shared a polite handshake before she joined me in the ring to start her own warm-up.

I tried to keep focused on myself, thinking about my footwork, the combinations I was throwing, keeping my head moving, but my gaze kept drifting over to Lauren. She moved around the ring easily. Lightly. And as she started throwing a few shots out, it seemed like her arms just kept extending further and further away from her body. With height comes reach. My brain automatically started to think about the best ways to deal with that.

'Concentrate, Ruqsana.' Salas was shouting at me from the edge of the ring. He always seemed to notice the exact moment I lost focus. 'Up the tempo!'

I started to throw a little faster. Picked up my feet a little quicker. Beads of sweat were starting to gather across my forehead.

'Tiiiiiiime.'

Salas called me over to the corner to glove up and get my headguard on, while Lauren and Steve did the same on the opposite side of the ring. I tried to slow my breathing, to bring my heart rate back down to normal, but the adrenaline was making it difficult. No matter how many deep breaths I took, I could still feel my heart pounding in my chest, as if I'd drunk ten espressos that morning.

'Just relax, Ruqsana,' said Salas. 'Relax, get used to the movement. I want you to keep it simple for the first few rounds – just jab and move. Throw the right hand if you see an opening but don't force it. And don't forget to move your head, okay?'

I nodded. Salas pulled my headguard down and tightened

the strap beneath my chin. 'You're talented, baby, remember that,' he whispered.

His words brought a smile to my face as I walked to the centre of the ring to touch gloves with Lauren. But the moment the buzzer sounded to begin the round, that smile was gone. Lauren started fast, throwing flurries of punches that were knocking my head from one side to the other.

'Feet, Ruqsana. Feet!'

I stepped off to the side and tried to find some space to gather myself. But Lauren was fast and clever at cutting off the ring. I tried to get my jab going but her reach meant that after every shot of mine, I was finding it difficult to get back out of range, to a safe distance.

So many times, I wished I could have kneed her like I would have done in Thai boxing. But I kept my control. Kept my discipline.

For six two-minute rounds (female boxers only do two-minute rounds, as opposed to the three that male boxers do), I tried to remember everything Salas had taught me in our short time together. But it was extremely difficult when the shots coming back at me were from distances and angles that I was so unused to.

As the buzzer sounded at the end of the final round, I breathed a big sigh of relief. I knew it hadn't been great technically and I'd taken more punches to the head than I was used to, but it was over. And I'd survived.

Salas was smiling at me as I waited for him to free me from my headguard and gloves. 'You definitely have something, you know?'

'Yeah?'

'You have a fighter's instinct. You're fighting out of instinct right now, I can see that. And just like all good fighters do, you're rising to the challenge that's in front of you.'

He was right, I was fighting on instinct. I didn't have any other choice. It was exactly the same in the next two spars. Looking back, I wouldn't even call them that – they were fights. I just had to go in there and do whatever I could to hold my own.

I was up against girls who had been learning the art of boxing for years, while I was still on the basic foundations of the sport. I didn't know how to slip shots or pivot away from my opponent. I didn't know how to move in and out of range or lean back so that shots would miss me by millimetres. I didn't understand those defensive methods yet.

And those spars didn't really give me the chance to learn them, either. I didn't have the capability to work on my technique or strategy – I was just focusing on trying to survive.

I held my own to an extent, but I was still taking more punches to the head than I was used to. I was leaning in too much – getting too hungry to box. My headguard absorbed most of the power, but the punches still had an impact. Sometimes I'd go home with a dull ache in my head that stuck around until the next day. Other times, I'd wake up the following morning with a stiff neck from taking a shot that had been heavy enough to knock my head right back.

But what I found hardest about boxing wasn't the punching – it was what to do before and after I threw a punch. A lot of the time I'd throw punches and then stand still because I'd exhausted myself or I didn't have the footwork to get out of range.

When I thought about how much I had to learn, it felt like

I was standing at the bottom of a huge mountain, wondering how on earth I'd ever be able to reach the summit. Whenever I felt disheartened, though, Salas was there to pick me back up. To tell me not to worry about the expectations of other people or what they might think of my boxing. (He had his own distinct way of phrasing it: 'Don't give a fuck about anyone else.')

He told me that it took him two years to train Jorge Linares (one of the world's top boxers, who has been a world champion in three different weight classes) from a basic level to being able to compete with the best. And that one of the foremost pound-for-pound boxers of the current era, Vasyl Lomachenko, started boxing at the age of four and took dancing lessons for three years to hone his exceptional footwork. The boxing skill sets were drilled into him from an early age. That's how long it takes.

Salas's point: I shouldn't be so hard on myself for taking longer than two months to learn the skills of boxing.

He's such a positive individual. And he always finds a way to give you some of that positivity – some of his light. To me, it's what marks him out as one of the great coaches. Most trainers can teach you the fundamentals – technique, strategy – but knowing how to bring the best out of someone is another skill altogether. And it's invaluable. In those moments when they're in your corner and you've got nothing left in the tank – when you've given it absolutely everything – it's knowing exactly what to say and how to say it that separates the good trainers from the great ones.

I remember talking to him once about negativity and people with negative auras. About how spending too much time with people who are very negative can drain you – actually make you feel tired. Salas then said something really powerful, which stuck with me: 'Remember, Ruqsana, you also have the power to put your positivity onto them.'

That's what Salas does. He projects his positivity onto you and it becomes this amazing circle where you're bouncing off each other.

As my first fight drew closer, I started asking a few questions about my opponent, Ivanka Ivanova. But no one seemed to know much about her. We didn't have any knowledge of her background and there wasn't any footage that we could find of her fighting, either. I was going in completely blind.

I wasn't worried, though. I felt reassured by my Muay Thai pedigree and was sure that, in Ivanka, my team had matched me up with an opponent designed to be a confidence-builder. Someone who would provide me with the opportunity to get in the ring and get my first bout out of the way.

Everyone around me seemed confident, too. They saw me train, saw how hard I could hit and they gave me the impression that whoever I came up against, I would have enough to destroy them.

It wasn't until the weigh-in, the day before the fight, that I actually got to lay eyes on Ivanka for the first time. And when I did, that was the moment I realised that, actually, we might have underestimated this girl. There was something about her presence, about the way that she held herself and her build, that told me: this girl hasn't had just one or two fights, she's had more than that. She reminded me of some of the girls that I'd faced in the Thai boxing world.

From that moment, I just knew that this wasn't going to be the easy fight that we'd all been expecting. It wasn't going to be a case of getting in there and knocking her out within one round. This girl was going to give me a few good rounds.

I wasn't nervous about taking her on, though. I was confident of being able to handle someone of my own weight and a similar height. What I was a little anxious about was being in my very first boxing fight after being out of the ring for more than a year. Ring rust is a phrase that's used a lot in boxing to describe the way a fighter looks when they've been inactive for a while. It often means they look a bit sluggish in the ring and aren't as sharp as usual in terms of their movement and reactions. I was about to take ring rust to a whole new level by combining it with my boxing debut.

But there was one note of familiarity about the whole event. The fight was taking place at York Hall – a legendary boxing venue in Bethnal Green, which was just down the road from the KO gym. I'd been to York Hall many times before to watch fights, so even though I'd never fought there myself, it felt like a place I knew well.

I also knew I was going to have good support there. My sister Ane was coming with my little niece, my brother Eklim and my uncle Mo. British athletes Christine Ohuruogu and Perri Shakes-Drayton, who I'd met at various events over the years, were coming. And a whole load of people from KO would be there, too – including Bill. We didn't have as much contact as when he was my coach, but we were still in touch. I'll always have an immense amount of respect for him and, as he'd been part of my journey for so long, I wanted him to feel he still had a role to play. I actually asked him to be in my corner that night, along with Salas and Ruben, and said he should join me and the team in the changing room before the fight.

But the two people who definitely wouldn't be there were my parents. They knew I was fighting that weekend, but I hadn't made a big deal out of it. We don't speak about these things. For me, the fact that they just let me get on with it is enough. I see that as their way of saying: 'It's fine with us . . . just don't talk to us about it.'

On the day of the fight, I met up with Salas and my agent Adam at the Park Plaza Hotel in Vauxhall (which is right next door to David Haye's gym) in the afternoon, to have a late lunch before Adam drove us to York Hall. The traffic was terrible, so by the time we got there it was about six o'clock.

Everything suddenly felt a bit rushed. David Haye was already there with Joe Joyce, who was also on the bill. I was due to box first, so Salas started by applying my hand wraps. It takes around forty-five minutes to apply all the padding, tape and wraps, but Salas had only been working on them for around ten minutes when he started being asked to 'hurry up with Ruqsana – remember, you have to do Joe's afterwards'.

Sitting in the changing room with my hands wrapped and fight-night outfit on (black leggings beneath my white and gold shorts), the nerves fully kicked in. I was excited too – I knew how privileged I was to be fighting on such a big platform so early in my career. But in those moments leading up to the fight, it was definitely the nerves that were taking centre stage.

The bouts had started at 6 p.m. so David was popping in and out of the changing room in between watching the other fights and meeting up with people from the television presenting team.

I hadn't seen Bill yet, so I gave him a call and told him to come into the changing room and join the team. About ten minutes later, he appeared. I said a quick hello but was in the midst of my warm-up and knew that, of all people, Bill would understand me not wanting to stop for a long chat. I was so focused on what I was doing that I didn't see him leave.

When I stopped shadow boxing to stretch out and take on some water, I looked around the room and realised there was no Bill. I asked Ruben where he'd gone and he just shrugged: 'He walked out.' I didn't see Bill again until after the fight, but, even then, I never really found out why he didn't stay, or take up my offer to be in my corner during the fight. Looking back, maybe it was just a bit strange for him, after all these years, not to be the one I was taking guidance from.

At the time, I had to follow Ruben's lead – shrug it off and focus on the job at hand. The advantage of being the first fight of the show to be televised is that you pretty much know what time you'll be in the ring. Nine o'clock was showtime.

The knock on the door came just before nine. As soon as it did, I felt the butterflies in my stomach settle. This was it; time to see whether I had what it took to make it as a boxer.

As I walked to the ring, I could feel the energy bouncing off a crowd that was already well into their night of boxing – warmed up by the five bouts that had taken place before the start of the television coverage. I didn't take my eyes off the ring, though. Didn't look around for my sister or for Bill – just tried to block everything out so that I could maintain a strict focus on the inside of that ring.

I knew it was going to go fast – four two-minute rounds are nothing, really. The men fight for rounds of three minutes and some women want to do the same, but personally I quite like the shorter rounds. It means I can be explosive and keep the intensity high. I've fought for three-minute rounds before and it means you have to conserve your energy more and pick your shots better to make sure you're not burning out before the end of the round. With two-minute rounds, I know I can go all out.

Salas's final words to me before the first bell were simple: 'Keep your guard up and don't forget to move your head.'

About thirty seconds later, I was in the middle of a war and my head was coming under heavy fire. Just as I'd suspected, Ivanka had come to fight.

I could hear Salas shouting at me from the corner: 'Move your head, Ruqsana. Move your head!'

If the first minute was filled with flurries of punches, from both of us, the second saw us both settle down just a little. Neither of us was scared to engage, though, and by the final bell we'd both landed a few good shots.

When the bell went, I walked back to the corner with the feeling I hadn't done enough to win that first round. But neither had she – to me, it felt like a 50:50 round. As I sat down, Salas looked at me and asked: 'How is everything? You all right?'

'Yeah, fine.'

'Okay, listen up: the only thing I need from you, Ruqsana, is just keep moving your head. Move your head and every-thing will be easy . . . You're doing great.'

I had to step it up in the second round, but I was still trying to work Ivanka out – trying to grasp exactly what her strat-egy was and figure out my range at the same time. Towards the end of it, she caught me with two big right hands – the hardest shots she had. And I took them. After that, I felt my confidence levels go up a notch. I knew: I can deal with this.

Now I just need to figure out how I can land my own shots without getting hit.

After the second round, I already knew what Salas was going to say before he said it . . .

'Only one thing, Ruqsana: you don't move your head, you get hit. But you're hitting her very good. So, listen up now: your right hook is very good – jab, jab and throw your right hook. Every time you throw that you hit her.'

I was listening but, at the same time, there were so many thoughts running through my head: I don't want to let people down – my parents; David, who's invested in me and took such a chance on signing me; myself and all the work I've done over the last few months. For these next two rounds I have to give it my all. I'm here to win.

With two rounds already gone, I knew what I had to do. I knew how to open Ivanka up: to go to the body, then to the head and keep my intensity high. I knew how to put myself in better positions. How to use my strength and fitness to get the better of her.

For two rounds, I piled on the pressure. But Ivanka was tough. Tougher than anyone had expected.

As the seconds ticked down at the end of the fourth and final round, I felt like I was just getting into my stride. When the final bell rang, I threw my hands in the air. I fully believed I'd done enough to get my first victory as a boxer. Salas and Ruben did too – they were all smiles as they took off my gloves and sent me back to the centre of the ring to wait for the result.

The referee held my left hand and Ivanka's right as the announcer spoke:

'We have the referee's score totals. He sees this contest 38–38: a draw, ladies and gentlemen.'

The referee raised both our hands in the air, but my face fell in the opposite direction. A draw? I looked over at Salas, who looked just as surprised as I was. It was gutting.

Everyone in my team reassured me that they also thought I'd won the fight. We knew straight away that there would be a rematch. Before we'd even left the venue, my management team, Adam and Sam, told me: 'Don't worry, we'll get this sorted.'

But it didn't ease the disappointment. As I went to bed that night, I could feel it festering deep in the pit of my stomach: it was the kind of feeling that you know isn't going away anytime soon.

I spent the next day at my parents' house with Ane and my niece Aleena – someone who always lifts my spirits. But it was something Ane told me that really made me feel good that day: she said that while she was at York Hall the previous evening, Dad had called her to ask which channel I was fighting on. I had no idea my parents were actually going to watch it. I didn't even think they were interested. It was crazy to think of them sitting in their living room and watching me fight!

It wasn't until later that evening that Dad actually said anything to me about it, though. He was dropping me off back at my flat when he just came out with it: 'Your opponent was really strong.' I just looked at him, stunned. I could see he'd been really engaged in my fight. Entertained, even. He went on about how tough she was and what the commentators were saying about me. I started to think he had nothing negative to say about it at all.

But, just as we pulled up outside my flat, he said: 'Couldn't you cover your arms, by the way?'

On Monday morning, I was back in the gym, desperate to start putting the low of Saturday night's result behind me as quickly as I could.

Salas did his best to buoy me up. He said that it wasn't a 'debut fight' in terms of the level of my opponent but that I'd risen to the challenge. He also admitted that he hadn't really had enough time to train me because, even though we'd had two months, most of his time had been invested in David and Joe's training – the two heavyweights (in every sense). So, he was pleased with my performance: 'You fought out of instinct. And considering you had almost no sparring and are learning a new sport, you did good.

'I'm proud of you, Ruqsana.'

I couldn't bring myself to watch it back until a few days later. Even then, it wasn't my idea. My aunt invited me over to her house one evening. She knew I was upset about the result and suggested we should replay the fight. I wasn't sold on the idea but she insisted: 'Listen to the commentators, they said really good things about you. You have to realise, this girl had already had four fights, she was much more experienced than you . . .'

Sometimes, it takes people from outside of the sport to really put things into perspective for you. My aunt made me realise that, instead of analysing what actually happened, I was being emotional about the outcome. Watching it back with a clearer mind, I could see there were moments where I was getting too close to Ivanka. Without being able to kick, like I could in Muay Thai, I was struggling to keep my range. And Salas was right – I wasn't moving my head anywhere near enough. I had a lot to work on.

Okay, a draw wasn't the best decision but it wasn't the worst either. It was something I could build on. Grow from. And it left me with the opportunity for revenge.

The rematch was scheduled for two months later, on the undercard of a huge fight: David Haye's own rematch with Tony Bellew at the O$_2$ Arena in London – a venue that holds 20,000 people. It was such an amazing opportunity to box on a huge stage and get the chance to put right that result from York Hall.

The gym was buzzing; the excitement tinged with a real intensity. Salas and Ruben were putting in twelve-hour days in the gym to make sure that nothing was left to chance when it came to David's preparation for his fight against Bellew. He'd lost the first one after picking up an injury halfway through the fight, but even he'd admitted afterwards that Bellew was the better fighter that night. This time, he was desperate to put that right.

I knew how he felt.

My own training was going well as we built towards my second meeting with Ivanka. I really thrived on the atmosphere in the gym – it was like getting a shot of adrenaline every time I went in there. Of course, I'd feel tired at the end of sessions, but it wasn't the same drained feeling that I used to get at KO. I just loved being in the gym and around the whole team; they inspired me.

We managed to find a better sparring partner this time, too. Josh was a young kid who was around my height and weight. The challenge he presented was much closer to my level than the one offered by the girls I'd been sparring before the first fight. He was strong enough to test me, but the fact he was a better match for me physically than those girls meant that I was able to learn from the spars while still being challenged.

It was working well. Even David was impressed. After watching me spar one afternoon a few weeks before the fight, he had a big smile on his face as he said: 'I love it when a plan comes together.'

Everything was going so well.

Until, with about three weeks to go, everything fell apart.

It was my last week of sparring before the fight and on the Tuesday I was back in the ring with Josh. We were a few rounds in when he caught me with a left hook. It wasn't anything special. Just another punch. No harder or more hurtful than any of the others he'd thrown over the previous month or so. But this time, it had an effect I'd never experienced before. As the shot landed on the left side of my chin, I felt my neck click. My instinct was to stop. To turn away from Josh and make sure nothing was seriously damaged. As I did that, Ruben called me over to the corner.

'You okay, Rox?'

I told him something felt funny in my neck. He carefully took off my headguard and had a feel around my neck and head. I could move everything fine and nothing really hurt. So, Ruben put my headguard back on and the spar continued.

Friday was due to be my final sparring session before we'd start to taper down for the fight. I still wasn't feeling quite 100 per cent, but there was nothing I could really put my finger on. Nothing physical that I could show to Ruben or Salas.

So, I got back in the ring.

The next afternoon, things started to deteriorate. It began with an intense headache. The kind of pain that renders you almost immobile. I couldn't get up from the sofa. I couldn't move. I couldn't look at the light. I was in so much pain.

The day passed by in a blur. I lay on the sofa until darkness fell, praying that, with rest, the pain would ease. When I woke up on Sunday morning, I was still in pain but told myself it had lessened since the previous day. I got up, showered and got ready to go to KO to teach my usual Sunday morning class.

I think I lasted about ten minutes. Once I was in the gym, the pain seemed to intensify once again. It got so bad I couldn't keep my eyes open. Couldn't hold eye contact with anyone or even stand up straight. I had to go home. Bill walked with me to the tube station, but before we could make it that far, I told him I needed to stop. To sit down for a bit. It wasn't only my head – I felt like I was going to be sick.

'Rox, I have to take you to A&E,' said Bill.

'No, I'll be fine. I just need to rest . . .'

'No, this is dangerous. If they put you in the ring again, what do you think is going to happen? You could already have a brain bleed. This could be your life.'

He was right. I knew he was. But I didn't want to do anything without the team's permission so I asked Bill to wait while I called Ruben. No answer.

'Okay, let's just go.'

I tried Ruben again while I was waiting to be seen at the hospital, but he still wasn't picking up.

Eventually, they took me through to see a doctor who asked me a long list of questions. When he was satisfied with those, he said they were going to do a CT scan to take a look at my brain and see if there were any signs of bruising or bleeding. I was terrified. What if it was really serious? I'd had black eyes from Muay Thai before and maybe mild concussion, but never anything like this.

Almost three hours after I arrived, I was in a taxi heading

back to my flat with a firm diagnosis: concussion. The relief was palpable. No bleeding on the brain and, in terms of the fight, I thought I'd be fine. I'd rest for a few days and then just take it easy for the next two weeks. The hard work was mostly done now, anyway.

I messaged Sam and Adam that night to let them know what was going on and then called Ruben again. This time, he picked up. I told him what the doctor had said and that I wouldn't be able to take any head shots for the next week or so; pad work only. I'd need another day or so to rest but I thought I'd probably be back in the gym by Tuesday or Wednesday. He said that was all fine.

About half an hour later, I got a phone call from Sam. 'Rox, have they definitely diagnosed you with concussion?'

'Yes, that's what it says on the doctor's notes.'

'Then you're out of the fight. If you've been diagnosed with a concussion, you're not allowed back in the ring for at least three weeks.'

'But it says on the notes: "Not permitted to box *unless* cleared by a physician." Maybe I can get a doctor's note . . .'

Sam said there was no chance. He, and the whole team, risked getting into huge trouble if they allowed me to fight.

I hung up the phone and lay down on the sofa, squeezing my eyes shut to try to stop the tears from forming. The throbbing in my head was now almost numbed by the feeling of crushing disappointment. It suddenly felt as though all the energy – all the life – had been sucked out of my body.

This amazing opportunity was right in front of me – just inches away. I could hardly bear the thought of not being able to take it.

Over the next twenty-four hours I kept going back and

forth in my head: should I have told them? Deep down, I knew it was the right thing to do. That my health had to come first, but there was always another voice in my head, one that said: 'You were so well prepared. Ready to go. This was your moment . . .'

I called my sister Ane and told her how I was feeling. She reassured me I'd done the right thing: 'What if something happens to you? Who's going to look after you? Our parents can barely look after themselves. Come on, is it really worth you taking this fight?'

Ane was right. I had no choice but to pull out.

Fight day came and went. I watched on television as David lost to Tony Bellew for a second time in front of a huge crowd at the O$_2$ Arena. After that, the gym was eerily quiet. It was dead. I was still going in and training, but there was no structure to it because everyone was taking a break. The build-up to David's fight had been so full-on that they needed a rest.

Everything lost a bit of focus after that. David announced his retirement from fighting and Salas left to go back to his training base in Las Vegas. All of which left me in limbo. The draw with Ivanka was still something I was desperate to rectify, but now I had no trainer to help me prepare for it and no fight date to even aim for. My boxing career had started in fifth gear, but now it felt like I was stuck in reverse.

I wasn't ready to give up on it, though. I felt like I hadn't even been tested yet. Okay, I'd drawn my first bout and then had a bit of a setback, but I still didn't know what I was really capable of in the boxing ring. Not knowing that was my driving force. Until I had the answer, I couldn't close this chapter of my life.

I managed to get in touch with Salas and spoke to him

about going over to Vegas to train with him. He had plenty of fighters out there keeping him busy, but he promised that, if I could get to Vegas, he would find the time to train me.

Before I did anything, I wanted to clear it with David. He'd believed in me enough to sign me up, so I felt I owed it to him to get his blessing, even though he didn't actually have a coach in London any more. I told him about Salas's promise and explained why I was so determined to keep on trying to progress: 'I can't give this up yet. If I knew that I'd given it my all and it wasn't good enough, then I'd be happy to walk away from this. But right now, I can't say that, not until I've been back in the ring and I've given it my all to see if I really belong there.'

I said to him: 'When the best coach in the world is willing to train you, it's a no-brainer.' David agreed. I walked out of the gym that day with my mind made up. I'd use my savings to pay for my own flight and accommodation in Vegas because I knew that what I was getting in return was worth far more. When I considered the value that Salas brought to me in terms of knowledge and experience, I knew that no money could add up to that. If I wanted to know what I was capable of, I had to do it.

A month or so later, I was on a plane to Las Vegas. But by the time I'd sorted out my travel and accommodation, Salas had taken on a new job, which meant he wouldn't have time to train me after all. Instead, I'd be training with his right-hand man.

It was a different experience from the first time I was there. At the time, I thought I was doing okay. But I look back now and think, God, I was so miserable. I found it really difficult to be out there on my own at that moment. I was giving it my all in the gym, but I was exhausting myself mentally and physically.

I didn't have any friends there – no one who could help to lift my energy when I was feeling low. The highlight of my day was the two hours I spent in the gym, when I was able to interact with other people. Other than that, I was alone. Isolated from the world. Just in my room resting and recovering.

It was challenging. But I knew, this is what makes a good fighter. This is the definition of getting to be a champion.

After three weeks, I came home with a renewed sense of confidence. Travelling alone forces you to gain knowledge. To find a new level of independence. It felt like a real accomplishment. But none of that was of any use to me unless I could find a way to get back into the ring.

Finding opponents in women's boxing isn't easy, especially at the lighter weights. There simply aren't that many females around at that weight who box. I was talking to David constantly about finding a fight, and trying to look at other promoters too – just searching for any avenue that I could explore that might help me secure a bout.

But every door I found kept shutting in my face. David was saying: 'No, there're no shows I can get you on,' and other promoters weren't responding to my messages. It felt like no one was giving me a chance and it was devastating. How could I keep moving forward when no one would offer me the opportunity to show what I could do?

For almost six months, I kept going. I just had to keep believing that something would come along. But it took a lot of strength. I remember saying to Bill once: 'I don't know why I'm doing this any more. I'm running out of funds. I'm running out of energy because I'm constantly training, trying to be ready in case something comes along.'

'Rox, one more roll of the dice. Let's see what we can do.'

One more roll of the dice. Why not?

When people ask what inspires me – why I've been so determined to get in the boxing ring after making my name in one sport – I tell them: it's not about money. Or fame. It's about challenging myself. Being stimulated. And being able to make a difference.

When I think about all the people who've told me how much my story has inspired them, and when I see the way my little niece Aleena looks up to me – how I give her hope and I inspire her – the thought that I might be able to do the same for others is what really stimulates me.

It's also the feeling that I have when I'm in the ring. It's one that I've never experienced anywhere else: the feeling that I've never been closer to God than I am in that moment. It's do-or-die inside that ring. To take on that challenge, you need that higher power – you need to connect with something greater than yourself. Because the physical is limited. The mental is limited. But the spiritual is never limited.

My religion has taught me that you should always be hopeful, because what is ahead of you is better than what is behind you.

It might have taken me some time to understand my religion, but now I know it's not there to judge me but to guide me. I understand that it doesn't have to be about wearing the hijab and praying five times a day. For some it might be, but for me, it's about your connection to God and living a good life – being kind and having good dealings in your day-to-day life.

That's how I see religion now – being the best version of myself. I'm just an ordinary girl, but I've always had this extraordinary desire to be the best version of myself, and in order to do that I found strength through God. That taught me discipline, focus, resilience, and to have good morals and values. Those things play a big part in how you feel about yourself.

It's about self-empowerment. Being comfortable with walking away from good opportunities because maybe they're not good enough, and trusting that later on you'll be presented with something even better. Having the courage and valuing yourself enough to know: I'm worth more than this.

I discovered my strength and my voice through finding God and I guess that has been my ultimate purpose – everything else has been a vehicle to get to that point. Even the boxing. Once I felt that connection to God, my mindset shifted. After so many years of questioning myself, questioning my life choices, I'm at peace because I know where I'm going and what my purpose is.

If you've taken anything from my story, I hope it is to know that there is always hope, even in those moments that might seem so dark you can't see a way out. When I think about everything that I've overcome, I realise that, actually, if you have faith you can overcome anything.

I've suffered from ME. Managed panic attacks. Been diagnosed with depression. Broken ribs. Torn my rotator cuff. But there is something beautiful you take away, even from those darkest moments. Life will always challenge you – it will beat you to the floor – but by having faith that you are doing the right thing and that something better is coming your way, you will find a way out.

When I look at where I came from and where I got to, sometimes I think: what the hell? How did I do this? Now I know, it's my roots that made me who I am. And it's by overcoming the challenges I have that I developed the resilience and self-worth that helped me to get here.

Where's here? A place that finally allows me to be at peace with who I am. With my purpose.

Epilogue

York Hall, 22 June 2019

One more roll of the dice.

The rematch with Ivanka was finally happening. Some fifteen months after our first fight, I was back at York Hall with Bill in my corner, friends and family in the crowd and a feeling that this was my time. I was convinced of it. After a month out in Vegas, working with one of Salas's right-hand men, Jorge Capetillo, I felt I'd done everything in my power to get myself into the best possible condition.

Mentally, spiritually and physically, I felt like I was in a good place. That everything was going according to plan. I felt a lot of inner peace. I was ready for this fight.

When we weighed in on the Friday afternoon, I was surprised to see that Ivanka came in a few pounds lighter than me. She's a little bit shorter but a stockier build, so, if anything, I expected her to be the heavier one.

On the morning of the fight, before I did anything else, I said a prayer. I asked God for protection, not only for me but for Ivanka too. I prayed that both of us would come out of the ring safe and well.

We were the second fight of the night, meaning we'd be in the ring by about 6 p.m. So, I met Bill at the venue at around 4.30 and started getting myself ready – physically and mentally – to get back in the ring.

I've been here before. I know what to do.

Anytime I started to feel my levels of anxiety rising, all I had to do was repeat these words to myself and any negative thoughts were cleared from my mind.

I was ready.

Ivanka was called into the ring first, but as I was about to climb through the ropes a few minutes later, I noticed she'd disappeared. I paused by the corner of the ring to bow my head and say another prayer, expecting Ivanka to have returned from wherever she'd gone by the time I opened my eyes. But no, there was still no sign.

I climbed into an empty ring and looked across at the referee, who shrugged his shoulders and said: 'She forgot her groin guard.'

She didn't want to wear it. She'd done the same thing in the first fight too – pretending that she didn't know it was necessary to wear one, so the referee had to send her back. In our first fight, I hadn't known I had to wear one, either, but that was my debut. At the time, I didn't even own one. When the referee sent me back to the changing room, I had to borrow a guard from a random guy. It was huge on me (not to mention a pretty disgusting thing to have to share . . .).

On this occasion, Ivanka would have known all too well she needed to wear one. Bill whispered in my ear: 'Rox, she's trying to throw you out.'

I nodded, not taking my eyes away from the opposite corner to look at him. I knew she was playing mind games. Trying to disrupt my focus by making me wait. But it was fine by me. I'd wait all night if I had to.

Finally, after three or four minutes, Ivanka reappeared. I took a few deep breaths, ran through the game plan in my head and waited for the first bell.

The first punch was a shock. I'd felt her power a year ago but this was something different. Something I'd never felt before – not from a female of that weight, anyway. I didn't know what had hit me.

The second punch was even worse. It was a big right hand that caught me flush on my right eye – it felt like her fist actually went right into my eye. Straight away, I knew there was damage. With every second that passed, I could feel my eye closing. From that moment on, I was just thinking about survival – about making it to the end of the round so that we could assess the damage and think about how to work around it. It was the hardest ninety seconds or so I think I've ever had inside the ring.

I was struggling to see from my right eye and that was throwing off my balance and range badly. I could handle the pain, but I was finding it hard to adjust to my impaired vision.

After what felt like hours, the bell finally sounded. I tried to catch my breath as I hurried to my corner, where the ring-side doctor was already waiting to look at my eye, which over the last minute and a half had swollen to almost golf ball size. He took a look and said the socket was okay – not broken – which was a huge relief. Damaged eye sockets can spell the end of a fighter's career. It was a case of managing the swelling and making sure I could see well enough to continue. I told him I could ... there was no way I wanted this to be over after just one round.

The second round was a blur of more heavy shots from Ivanka – most of them targeting my right eye. It didn't feel like she was just there to win – it felt like she wanted to kill me. She was playing pretty dirty, too – a few times she caught me with an elbow or around the back of my head (which is actually illegal). She even hit me after the bell had gone at the end of the second round.

Looking back, I don't know how I carried on.

With two rounds left, I knew I had to do something if I was going to stop the fight from being a totally one-sided affair. When I was training in Las Vegas, the coaches had told me to manage the distance between me and my opponent – to jab and move, and not get caught up in a war. And that had been my plan. But now, Bill was saying: 'You're throwing ones and twos, you need to get combinations in there to stop her from coming forward.'

He was right. In the next round I started letting my hands go. But she was so strong, she was walking straight through my punches. It wasn't that she had more skill than me. She wasn't dodging my punches, or using her angles; there was nothing clever about what she was doing. It was just the fact that she had the sheer strength – she'd absorb two of my shots just to get in and close the distance so that she could unload on me.

It didn't seem to matter how much power I had – she didn't feel it and just kept coming forward. Somehow, she was not the same girl I fought a year earlier, when, every time I punched her, I knew that she felt my shots.

The fight was gone. I knew it before the final bell had rung. Four rounds were simply nowhere near long enough for me to recover from the shock of the eye injury I suffered in the first round and get myself back into the fight. Bill knew it, too. But as he took off my gloves he said: 'Most guys would have given up after the second round. But you carried on. That showed tremendous courage.'

The feeling of disappointment was immense, but at the same time, I felt proud. I got in there and fought the best I could – there was nothing more I could have done. I felt a sense of gratitude as well; grateful that I'd left the ring with nothing worse than a swollen eye. Grateful that so many people – friends, family, people from KO – had come out to support me. I stayed to chat to a few of them, holding an ice pack against my eye, which was almost entirely closed by that point. But I really just wanted to get home and have some time to think.

Before the fight I'd thought: if I win, then I continue. If I don't, then I gave it my all and it wasn't enough.

Now I had to decide: is it over?

Honestly, that night I wished that I could say, 'Yes. It's over.'

But I couldn't. I couldn't even find any tears.

On the train home from York Hall, I talked to my aunty about it: 'I wish I could cry and say that this is the end of the road. That I don't have what it takes. But I just don't feel like it is.

'You don't know how badly I want to give this up now. But I don't feel like I can.'

I realise that's a hard thing to understand.

That night, my sister decided to stay in the flat with me,

just in case I suffered any effects of concussion. Luckily, I didn't – but my eye was completely shut. All I could do was ice it and apply arnica gel to try to help with the swelling.

I knew I'd have to see my parents at some point, but I was scared of their reaction. I didn't dare go until my eye was looking at least a little better.

On the Monday evening, two days after the fight, I was at home in the flat but decided to go to my mum's for the night. I hadn't slept well since the fight and thought it might help me to get a good night's sleep if I went back to my old room. I called my sister and told her I was coming round: 'Just open the door for me so I can come in and go straight upstairs, then I'll go home in the morning.'

It worked that night – no one saw me arrive. But the next morning, Mum walked into the room and saw me – my dark glasses sitting on the bedside table. For the next hour or so I sat and listened to both my parents. The key question? 'When are you going to give this up?'

They did all the talking. I didn't say anything – just listened and let them say what they wanted to say. From their point of view, of course I understood it. I was even having that battle with myself.

Why don't I want to give this up? I've already become a world champion in one sport, why do I need to continue? I can do other things that can still help me make a living. I can do community work that helps other people and can help to inspire me – give me the motivation to get out of bed in the morning.

For the next few days, I gave it a lot of thought. Over and over again, I asked myself: why? Why am I doing this?

When you're beaten up that badly it's scary – I could have

lost my vision that night. That's not temporary – it's not a bruise – it's for ever.

And it's not that I don't have anything else to do, or that I don't have other goals.

But nothing makes me feel as passionate and alive as boxing. Even though there are so many hard truths to it, it's the sense of fulfilment that it gives me. The fact that this is one of the hardest things I'm doing in my life and that nothing else is going to challenge me as much.

I love to know that I'm overcoming my fears and every single barrier that's put in front of me. And knowing what that does for other people – that I can really inspire them and give so many others hope. That's what makes me feel fulfilled.

It's funny, the one person who encouraged me to continue was my 7-year-old niece, Aleena. She was at the fight. She saw everything. When I went to my mum's a few days later she took me aside: 'Aunty, we need to have a private conversation away from Mummy.'

She took me to the stairs, sat me down on a step and said: 'Aunty, that girl cheated. You can't give up. You need to come back and go for it again and beat her. You can't let her win.'

It's easy for other people to say: 'Just give up.' They have a right to their opinion and I do hear what they're saying, but I don't absorb it. Not until I'm ready to.

Because, for me, being successful means that sometimes you have to go through the darkest hours first. I already know this. I've been there so many times before. In a way, the problem is that all those people telling me to quit haven't been through what I have. They don't know the depths that I've already encountered.

For me, the defeat was just a contrast with what's about to come for me: the lower I go down, the higher I will go up.

I want victory, but it's also about whatever God feels is a victory for me. I've been here before in other aspects of my life, where I've felt like victory can come in so many ways. Maybe God has already given me a victory in the fact that I survived. I'm healthy.

Who knows what's around the corner? In my life I've sometimes been in situations where I've thought: I really wanted this, how could God let me down? Only to realise, a year or two later, that there was a reason for that.

But it takes time. Sometimes you have to go through low, dark moments before you get there, and it's about how you rise from those.

When I look back over my time as a fighter – almost eighteen years now – I know that it has been responsible for shaping my outlook on life. That I'm the result of a combination of my faith, my religion and the experiences that I've faced in Muay Thai and now boxing.

I spent so many years desperate simply to belong somewhere. I wanted to belong at KO. I wanted to belong at family functions. But I never belonged anywhere.

My sister belonged to the family unit. At weddings she was always part of everything, whereas I would just turn up on the day and no one would even notice me. It was the same at KO. For years I was bullied. I wanted to belong but I knew that I didn't; that I wasn't part of the unit either.

Now, I've learned that I don't need to belong anywhere. And I embrace that.

I'm going to be wherever I want to be and achieve whatever I need to achieve to feel fulfilled. Freeing myself of that need to belong has opened my horizons to so much more, because I just enjoy what is good and what makes me happy.

It has given me the confidence to be who I want to be.

And, for now, that's still Ruqsana Begum: fighter.

Acknowledgements

I would like to thank God for all my blessings in life. I can honestly say that I'm living my dream.

The sacrifice comes with great rewards.

I'm fortunate enough that my family have accepted me and my life choices. I'm truly grateful that they allowed me to fulfil my potential, even though it might have been extremely difficult for them to understand my choice to become a full-time Thai boxer.

I want to say a special thank you to my younger sister who has always been like a best friend to me and supported me throughout my university life and beyond. And to my dear nieces Khairah and Aleena who are my biggest inspiration; they allow me to see how my vision can inspire a whole new generation and the impact that being authentic and following your dream can have.

To my coach Bill who took me on as a teenager, helped me to become a world champion and taught me life lessons along the way – through good and bad. Life is all about change and adaptation, growing and evolving – not resisting, but embracing the changes and turning them into a positive.

Thank you to David Haye, for signing me and helping me to start on my new path.

I also want to thank my ghost writer Sarah Shephard – a Muslim and a Jew working together. We had lots of fun getting to learn more about each other's faith and culture.

Finally, I want to thank Ian Marshall and Kaiya Shang at Simon & Schuster for their hard work, and Charlotte Atyeo, without whom this book might not be in your hands right now. Thank you for believing in it and in me.